THE
BOLIVIAN REVOLUTION
AND THE
UNITED STATES,
1952 TO THE PRESENT

JAMES SIEKMEIER

THE
BOLIVIAN REVOLUTION
AND THE
UNITED STATES,
1952 TO PRESENT

THE PENNSYLVANIA STATE UNIVERSITY PRESS
UNIVERSITY PARK, PENNSYLVANIA

Earlier versions of chapters 2, 3, and 5 were published as "Trailblazer Diplomat: Victor Andrade Uzquiano's Efforts to Influence U.S. Policy, 1944–1952," *Diplomatic History* 28, no. 5 (2004); "Limits of Dependency: Bolivian–United States Relations in the Early Alliance for Progress Years, 1961–1963," *Bolivian Studies Journal* 12 (2005); and "A Sacrificial Llama? The Expulsion of the Peace Corps from Bolivia in 1971," *Pacific Historical Review* 69, no. 1 (2000), respectively.

Library of Congress Cataloging-in-Publication Data

Siekmeier, James F.
The Bolivian revolution and the United States, 1952 to the present / James F. Siekmeier.
p. cm.
Includes bibliographical references and index.
Summary: "A study of United States-Bolivian in the post–World War II era. Explores attempts by Bolivian revolutionary leaders to both secure United States assistance and to obtain time and space to develop their policies and plans"—Provided by publisher.
ISBN 978-0-271-03779-0 (cloth : alk. paper)
ISBN 978-0-271-03780-6 (pbk. : alk. paper)
1. United States—Foreign relations—Bolivia.
2. Bolivia—Foreign relations—United States.
3. United States—Foreign relations—Bolivia.
4. Bolivia—Foreign relations—United States.
5. Bolivia—Politics and government—1952–1982.
6. Bolivia—Politics and government—1982–2006.
7. Bolivia—Politics and government—2006- .
I. Title.

E183.8.B6S54 2011
327.73084—dc22
2010036078

Copyright © 2011 The Pennsylvania State University
All rights reserved
Printed in the United States of America
Published by The Pennsylvania State University Press,
University Park, PA 16802-1003

It is the policy of The Pennsylvania State University Press to use acid-free paper. Publications on uncoated stock satisfy the minimum requirements of American National Standard for Information Sciences—Permanence of Paper for Printed Library Material, ANSI Z39.48-1992.

TO *Catherine* AND *Claire*

CONTENTS

Acknowledgments ix

Introduction 1

1
The Early Years 13

2
The Bolivian Revolution and the United States 38

3
The Splintering of the Revolution 73

4
The Rebellion in the Countryside 103

5
Bolivia's Line in the Sand 133

6
The Revolution's Long Shadow 152

Conclusion:
Another Round of Tension 172

Appendix:
U.S. Economic Assistance to Bolivia 180

Bibliography 182

Index 202

ACKNOWLEDGMENTS

I would like to thank the teachers who inspired my love of learning and the past—Larry Buell, Susan Copley, Ronald DiCenzo, Elida Giles, Peter Katzenstein, Clayton R. Koppes, Gary Kornblith, Joel Silbey, and David Young, and of course my doctoral dissertation committee, Thomas Holloway, Walter LaFeber, and the late Eldon "Bud" Kenworthy. These scholars, excellent teachers all, and others, inspired in me a sense of inquiry about the past and helped me improve the clarity of my writing. My gratitude to them is deeply heartfelt.

In addition, I would like to thank supportive friends and colleagues over the years. They probably could not figure out why I was so interested in Bolivia and regretted asking me, but I benefited greatly from their intellectual stimulation and friendship nevertheless. At Luther College (Decorah, Iowa), Nancy Berry, Jyothi Grewal, Jaime Gomez, Eduardo Guizar, Lawrence Mbogoni, Benjamín Milano, and Edward Tebbenhoff were the best of colleagues. Two people I met there, Perry-O and David Sliwa, provided me with not only intellectual stimulation but supportive friendship. I would like to acknowledge an intellectual debt to Jack Barbour, Arnoldo De León, Charles Endress, Shirley Eoff, Roberto Garza, E. James Hindman, E. James Holland, Paul and Sandy Love, William Montgomery, Ed Olson, Dennis Pate, the late Jim Ward, John Wheeler, and Guoqiang "Joe" Zheng, at Angelo State University (San Angelo, Texas). I would also like to thank them for being excellent colleagues and good friends. I would like to thank Monica Belmonte, Michael Todd Bennett, Bradley Coleman, Craig Daigle, Steven Galpern, Mark Hove, Adam Howard, David Humphrey, Andrew Johns, Hal Jones, Edward C. Keefer, the late Peter Kraemer, Douglas Kraft, Robert Krikorian, Erin Mahan, Richard Moss, David Nickles, Kathy Rasmussen, Douglas Selvage, Louis "Luke" Smith, and James and Laurie Van Hook, among others, at the Office of the Historian, U.S. Department of State, for their intellectual stimulation and friendship. At West Virginia University (Morgantown), Katherine Aaslestad, Mary Angel Blount, Tyler Boulware, Peter Carmichael, Joel Christenson, Mike Ennis, Josh Esposito, Elizabeth and Kenneth Fones-Wolf, Jack Hammersmith, Joseph Hodge, David Krech, Melissa Latimer, Jordan

Lieser, Brian Luskey, Maria Miro-Quesada, Maryanne Reed, Dan Renfrew, Forrest Schwartz, SilverMoon, Angel Tuninetti, and Matt Vester, have been supportive colleagues and friends.

My friends in Bolivia who offered crucial help and support are too numerous to mention. However, I would like to acknowledge those who went beyond the call of duty in helping me. They include members of the carrera de historia at the Universidad Mayor de San Andrés (UMSA) in La Paz: Magdalena Cajias de la Vega, Juan Cordero Jauregui, and Raúl Calderón Jemio, who helped me early on in my research process in finding sources and refining my ideas and organizing an opportunity to share my ideas with fellow *bolivianistas* in La Paz. I would also like to thank Luis Oporto Ordoñez, of the Biblioteca Nacional de Bolivia, for sharing his ideas and suggesting good sources and organizing an opportunity for me to speak. Others in La Paz who have helped me with my work include Hans Huber Abendroth, Gregorio Loza Balsa, Aida Choquetaxi de Loza, Peter and Wendy McFarren, Julio Sanjines Goitia, and Harry Sojka.

I cannot thank them enough for the doors they opened to me. In particular, Hans has helped me with translations, and for that I am very grateful. In Cochabamba, I would like to thank Pamela Calla, Tom Kruse, Kathryn Ledebur, Fernando Mayorga, Raúl Barrios Morón, Gustavo Rodríguez Ostria, and colleagues at the Universidad Mayor de San Simón, who were helpful to a fault. One person in Bolivia stands out for special mention. Lupe Andrade generously shared not only her time but allowed me access to her father's papers, a very useful resource for this project.

My *bolivianista* friends in the United States are an important network of intellectual and moral support. They include Mary Jo Dudley, Linda Farthing, Thomas Fields, Eduardo Gamarra, Matt Gildner, Kevin Healy, the late Fred Hendel, Benjamin Kohl, Katrina Lehman, John Powers, Lynn Swartley, Donna Lee Van Cott, and Robin Wierum. Mary Jo cheerfully let me stay in her house in Ithaca one summer. Eduardo has helped me many a time with help adjusting "on the ground" in La Paz—and taken me out to dinner in Miami after returning from Bolivia. Kevin has been an excellent source of information on all things Bolivian, and was a fine colleague at George Washington University and remains a good friend. I would like to extend a special thanks to Jerome Crowder and Alicia Krouse, with whom I've enjoyed many a good meal, great conversation, and in generally good times in La Paz, Austin, Houston, San Angelo (Texas), and Washington, D.C., among other places.

Also too numerous to mention are those who read drafts of all or part of my manuscript. However, I would like to highlight five people who went beyond the call of duty in this regard: Arnoldo De León, Erick Langer, Catherine Tall, and two outside reviewers. The manuscript greatly benefitted from their input. Arnoldo has proven to be an excellent mentor for me for research and writing. Not only is he a model scholar and human being, he has spent a lot of time going over not only drafts of this book, but drafts of my other work as well. Of special note, Erick provided important and useful help regarding how to operate in Bolivia early on in my research in that country. He has also introduced me to numerous people in the Washington, D.C., area who are interested in Bolivia. In addition, I would like to thank those who went over parts of the manuscript: Bradley Coleman, Manuel Contreras, Jerome Crowder, James Dunkerley, Eduardo Gamarra, R. Matt Gildner, Jyoti Grewal, Elizabeth Cobbs Hoffman, Thomas Holloway, Andrew Johns, Peter Klarén, Benjamin Kohl, Walter LaFeber, Lester Langley, Kenneth Lehman, Jane Mangen, Chester Pach, Stephen Rabe, Kathryn Statler, Stephen Streeter, and Don and Christine Tall.

I would also like to highlight the unsung heroes of the research profession: librarians and archivists. These persons work hard day in and day out to make the research process easier. Although I cannot mention all of them here, I would like to highlight, in Bolivia, René Danilo Arze Aguirre, Laura Escobari de Querejazu, and Marta Paredes. In Washington, D.C., I would like to thank Ed Barnes, David Langbart, and John Powers, who tirelessly and cheerfully explained the sometimes confusing system at the National Archives, and helped me find resources I otherwise would not have found. Librarians at the Eisenhower Presidential Library, the Kennedy Presidential Library, the Johnson Presidential Library, and the Nixon Presidential Materials Project helped me immensely. Librarians at Cornell University, the University of Pittsburgh, Luther College, Angelo State University, and West Virginia University, among others, have helped me tremendously in finding sometimes obscure sources. Another group of people who often go unacknowledged are those who are willing to give their time to be interviewed. Although too numerous to name here, I would like to thank them *en masse* for their selfless giving of their time.

A project of this scope involves a number of research trips. I would like to thank Luther College, Angelo State University, and West Virginia University for providing the necessary funding for these trips. In addition, I received two Fulbright Awards for Bolivia. The teaching experiences they provided, one at the Universidad Mayor de San Andrés, in La Paz, and the second at the Universidad Mayor de San Simón, in Cochabamba, proved to be very enriching. Moreover, I would also like to acknowledge Bolivians who have provided me with housing in Bolivia: Peter and Sonia Sojka in La Paz, Maria Choquetaxi in Cochabamba, and Jane Mangan and Robert Phocus in Sucre. Without this help, my stay in Bolivia would have been much more taxing, and prohibitively expensive. In addition, I would like to thank Maria for her help with translation and for sharing a number of meals with me in La Paz and Cochabamba. In Vienna, Virginia, college friends James and Anna Bradford and their families, opened their doors to me many a time when research called me to Washington, D.C. In Austin, Texas, Aleta Riccardi and Michael Ogg were kind enough to let me stay with them while I did research there. Good friends all, they put me up with good cheer, and in addition provided an intellectually stimulating place to study, research, and write. Heartfelt thanks go out to all of you.

As a Fulbright scholar, I enjoyed the support of many people then at the American Embassy in La Paz. Some of the more important included Carlos Aranaga, Diego Ballivián, Carmen Pardo, and Philip Parkerson. I would like to thank your for taking time from your busy schedules to help me "learn the ropes" of La Paz and Bolivia. In addition, I would like to thank them for organizing opportunities to speak in Bolivia, allowing me to learn from the Bolivia experts in that country.

Over the years I have benefited from conversations with those who have dedicated a part of their lives to the study of the history of U.S. foreign policy and U.S.–Latin American relations. These people include Susan Brewer, Frank Costigliola, Brian Etheridge, Anne Foster, Max Paul Friedman, Mark Gilderhus, Robert Good, Sayuri Shimizu Guthrie, Anthony Harkins, Elizabeth Cobbs Hoffman, Clark Joel, H. Matthew Loayza, Daniel Michael, Christopher Lance Murchison, Lorena Oropeza, Jason Parker, David Ryan, Timothy Scarnecchia, Thomas Schoonover, Shannon Smith, Jeff Taffett, and Elizabeth Murphy Weithman, among others. You all have enriched my life in numerous ways. Also, I would like to thank former students (some of whom were also research assistants) who suffered under my tutelage and have gone to bigger and greater things beyond my classroom: Alex Cano, Ben Coltvet, Dana McGill Cooper, Darryl Hansmeier, Anthony Rogers, and Keith Sauer.

I would like to thank the editorial staff at Penn State University Press, in particular Sanford Thatcher, Kathryn Yahner, and Andrew B. Lewis, for shepherding the manuscript through the editorial process with unique efficiency and unflagging good cheer.

Finally, I would like to thank my family, my parents, Donald and Jessie Siekmeier, and my brother and sister-in-law, Peter Siekmeier and Maria Stalford, as well as my parents-in-law, Christine Tall and Don Tall. They have been very supportive of my academic career and, more important, the best family I could ever have. Most importantly, I dedicate this book to my wife, Catherine Tall, and our daughter, Claire Elizabeth. Catherine not only went over the book line by line, but did so with good cheer, even if U.S. diplomatic history is not the most simulating of subjects for her (to say the least). In addition, she has supported me in countless ways in my pursing an academic career. She has done a tremendous amount for me, while juggling her own career and child-rearing along the way.

INTRODUCTION

Explaining a Unique Relationship

Evo Morales, Bolivia's first indigenous president, called upon the leaders of South America to oppose the U.S.-sponsored Free Trade Area of the Americas (FTAA), blasting it as a "neocolonization project." He concluded that "for the first time in Latin America the [U.S.] Empire could be defeated."[1] Morales's rhetoric tapped into a deep well of resentment against the United States, but overstated the extent of its power. In its relationship with the so-called colossus of the North, Bolivia has managed to exert a degree of control. Bolivia's ability to get what it wanted from the United States was particularly evident during the Bolivian revolution, arguably the nation's most significant event in recent times.

Along with the revolutions in Mexico (1910), Cuba (1959), and Nicaragua (1979), the Bolivian revolution marked a distinctive turning point in Bolivian history and stands as one of the great twentieth-century social revolutions in Latin America. It deepened Bolivia's democracy and made Bolivian society more inclusive. The early 1950s, however, also represented a turning point in U.S. history. After 1945, U.S. interests had multiplied worldwide, and it began to employ new policy techniques to pursue its interests. One of these techniques, economic assistance, had a large impact on the Bolivian revolution and on the trajectory of U.S.-Bolivian relations. Washington's policy toward Bolivia proved to be a pioneering test case of U.S. attempts at nation-building in the developing world.

1. Michael Radu, "A Matter of Identity: The Anti-Americanism of Latin American Intellectuals," in *Understanding Anti-Americanism: Its Origins and Impact at Home and Abroad*, ed. Paul Hollander (Chicago: Ivan R. Dee, 2004).

This book analyzes U.S.-Bolivian relations from 1952 to 1971. In doing so, it describes and analyzes the formation and implementation of U.S. policy, as well as Bolivia's response to U.S. policy.[2] This study breaks new ground in three ways. Unlike most other existing studies, it carries the saga of the revolution through the beginning of the 1970s and provides a more up-to-date analysis of the revolution's political dynamics.[3] It explores the political, social, and cultural transformation of Bolivia during the revolutionary years between 1952 and 1971 and explains how that transformation emanated from a process in which a relatively poor and nonindustrial nation moved in momentous revolutionary directions.

Because Bolivia represents the earliest example of attempted U.S. nation-building in the nonindustrialized world, studying U.S.-Bolivian relations is key to understanding Washington's relationship with the Third World. This monograph will focus on two key aspects of U.S.-Bolivian relations: the attempts by U.S. leaders to influence Bolivian policy, often without adequate understanding of Bolivian society and culture, and Bolivia's role as an active player in crafting a series of workable compromises over time with U.S. government officials, which has not been adequately addressed in the literature. Part of the story is how Bolivia reacted to U.S.

---

2. For general treatments of the Bolivian revolution, see Robert Alexander, *The Bolivian National Revolution* (New Brunswick: Rutgers University Press, 1958); James Dunkerley, *Rebellion in the Veins: Political Struggle in Bolivia, 1952–1982* (London: Verso, 1984); Luis Antezana Ergueta, *Historia secreta de la Moviemiento Nacionalista Revolucionario*, 8 vols. (La Paz: Librería Editorial, 1986); Manuel Frontaura Argandoña, *La revolución nacional* (La Paz: Editorial Los Amigos del Libro, 1974); James Malloy, *Bolivia: The Uncompleted Revolution* (Pittsburgh: University of Pittsburgh Press, 1970); and Quebracho (Liborio Justo), *La revolución derrotada* (Cochabamba: n.p., 1967). For treatments of U.S.-Bolivian relations in this crucial time for both nations, see Laurence Whitehead, *The United States and Bolivia: A Case of Neocolonialism* (Oxford: Haslemere Group, 1969); Carlos Navia Ribera, *Los Estados Unidos y la revolución nacional: Entre el pragmatismo y el sometimiento* (Cochabamba: Centro de Información y Documentación para el Desarollo Regional, 1984); Kenneth Lehman, "The United States and the Bolivian Revolution, 1952–1961: The Pragmatics of a Patron-Client Relationship" (Ph.D. diss., University of Texas, 1992), and more recently, his *Bolivia and the United States: A Limited Partnership* (Athens: University of Georgia Press, 1999); and Naoki Kamimura, "Liberal America and Revolution: U.S. Cold War Policy and the Bolivian Revolution of 1952" (paper prepared for presentation at the 1997 Society of Historians of American Foreign Policy Annual Conference, Georgetown University, June 19–22, 1997). The most recent published survey of these relations is Francisco Roque Bacarreza, *Los años del cóndor: Sesenta crónicas del triunfo revolucionario boliviano en plena Guerra Fría* (La Paz: Mundy Color, 1995), a journalistic, though useful, treatment.

3. A few synthetic treatments of the Bolivian revolution exist, but they focus mainly on the politics of the early years of the revolution. See the previous note for citations. There is one recent book that emphasizes the latter years of the revolution: René Zavaleta Mercado, *La caída del MNR y la conjuración de noviembre: historia del golpe militar del 4 de noviembre de 1964 en Bolivia* (Cochabamba: Editorial Los Amigos del Libro, 1995).

initiatives. Some scholars, such as Eduardo Gamarra, discuss this side of Bolivia's relationship with the United States.[4] However, Bolivia also influenced U.S. policy on its own initiative, not reacting to specific U.S. policy decisions. A study of the course of the Bolivian revolution in the context of its relations with the United States shows how a nation can make a revolution work in the midst of a rapidly globalizing world.[5]

Despite Bolivia's success at moderating Washington's intentions, U.S. influence forced a partial retreat from the revolution on the part of Bolivia's powerful Left as early as 1960. Later, in 1964, a coup d'état or *golpe de estado* by the military removed the revolutionaries from power—a coup in which some observers have implicated the United States.[6] In any case, by the late 1960s, the legacy of U.S. policy was a heightened dislike for the "colossus of the North." In early 1970s, however, U.S.-Bolivian relations became cordial, and after a rocky period in the late 1970s and early 1980s, remained largely so for over thirty years. In 2006, Bolivian voters elected leftist Evo Morales as president. Morales called for rapid reform, including increasing taxes on the profits of foreign-owned oil and gas companies, and promoting non-cocaine uses of the coca leaf, one of Bolivia's more common agricultural products. Washington officials disagreed with much of Morales's program, which led to a deterioration of U.S.-Bolivian relations.

A Most Important Revolution

Morales's rise was not the first time in recent Bolivian history a candidate swept into power on a platform of rapid economic, social, and political

---

4. Eduardo A. Gamarra, "The United States and Bolivia: Fighting the Drug War," in *The United States and Latin America: The New Agenda*, ed. Victor Bulmar-Thomas and James Dunkerley (Cambridge: David Rockefeller Center for Latin America Studies, Harvard University Press, 1999), 177.

5. Good theoretical works on how relatively weak historical actors can influence stronger ones include James C. Scott's *Weapons of the Weak: Everyday Forms of Peasant Resistance* (New Haven: Yale University Press, 1985) and *Domination and the Arts of Resistance: Hidden Transcripts* (New Haven: Yale University Press, 1990). For an analysis of recent U.S.–Latin American relations that displays how a relatively weak nation, Costa Rica, influenced U.S. policy toward it during the cold war, see Kyle Longley, *The Sparrow and the Hawk: Costa Rica and the United States During the Rise of José Figueres* (Tuscaloosa: University of Alabama Press, 1997).

6. Lehman, *Bolivia and the United States*, concludes that the United States could have quietly spurred the coup plotters into action; however, Robert O. Kirkland, *Observing Our Hermanos de Armas: U.S. Military Attachés in Guatemala, Cuba, and Bolivia, 1950–1964* (New York: Routledge, 2003), concludes that there is no evidence of U.S. complicity.

change. A similar event occurred in 1952. Income inequalities and the unjust treatment of the indigenous majority led many to call for a total reorganization of the power relationships in the country. Indigenous persons, or Indians, had little access to land and few civil rights. The economy was dependent on the export of valuable minerals, in particular, tin; and three large (and all foreign-owned) mining companies controlled the market for minerals in the nation. These conditions were a compelling argument to many for revolution. With the 1952 revolution, Bolivia, despite its isolation and its status as an economic and cultural backwater, became an important part of the worldwide nationalist, democratic, and anticolonialist fervor that was sweeping the developing world in the late 1940s and 1950s.[7]

The revolution was a "total social fact": it touched all social, cultural, and economic aspects of Bolivian life and changed many of them irrevocably.[8] It was a dramatic social upheaval that resulted in a major reorganization of society that, among other things, empowered the less privileged. The literacy requirements for the franchise were dropped. The franchise was extended to Indians; and although some anti-Indian discrimination has remained to this day, postrevolutionary indigenous members of Bolivian society now have a significant voice. The franchise was also extended to women. The important role that women had played in the revolution radically altered gender relations.[9] Bolivia committed itself to education reform,[10] national integration, and economic development, issues hardly discussed before the revolution. In their pursuit of national integration and economic development, the revolutionaries nationalized the holdings of the three large mining corporations and in 1953 passed a land reform to benefit poor, landless *campesinos* (farmers with small holdings).

Up through the 1970s, Bolivia's economy remained largely dependent on the export of minerals.[11] But this dependence did not prevent it from

---

7. Luis Antezana Ergueta, *La clase media y la clase obrera en la revolución nacional del MNR* (n.p.: n.p., 1987), 6.

8. For a definition of "total social fact," see Alison L. Spedding, "The Coca Field as Total Social Fact," in *Coca, Cocaine, and the Bolivian Reality*, ed. Madeline Barbara Leóns and Harry Sanabria (Albany: State University of New York Press, 1997).

9. Lidia Gueiler Tejada, *La mujer y la revolución* (La Paz: Editorial Los Amigos del Libro, 1983).

10. An early journal that addressed educational reform was *Minkha*, which began in 1956 and was edited by César Chávez Taborga.

11. Although the Bolivian economy has diversified since the revolution, significant economic diversification did not occur until the 1970s. Herbert S. Klein, *Bolivia: The Evolution of a Multi-ethnic Society*, 2nd ed. (New York: Oxford University Press, 1992), 259–61.

exerting a degree of influence over its relationship with the United States. The U.S. decision to use economic assistance as means of promoting its interests in Bolivia represents an early example of nation-building in the Third World and thus was an important test case for U.S. policy. Once the economic assistance began to flow, Bolivian leaders realized they could use this assistance to assert a degree of agency over their relationship with the United States. Bolivia leaders discovered that they could increase the flow of assistance either by claiming outright that more assistance would prevent the nation from falling to communism or by quietly reaching out to the East bloc.

The Revolution and a New U.S.-Bolivian Relationship

U.S. economic involvement in Bolivia during the revolution proved to be a new departure for U.S.–Latin American relations. Instead of using force, Washington turned to economic leverage to influence the revolution, in part because of the logistical difficulty of deploying the U.S. military to Bolivia. This restraint is striking for two reasons. First, the use of force had featured prominently in U.S. efforts to channel, constrain, or attempt to overthrow twentieth-century Latin American social revolutions whose leaders called for rapid, thoroughgoing social change, such as in the Mexican, Cuban, and Nicaraguan upheavals. In fact, the Good Neighbor Policy of the 1930s and 1940s, in which the United States formally pledged not to intervene in Latin America militarily, proved to be but a brief pause in the use of U.S. force in the hemisphere.[12] This pause ended when U.S.-backed paramilitary forces overthrew the constitutionally elected government of Guatemala in 1954.[13] Second, the Bolivian revolution, while unusually complex and sharply divided along ideological lines, had a strong radical, even communist, dimension to it, which made it the sort of revolution the United States most opposed.[14]

---

12. Bryce Wood, *The Dismantling of the Good Neighbor Policy* (Austin: University of Texas Press, 1985).

13. Publications on the Guatemalan intervention are numerous. See Stephen C. Schlesinger and Stephen Kinzer, *Bitter Fruit: The Untold Story of the American Coup in Guatemala*, rev. and expanded ed. (Cambridge: David Rockefeller Center for Latin American Studies, Harvard University Press, 2005); Richard Immerman, *The CIA in Guatemala* (Austin: University of Texas Press, 1982); and Kenneth Lehman, "Revolutions and Attributions: Making Sense of Eisenhower Administration Policies in Bolivia and Guatemala," *Diplomatic History* 21 (Spring 1997): 185–213.

14. Lehman, "Revolutions and Attributions," 192; Klein, *Bolivia*, 221–22.

Why did the United States eschew the use of force? Some interpretations of U.S.-Bolivian relations argue that when the United States realized that it could control the Bolivian revolution through economic means, it knew that force would not be necessary.[15] Some historians have also highlighted the role of Milton Eisenhower, the brother of President Eisenhower, who served as an important adviser to the president on Latin American affairs. According to this school of thought, Milton Eisenhower's well-publicized tour of South America from May 21, 1953, to June 6, 1953, proved instrumental for the Bolivians. During his Bolivian stop he met the new revolutionary leaders, who apparently convinced him that the revolution was something the United States should support. Other interpretations emphasize the decision of the leadership of the Movimiento Nacionalista Revolucionario (Nationalist Revolutionary Movement, MNR) to take a pro-U.S. stance.[16]

I argue that the policymakers avoided the use of force and opted for economic assistance because they thought that only through such assistance could they maintain a friendly regime in La Paz. Washington leaders feared that if the Bolivian revolutionary government fell, a government further to the left and even more hostile to U.S. interests would come to power.[17] The MNR, which started out as a social movement in the 1940s, coalesced as a political party with a broad coalition, from leftists to conservatives, by the early 1950s. Soon after the triumph of the revolution in 1952, Washington leaders realized that the MNR's victory was near total, and no other viable option remained to contest the revolutionaries. Although U.S. leaders disliked Bolivia's nationalist economic policies—the nationalization of the three largest mining companies into a state-run mining company, the Corporación Minera de Bolivia (COMIBOL)—there was little Washington could do about it.

---

15. Navia Ribera, *Los Estados Unidos y la revolución nacional*; Whitehead, *The United States and Bolivia*; John Stephen Zunes, "The United States and Bolivia: The Taming of a Revolution, 1952–1957," *Latin American Perspectives* 28 (September 2001): 33–49.

16. See Roque, *Los años del cóndor*, 291–312; Cole Blasier, *The Hovering Giant: U.S. Responses to Revolutionary Change in Latin America, 1910–1985*, 2nd ed. (Pittsburgh: University of Pittsburgh Press, 1986), 101–50; and James W. Wilkie, *The Bolivian Revolution and U.S. Aid Since 1952* (Los Angeles: Latin American Center, University of California, 1969), 8. For Milton Eisenhower's own view, see Milton Eisenhower, *The Wine Is Bitter: The United States and Latin America* (Garden City, N.Y.: Doubleday, 1963), 67–68. Kenneth Lehman emphasizes the pro-U.S. orientation of the revolution's leadership. Lehman, "Revolutions and Attributions," 189, 194.

17. Lehman, "Revolutions and Attributions"; Kamimura, "Liberal America and Revolution"; James F. Siekmeier, "'[T]he most generous assistance': U.S. Economic Aid to Guatemala and Bolivia, 1944–1959," *Journal of American and Canadian Studies* 11 (Spring 1994): 1–44.

Realizing, however, Washington's discomfort at the creation of COMIBOL, and desiring U.S. assistance, the MNR (at least its centrist, middle-class strain) worked to help solidify U.S. support for the regime.[18] These efforts help to explain the large distributions of U.S. aid to the nation during the revolution—Bolivia received the highest amount of U.S. government foreign assistance during the 1950s (measured in per capita terms).[19] U.S. policymakers quickly learned that the revolutionaries had a long list of economic needs, and the willingness of Bolivia's middle-class leadership to accept assistance (on behalf of the entire nation) gave Washington policymakers leverage over Bolivia's economic policy, which had a significant impact on Bolivian politics—U.S. aid gave the moderates the means to "deliver the goods" to their constituency, which strengthened their hold on the MNR and the country as a whole.

It is important that the MNR featured both centrist and left-wing groups. The centrist element (nearly all if its members were middle class) concentrated on national integration and economic diversification. The Left demanded *co-gobierno*—that labor should have a say in governance and in managing state-run industries and that labor leaders sit on the boards of state-run corporations—and were pressing hard for agrarian reform. The centrist leaders, however, proved adept at reminding U.S. officials that they shared the same assumptions regarding how Bolivia should develop economically—through private sector investment. The tacit message of the centrist leaders to Washington officials was that if they cut off assistance, the MNR might collapse. Given the atrophy of the cautious moderates and the severe reduction of the size of the military in the early revolutionary period, such a collapse would have very negative ramifications—from the perspective of Washington's "cold warriors." Centrist MNR leaders were fully cognizant that Washington feared that if the MNR collapsed, a radical regime hostile to the United States would take power in La Paz. To avoid that, Washington gave and gave generously.

18. Lehman, "Revolutions and Attributions," 198; Blasier, *Hovering Giant*, 132; James F. Siekmeier, "Trailblazer Diplomat: Víctor Andrade Uzquiano's Efforts to Influence U.S. Policy Towards Bolivia, 1944–1962," *Diplomatic History* 28 (June 2004): 385–405.

19. According to Statistics and Reports Division, Office of Programs and Policy Coordination, U.S. Agency for International Development (AID), *U.S. Overseas Loans and Grants: Obligations and Loan Authorizations* (Washington, D.C.: U.S. Government Printing Office, 1985), 41, the amount was $192.5 million for 1953–61. For a detailed quantitative analysis of the Bolivia aid program that focuses on the impact of U.S. economic aid on the Bolivian national budget, see Wilkie, *Bolivian Revolution and U.S. Aid*, 48. Wilkie says that the total aid given during this period was $198.2 million.

One important middle-class MNR leader, Víctor Andrade Uzquiano, Bolivia's ambassador to the United States at various times from 1944 to 1962, wanted U.S. aid and the policy changes that would come with it.[20] One prominent scholar of U.S.–Latin American relations has characterized Andrade as a "raconteur."[21] Indeed, his personal charm proved an important asset in his efforts to secure aid for the Bolivian government. However, I argue here that he was far more than a charming diplomat. He systematically used his abilities as a public speaker and behind-the-scenes negotiator, as well as his extensive knowledge of U.S. culture, to impress upon Washington officials the benefits of bulwarking the centrist elements of the MNR.[22]

By 1960, the middle-class leadership of the party had triumphed over the Left. Certainly U.S. power played a part, but one cannot discount Andrade's behind-the-scenes efforts. Although his actions reinforced preexisting tendencies among Washington officialdom, he proved to be a trailblazer when it came to Bolivian leaders influencing U.S. policy.

By the end of the 1950s, then, U.S. officials had exerted a significant degree of control over Bolivia's economic policy and helped to exacerbate already heightened political divisions in the nation.[23] When Bolivia entered a period of rapid inflation, in 1956, the United States, in tandem with the International Monetary Fund (IMF), threatened to cut off economic aid unless the Bolivians rescinded some of their nationalist economic policies, which were designed to control foreign economic activity and promote diversified economic development. Washington's policy in this regard marked a reversal: an earlier U.S.-sponsored mission, headed by Merwin Bohan in 1941–42, called for Bolivia to take measures to diversify its economy. The austerity plan of 1956–57 marked the first instance in which the IMF applied an austerity/stabilization program in the Third World. Washington leaders firmly believed that if they forced Bolivia to reduce the role of the state in the economy, foreign investment would flow in, thereby stimulating growth, and ultimately, benefiting all Bolivians. The MNR responded to this pressure by reducing its subsidies for government-run mining and oil and gas industries and shelving some, but not all, of its hydroelectric and economic diversification projects.[24]

---

20. He served as ambassador to the United States in 1944–46, 1952–58, and 1961–62.

21. Steven Rabe, *Eisenhower and Latin America: The Foreign Policy of Anticommunism* (Chapel Hill: University of North Carolina Press, 1988), 82.

22. Siekmeier, "Trailblazer Diplomat."

23. Dunkerley, *Rebellion in the Veins*, 85–87.

24. Catherine M. Conaghan, "Reconsidering Jeffery Sachs and the Bolivian Economic Experiment," in *Money Doctors, Foreign Debts, and Economic Reforms in Latin America: From*

U.S. pressure by the end of the 1950s, therefore, had prodded Bolivia to open itself up economically. The costs of this opening fell most heavily on the nation's working class and poor. The Left had feared increasing U.S. intervention in the nation since the beginning of the revolution. It sharply criticized Washington's role in slowing down the implementation of the goals of the revolution and stepped up its denunciations of the MNR's centrist wing. The centrists found themselves relying more and more on the Bolivian military to remain in power—a military that had become more powerful as U.S. military assistance (at the behest of the centrists) began to flow in 1958. The dependence of the centrists on the military only fueled the desire of the armed forces to rule the nation directly. The divisions between the left and centrist wings of the MNR paved the way for the military *golpe de estado* in 1964.

After the MNR: Changes in U.S.-Bolivian Relations

The military *golpe* brought fourteen years of democracy in Bolivia to a close, but not before dramatic, even irreversible, changes had occurred. Although Bolivia still remained largely dependent on the export of tin, the revolution had empowered new groups, attempts at economic diversification had taken place, and national integration had proceeded apace. In addition, U.S.-Bolivian ties had changed. The coup in Bolivia capped a process by which the centrists had solidified their power in Bolivia—and the United States had become more assertive in promoting pro-U.S. regimes in the region. By the late 1950s, the United States feared that the rise of nationalism in Latin America would lead to increasing anti-Americanism. Consequently, Washington took measures to attempt to jump-start economic growth in the region, and to dispense more foreign assistance.[25] While U.S. relations with the Paz Estensorro government were fairly close, by the mid-1960s Washington's ties with military governments in Latin America were tighter than U.S. ties with civilian governments, because Washington saw military governments as firmer

---

the 1890s to the Present, ed. Paul W. Drake (Wilmington, Del.: Scholarly Resources, 1989), 238–40; Siekmeier, "'[T]he most generous assistance,'" 31–37; John Stephen Zunes, "Decisions on Intervention: United States Responses to Third World Revolutionary Movements" (Ph.D. diss., Department of Government, Cornell University, 1990), 121–234.

25. James F. Siekmeier, *Aid, Nationalism, and Inter-American Relations: Guatemala, Bolivia, and the United States, 1945–1961* (Lewiston, N.Y.: Edwin Mellen Press, 1999), 345–83.

bulwarks against the spread of communism.[26] By 1964, with the coming to power of the Bolivian military, then, U.S.-Bolivian relations became more cordial.

But despite closer ties with the United States after 1964, Bolivia made it clear that Washington could not control Bolivia, and relations between the two countries eventually soured. In this context, sharply increased U.S. assistance gave Bolivian leaders more influence over U.S. policy than Andrade had exerted. While the United States did not control the nation in the 1950s, close working relationships between the MNR's middle-class leaders and Washington political leaders gave the United States at least the appearance of considerable control over Bolivian policy. After 1964, however, Washington leaders frequently agonized over their seemingly fruitless efforts to produce pro-U.S. stability in the South American nation. Bolivian officials understood Washington's terror regarding a possible collapse of Bolivia, which borders all of the major nations of South America's southern cone. Showing considerable political skill, Bolivian military leaders convinced Washington that economic and military aid was necessary to keep their nation from disintegrating. Such assistance flowed in record amounts in the 1960s as the Kennedy and Johnson administrations funneled military assistance to friendly Third World militaries in order to make them more effective counterinsurgency fighters. The military assistance to Bolivia—including funds for civic action programs and an internal security program directed at the Bolivian people—closely served Bolivian military interests.

By the 1969–71 period, Bolivia's connections with the United States swiftly and dramatically changed. Rising anti-American sentiment in Bolivia provoked crises that sent relations between the two nations to their lowest point in a generation or more. A lack of U.S. understanding of Bolivia's society and culture proved to be the crux of the problem.

Bolivia forced changes in U.S. policy in the late 1960s and early 1970s by nationalizing the holdings of a key U.S. company, Gulf Oil, and by expelling the U.S. Peace Corps. Expropriation was not a new problem in U.S.-Bolivian relations—Bolivia's expropriation of Standard Oil in 1937 roiled relations with Washington. However, the expulsion of a relatively

26. Joseph S. Tulchin, "The Promise of Progress: U.S. Relations with Latin America During the Administration of Lyndon B. Johnson," in *Lyndon Johnson Confronts the World: American Foreign Policy, 1963–1968*, ed. Warren I. Cohen and Nancy Bernkopf Tucker (Cambridge: Cambridge University Press, 1994), 211–44.

new player in the foreign policy arena, the Peace Corps, proved to be particularly interesting. This episode shows that U.S. officials did not understand Bolivian society and culture.

Bolivians tended to perceive the United States as generally insensitive toward Bolivian culture and saw the Peace Corps as a symbol of that insensitivity. Many Bolivians believed that the Peace Corps workers constituted an actual danger to Bolivian culture. For example, Peace Corps volunteers helped Bolivian government officials in (quietly) distributing various forms of birth control and instructed the recipients on how to use it. U.S. contraceptive policy combined in a volatile mix with rising anti-Yankee sentiment to produce the 1971 expulsion of the U.S. Peace Corps from the nation. Washington was unprepared for this assertive Bolivian reaction to U.S. policy. Popular protest in Bolivia was fueled by a fear that U.S. personnel were sterilizing Indian women (there was no solid evidence of this, however). This incident illustrates how rising anti-U.S. sentiment can affect the nexus between the United States and other nations—indeed, anti-Americanism was a staple of U.S. relations with Latin America in these years.[27] The end of the Peace Corps experiment in Bolivia also reveals that nations with very different cultures often have a hard time spanning their cultural differences. U.S. officials had little idea of the value Bolivians attached to their children; for many Bolivians, offspring are their only form of wealth. In addition, children are the only conveyors of history and culture in indigenous cultures with strong oral traditions.

The right-wing dictatorship of Hugo Bánzer Suarez (1971–78) represents a turning point in recent Bolivian history. First, Banzer slammed the brakes on the political and social reforms that flowed from the revolution. (Economic diversification proceeded apace, in part because of investments in infrastructure made since 1952.) Second, after 1971, relations between the United States and Bolivia warmed noticeably.[28] In part because of its continuing need for foreign investment funds to ensure its economic diversification, Bolivia, most notably in the 1980s and 1990s, increasingly accepted the U.S. argument that more foreign (most notably U.S.) investment was necessary for continued economic growth.

Studying the history of U.S.-Bolivian relations helps us understand a key aspect of U.S.–Latin American relations. All too often observers conclude that the United States dictates the terms of its relationships with the

27. Alan McPherson, ed., *Anti-Americanism in Latin America and the Caribbean* (New York: Berghahn Books, 2006).
28. Lehman, *Bolivia and the United States*, 147.

various countries of Latin America. However, it is important to understand that the Latin Americans also play an active role in the making of the inter-American relationship. Unquestionably, the United States used its considerable economic clout to force changes in Bolivia's economic policy. Nonetheless, Bolivia did not unquestioningly accept U.S. policy actions. In some instances, Bolivia managed to get U.S. officials to produce policy according to Bolivia's calculation of its interests. Because Bolivia has been a dependent nation for so long, the Bolivians have learned the ins and outs of being on the receiving end of a dependency relationship. They have used this knowledge to influence U.S. policy. In general, because the United States does not have a long history of dependency on a foreign power, Washington was not fully cognizant of how the dependent government in a patron-client relationship can subtly manipulate its more powerful benefactor. The U.S. lack of understanding in this regard, then, provided an opportunity for Bolivia to slant U.S.-Bolivian relations in a way favorable to Bolivia.

1

THE EARLY YEARS

In 1848, U.S. Secretary of State (and later president) James Buchanan instructed his chargé d'affaires to Bolivia, John Appleton, that "the enemies of free Government throughout the world point with satisfaction to the perpetual revolutions in the South American Republics. They hence argue that man is not fit for Self Government." Buchanan continued, "Liberty cannot be preserved without order; and this can only spring from a sacred observance of the law. So long as it shall be in the power of successive military chieftains to subvert the Governments of the Republics by the sword, their people cannot expect to enjoy the blessings of liberty." He concluded, "You will omit no opportunity of pressing these truths upon them, and of presenting to them the example of our own country, where all controversies are decided by the ballot box."[1]

Appleton was the first official representative of the United States to Bolivia; and Bolivia was the second-to-last (after Paraguay) Latin American nation upon which the United States had bestowed this honor.[2] Buchanan's instructions to him provide a rare insight into a key aspect of the motives of the U.S. government vis-à-vis Bolivia. In general, the United States viewed itself as the leader of the hemisphere and, since the declaration of the Monroe Doctrine in 1823, its chief defender against the imperialist powers of Europe. In the short run, the United States, because of its

---

1. Buchanan, quoted in James Dunkerley, "The United States and Latin America in the Long Run (1800–1945)," in *The United States and Latin America: The New Agenda*, ed. Victor Bulmer-Thomas and James Dunkerley (Cambridge: David Rockefeller Center for Latin America Studies, Harvard University Press, 1999), 3.

2. Lehman, *Bolivia and the United States*.

relatively weak military, could do little to prevent European expansion in the hemisphere. However, by the late nineteenth century the United States was rapidly expanding in terms of territory and commerce, and thus confidently viewed itself as the only nation with the ability and political desire to promote what it concluded was the proper economic and political development it thought that the rest of the Americas, among them Bolivia, needed to pursue.[3] By the early twentieth century the United States was attempting to dictate the boundaries of acceptable political and economic behavior not only to Bolivia, but to the hemisphere as a whole. Before World War II, the United States saw Bolivia first as a source of raw materials (principally strategic minerals) and, second, as a nation in need of political and economic reform. Officials in Washington wanted Bolivian leaders to embrace a free-market system open to outside foreign investment and trade and a liberal (in the nineteenth-century sense) democracy that modeled itself on the U.S. political system.[4]

U.S. investors were primarily interested in the mineral-rich mountains in the western portion of the nation, where the bulk of the population had lived since before the days of the Inca. American travelers in the region, such as U.S. citizen and adventurer Lardner Gibbon, viewed Bolivia's inhabitants as racially inferior to whites from North America or Europe and thus lacking both the will and wherewithal to exploit Bolivia's potentially vast resources. The British were also interested in Bolivia's economic potential, in particular in mining. J. B. Pentland's report of 1827 outlines in remarkable detail the vast potential of Bolivia's mines if they could attract significant foreign investment.[5]

---

3. Richard Hofstadter noted that many Americans view their past in very rosy terms: "American history, presenting itself as a rich and rewarding spectacle, a succession of well-fulfilled promises, induces a desire to observe and enjoy, not to analyze and act." *The American Political Tradition* (New York: Knopf, 1948), v.

4. The classic study of U.S. government attempts to shape foreign nations in the image of the United States is Robert A. Packenham, *Liberal America and the Third World* (Princeton: Princeton University Press, 1973). A more recent study of U.S. attempts to mold Third World (in particular Latin American) nations in the image of the United States is Michael E. Latham, *Modernization as Ideology: American Social Science and "Nation-Building" in the Kennedy Era* (Chapel Hill: University of North Carolina Press, 2000).

5. Lardner Gibbon, quoted in Lehman, *Bolivia and the United States*, 180. For overviews of Bolivian history, see Klein, *Bolivia*, and J. Valerie Fifer, *Bolivia: Land, Location, and Politics Since 1825* (Cambridge: Cambridge University Press, 1972). For an overview of mining in the early twentieth century, see Manuel E. Contreras C., *The Bolivian Tin Mining Industry in the First Half of the 20th Century* (London: Institute of Latin American Studies, University of London, 1993). During the nineteenth century, about 75 percent of Bolivia's population consisted of indigenous peoples. J. B. Pentland's "Report on Bolivia, 1827," edited by J. Valerie Fifer, can be found in the Camden Fourth Series, volume 13, pages 169–267, which is in volume 25 of *Camden Miscellany* (London: Royal Historical Society, 1974).

Visions of Economic Modernization

By the late nineteenth century, the United States was investing more in Bolivia than Britain was. This shift in the pattern of investment reflected the shifting power relations between Britain and the United States in the Western Hemisphere.[6] U.S.-British competition came to a head in 1894–95 when a controversy erupted over the boundary between Venezuela and British Guyana. Citing the Monroe Doctrine, but asserting a hemispheric police power not found in the original version of that statement of U.S. policy toward the Western Hemisphere, U.S. leaders used the threat of force to compel the British to send the dispute to an arbitration board friendly to U.S. interests. As a result, the boundary dispute was settled in Venezuela's favor.[7]

As British power in the hemisphere waned, U.S. influence grew. U.S. investment proved extremely important in the development of Bolivia's infrastructure and—later—the petroleum industry.[8] The presidency of Ismael Montes (1904–9 and 1913–17) represented an important turning point in that Bolivia would intensify its search for foreign loans. In 1906, loans from the United States (not Britain) allowed Bolivia to complete rail connections between a number of Bolivian cities, and even with Peru.[9]

Both Bolivian and U.S. elites shared dreams of economic modernization by means of foreign lending. Unfortunately, the dreams turned to nightmares in only two decades. In 1908, Bolivia had virtually no foreign debt. By 1927, it had $40 million of foreign debt and was struggling to make the interest payments on that mountain of obligations.[10]

---

6. Symbolic of Britain's loss of influence in Bolivia was the (probably apocryphal) story of one British ambassador John Lloyd, whom President Manuel Belzú expelled from the country by having him tied backward to the back of a mule and driven out of La Paz in 1853. See James Dunkerley, *Americana: The Americas in the World Around 1850 (or "Seeing the Elephant" as the Theme for an Imaginary Western)* (London: Verso, 2000), 454n24.

7. Walter LaFeber, "The Evolution of the Monroe Doctrine from Monroe to Reagan," in *Redefining the Past: Essays in Diplomatic History in Honor of William Appleman Williams*, ed. Lloyd C. Gardner (Corvallis: Oregon State University Press, 1986), 121–41.

8. Lehman, *Bolivia and the United States*, 66–67, 70. Lehman makes the important point that British and U.S. influence overlapped in key ways—for instance, increasingly in the late nineteenth and early twentieth centuries, U.S. financiers funded the British companies that built many of Bolivia's railroads.

9. Herbert Klein, *A Concise History of Bolivia* (Cambridge: Cambridge University Press, 2003), 162. For a detailed analysis of the 1906 loan, see Hans Huber Abendroth et al., *La deuda externa de Bolivia: 125 años de renegociaciones y ¿cuántos más?* (La Paz: Centro de Estudios para el Desarollo Laboral y Agrario, 2001), 95–99.

10. Margaret A. Marsh, *Bankers in Bolivia: A Study of Foreign Investment* (1928; repr., New York: Vanguard, 1970), 90.

Economics, however, was not the only motive behind U.S. policy toward Bolivia in the early twentieth century. Washington leaders, imbued with a sense of mission, dreamed of reforming aspects of the governmental and economic systems of Latin America, including Bolivia's. Bolivia was the subject of an early attempt by the U.S. government to promote economic and political reforms in a handful of Latin American nations. For Bolivia's part, it decided, in order to spur infrastructure development, to avail itself of what one author has termed an "El Dorado that had been found on Wall Street."[11] However, in order to receive loans, the Bolivian government needed the imprimatur of the dean of what a future generation would call "developmental economics," Edwin Kemmerer. One of the most prominent economists of his day, Kemmerer traveled to Bolivia to prod the Bolivian leadership to implement reforms that would theoretically increase the confidence of foreign investors in the Bolivian economy.[12] Although Kemmerer's visit did not result in significant reforms, the mere fact that he made the visit instilled confidence in foreign investors who probably would not have invested in Bolivia otherwise.[13]

Beset by financial crises, the Bolivian leadership made the calculation that accepting the mission would be in its interests. Bolivia's acceptance of Kemmerer's assistance bespoke its overall foreign policy toward the United States. Bolivia saw its relationship with the United States as that of a client with a patron, with themselves on the receiving end.[14] The Bolivian leadership surmised that the quickest path to economic development was through working with U.S. officials, who in turn would smooth the way toward future U.S. private sector investment in their country.

As in much of the rest of the region, financial crises evolved into political crises in the 1930s. Bolivia provoked a war against Paraguay in 1932

---

11. Frederick B. Pike, *The United States and the Andean Republics; Peru, Bolivia, and Ecuador* (Cambridge: Harvard University Press, 1977), 197.

12. Robert N. Seidel, "American Reformers Abroad: The Kemmerer Missions in South America, 1923–1931," in *Money Doctors, Foreign Debts, and Economic Reforms in Latin America from the 1890s to the Present*, ed. Paul Drake (Wilmington, Del.: Scholarly Resources, 1994), 85–109; Barry Eichengreen, "House Calls of the Money Doctor: The Kemmerer Missions to Latin America, 1917–1931," in Drake, *Money Doctors*, 110–31.

13. Emily S. Rosenberg and Norman L. Rosenberg, "From Colonialism to Professionalism: The Public Private Dynamic in United States Foreign Financial Advising, 1898–1929," in *Money Doctors, Foreign Debts, and Economic Reforms in Latin America from the 1890s to the Present*, ed. Paul Drake (Wilmington, Del.: Scholarly Resources, 1994), 76.

14. Glen Rotchin, *The Clientelist State and International Patronage: The Case of Revolutionary Bolivia, 1952–1964* (Geneva: Institut Universitaire de Hautes Études Internationales, 1994), 1–45, describes patron-client relations as informal, mutually beneficial, voluntaristic, and unequal.

over a boundary dispute—the Chaco War. The war, which lasted for three years, turned into one of the biggest debacles in Bolivian history. The country lost about one-third of its territory and suffered psychological wounds that would not heal for decades. A number of Bolivians faulted the United States for not making an effort to prevent Bolivia's loss of territory in the peace settlement.[15]

The relationship between Bolivia and the United States in the years before 1952 proves to be an interesting prelude to their future relations.[16] The entente between the United States and the Bolivian revolutionaries in 1952 was not the culmination of years of harmonious relations. On the contrary, relations between the United States and Bolivia were rocky in the years leading up to 1952, primarily because U.S. leaders aimed to suppress economic nationalism in Bolivia, and Bolivia resisted, with some success, the attempts by the United States to shape its economic development in the way that Washington thought best.

Economic Nationalism and U.S.-Bolivian Relations

Economic nationalism was a set of policies that aimed to assert state control over some sectors of the economy to stimulate their development. Latin American economic nationalists wanted to grant the state greater authority in economic policy decision-making to ensure that foreign investors did not disproportionately benefit from the exploitation of the nation's resources.[17] In addition, these nationalists advocated increased economic self-sufficiency. They believed that economic self-sufficiency would insulate a country's domestic economy from the vicissitudes of the world marketplace and pave the way for diversifying the economy, which would lead to long-term prosperity and economic power.[18]

Such ideas had deep roots in Latin America. One important and early manifestation of Latin American economic nationalism flowed from the

---

15. The U.S. government's reluctant participation in the peace process is described in Bruce W. Farcau, *The Chaco War: Bolivia and Paraguay, 1932–1935* (New York: Praeger, 1996), III, 200, 234.

16. For a good overview of Bolivia's foreign policy from 1936 to 1946, see Emmett James Holland, "A Historical Study of Bolivian Foreign Relations, 1935–1946" (Ph.D. diss., American University, 1967).

17. David Green, *The Containment of Latin America* (Chicago: Quadrangle, 1971), 35.

18. Robert H. Swansbrough, *The Embattled Colossus: Economic Nationalism and United States Investors in Latin America* (Gainesville: University of Florida Press, 1976), 11.

pen of Carlos Calvo, an Argentine diplomat and scholar of international law. Between 1868 and 1896, he worked out what came to be known as the Calvo Doctrine. It stated that no foreign national could call upon his own government to intercede on his behalf in a dispute with the host country.[19] Foreign nationals, according to Calvo, had no right to invoke "extraterritoriality," which allowed them to seek redress under their home country's legal system.[20]

Latin American economic nationalism hurt U.S. economic interests, which were based on access to Latin American raw materials and the search for markets and investments in the region. Not surprisingly, an important theme of U.S.–Latin American relations in the twentieth century is the attempt by the United States to limit economic nationalism in Latin America. In addition to ensuring U.S. access to raw materials, suppressing economic nationalism also helped to ensure that Latin America's economic development would be open to outside (in particular U.S.) private sector investment and trade. Maintaining private sector investment and trade was very important to both the U.S. government and U.S. businessmen as the presence of U.S. multinational corporations in Latin America became much more pronounced in the early twentieth century. (Standard Oil of New Jersey moved into Bolivia in 1921.) The growth of U.S. economic power in the region was abetted by growing U.S. (private sector) loans there. Between 1914 and 1929, U.S. loans to Latin America grew from $350 million to $1.5 billion.[21]

But quashing economic nationalism was important for another reason. It gave the United States a degree of control over the development of Latin America. Washington used that control to attempt to promote its own ideology with regard to stimulating economic prosperity. Policymakers thought that only private sector growth could provide enough resources for a growing population and the increasing expectations among the Latin Americans for a better standard of living. By suppressing economic nationalism, the United States could export its products, but also its way of life. Since U.S. leaders saw their way of life as superior, suppressing economic nationalism was part of the U.S. mission of promoting sound government and what it saw as rational policies in the region.[22]

19. Ibid., 54.
20. Robert Freeman Smith, *The United States and Revolutionary Nationalism in Mexico, 1916–1932* (Chicago: University of Chicago Press, 1972), 27.
21. Thomas F. O'Brien, *The Century of U.S. Capitalism in Latin America* (Albuquerque: University of New Mexico Press, 1999), 45.
22. Thomas F. O'Brien, *Making the Americas: The United States and Latin America from the Age of Revolutions to the Era of Globalization* (Albuquerque: University of New Mexico

Thus suppressing economic nationalism was a key part of U.S. policy toward Bolivia. U.S. leaders saw economic nationalism as counterproductive: an unwarranted governmental intrusion into the economy, inhibiting the marketplace's determination of where the free flow (or at least freer flow) of trade and investment would go.[23] The only way for Latin America to prosper, the argument went, was for it to make itself a friendly environment for foreign capital. Therefore, Washington policymakers concluded, Latin American leaders needed to stimulate private sector growth through participation in a hemispheric economic system where the Latin Americans would sell raw materials and partly assembled goods to the North Americans and use the foreign exchange earned to further industrialize their countries.[24]

The view from the South was different. Economic nationalism, as in the rest of the Latin America, had for many years been a staple of Bolivian policy. During his brief presidency, from May 1936 to July 1937, General José David Toro Ruilova nationalized the U.S. holdings of the Standard Oil Company in Bolivia. Toro was part of an increasingly important group of "military socialist" leaders whose politics had been forged in the dual crucibles of the Great Depression and the Chaco War. Not only had the Great Depression soured many in Latin America (in particular in Bolivia) on the benefits of export-led capitalistic growth; many observers in Bolivia thought that rivalry over possibly rich oil reserves in the Gran Chaco had caused oil companies to spur on the antagonists in the Chaco War. (The evidence for this position is thin, but the idea was widely held at the time.) Toro's nationalization preceded the much better known Mexican nationalization of its foreign oil companies' assets the following year.[25]

A good summary of Bolivia's policy during the 1930s through the early 1950s would be that it attempted to maintain its traditional economic nationalist policies in the face of U.S. opposition, while carefully maintaining and nurturing its clientelistic relationship with the United States. However, economic nationalism in Bolivia intensified in the late 1940s and

Press, 2007), 87. See also Emily S. Rosenberg, *Financial Missionaries to the World: The Politics and Culture of Dollar Diplomacy, 1900–1930* (Cambridge: Harvard University Press, 1999).

23. Michael Krenn, in his *Economic Nationalism in Latin America* (Wilmington, Del.: Scholarly Resources, 1990), provides a good survey of U.S. attempts to quash economic nationalism in Latin America in the early twentieth century. See also Green, *Containment of Latin America,* for the 1940s, and Siekmeier, *Aid, Nationalism, and Inter-American Relations,* who takes the argument up through the 1950s.

24. Secretary of State Elihu Root, quoted in *Papers Relating to the Foreign Relations of the United States* (hereafter *FRUS*), *1906,* vol. 2, "Venezuela," 1456–65. See also Emily Rosenberg, *Spreading the American Dream: American Economic and Cultural Expansion, 1890–1945* (New York: Hill and Wang, 1982).

25. Malloy, *Bolivia: The Uncompleted Revolution,* 94.

early 1950s to such a degree it helped to cause a significant rupture in Bolivian history—the 1952 revolution—a rupture that reshaped the traditional patron-client relationship.

Two attempts by the United States to suppress Bolivian economic nationalism and foster a model of economic development amenable to U.S. interests are especially important for understanding Bolivia's relationship to the United States in the 1930s and 1940s. The first, just mentioned, involved what many Bolivians considered the national patrimony: oil. In the late 1930s Bolivia expropriated the holdings of Standard Oil. The second case—which flowed from the expropriation—was an early attempt at economic diversification, the Bolivia Development Corporation (Corporación Boliviana de Fomento, CBF), formed in 1942.

In March 1937 the government of Bolivia, headed by General José David Toro Ruilova, expropriated the Bolivian holdings of Standard Oil of New Jersey. After requesting compensation for the expropriation from the Bolivian government, Standard Oil asked the State Department if it would demand indemnification. The State Department pressured the Bolivians to compensate the company by attempting to prevent the Bolivians from exporting oil abroad by notifying potential buyers, especially the Argentines, that the U.S. government was unhappy with Bolivia's expropriation. In addition, the State Department delayed U.S. Export-Import Bank loans to Bolivia.[26]

The Bolivians and the oil company disagreed over the terms of an agreement for over four and a half years. At first, the State Department refused to argue Standard Oil's case with the Bolivians. By 1941 both sides felt the impasse had dragged on long enough; moreover, the clouds of war in Europe helped to push the two countries to reach an agreement. Although the timing of the eventual agreement—January 1942—can be partially explained by the U.S. entry into World War II, the main reason the disputants resolved their differences was that the United States wanted to foster a propitious climate for foreign investment in Bolivia and the Bolivians were interested in economic aid from the *norteamericanos*. The State Department offered Bolivia $25 million in economic aid, if Bolivia would break off relations with the Axis powers and indemnify Standard Oil for its losses. Although Standard Oil had estimated the value of its holdings

---

26. The Export-Import Bank, set up in 1934, was a U.S. government agency that lent funds to U.S. companies that exported products overseas or invested in foreign nations. Navia Ribera, *Los Estados Unidos y la revolución nacional*, 44–45.

to be around $17 million, Bolivia offered $1.5 million to the oil company.[27] While Washington leaders quietly urged Standard Oil businessmen to accept Bolivia's indemnity, U.S. officials exerted more pressure on the Bolivian leadership. U.S foreign policymakers made it clear that an indemnity had to be paid for Bolivia to receive the assistance: State Department officers stated that they "made known to important political circles in Bolivia . . . that this government expects the cooperation to be unqualifiedly bilateral."[28]

In a narrow sense, the agreement represented a quid pro quo. By promising to "cooperate" with U.S. officials, Bolivian officials were tacitly agreeing to curtail future expressions of economic nationalism—such as expropriations—in exchange for economic assistance.[29] More broadly and fundamentally, the economic aid granted to Bolivia constituted the first time Washington granted a significant amount of economic aid, or aid for economic development, to a nation in the developing world.[30] From this point forward, Bolivian requests of assistance, and U.S. assistance projects, would be an integral (if not the most important) part of the U.S.-Bolivian relationship.

U.S. Economic Assistance and the Bolivian Development Corporation

The assistance was not only significant with regard to the relationship between the United States and its poorer Andean "neighbor." The aid was a means of implementing a key component of U.S. policy toward the entire

---

27. Chargé Dawson to the Secretary of State, February 2, 1942, *FRUS, 1942*, vol. 5, *American Republics*, 520–25. For more on Bolivia's indemnity, see Bryce Wood, *The Making of the Good Neighbor Policy* (New York: Columbia University Press, 1961), 197–98. The U.S. aid was in the form of technical assistance—U.S. experts would help Bolivia exploit its resources more efficiently. Donald W. Rowland, *History of the Office of the Coordinator of Inter-American Affairs* (Washington, D.C.: U.S. Government Printing Office, 1947), 18.

28. State Department official, quoted in Wood, *The Making of the Good Neighbor Policy*, 196.

29. In addition to receiving assistance, Bolivia was not required to make payments on bonds sold to U.S investors that the Bolivians had defaulted on. One U.S. official estimated the amount defaulted on was around $100 million. Minister Jenkins to the Secretary of State, April 4, 1941, *FRUS, 1941*, vol. 6, *American Republics*, 468–74.

30. This is due in part to the historical context in which the aid was given—World War II. Latin America, during the war, was seen as an important source of raw materials. In late 1941, U.S. officials began to draw up a blueprint for technical assistance to Latin America. U.S. officials wanted Latin American efforts to stimulate the production of raw materials and foodstuffs for the war effort and to produce "items for which there was a possible market in the United States or the other American republics." Rowland, *History of the Office*, 18.

region—the policy of thwarting or at least limiting economic nationalism. It is interesting and telling that the aid was granted in exchange for compensation for an expropriation of a foreign industry's assets and a Bolivian promise it would accept a policy of "cooperation." "Cooperation" is a vague term. Most prominently, it meant that Bolivia would not pursue economic nationalistic policies.

The economic aid was used to help stimulate the economic development—in particular the economic diversification—of the country. This was the second attempt by the United States to suppress Bolivian economic nationalism and foster a model of economic development amenable to U.S. interests, and it was carried out under the auspices of the CBF.[31] The CBF was established at the recommendation of the U.S. Economic Mission, or Bohan Mission, a team of economists headed by U.S. economist Merwin Bohan that went to Bolivia in late 1941 to study the economic problems of the country and devise a solution to them. The Bohan Mission focused mainly on the economic problems of Bolivia and did not, generally, confront the political problems.[32] In its report, the Bohan Mission described Bolivia as a resource-rich country that was hard-pressed to feed its relatively small population, but ignored the main reason for this condition, the fact that Bolivia had an archaic, perhaps even feudal, agricultural system where a small group of elite owned the vast majority of the land, which was tended mostly by unpaid laborers, some of whom were tied to the land through debt peonage.

The report of the Bohan Mission discussed the need for economic diversification and development in Bolivia, specifically how Bolivia could reduce its imports and stimulate its exports. Further, it argued that agricultural production needed to be stimulated as well—this included increased irrigation—and concluded that Bolivia could no longer afford to spend valuable foreign exchange to import food.[33] The report also argued that Bolivia should avoid allocating government resources (loans or subsidies) to increase metals exports—it needed to broaden its economic base somewhat. This, however, seems to contradict the central tenet behind Bohan's recommendations—that for Bolivia to further develop economically it needed to generate foreign exchange.

31. The agreement outlining the CBF can be found in Undersecretary of State Sumner Welles to Bolivian foreign minister Arce Matienzo, January 27, 1942, *FRUS 1942*, vol. 5, *American Republics*, 592–95.
32. Siekmeier, *Aid, Nationalism, and Inter-American Relations*, 230–31.
33. La Corporación Boliviana de Fomento, *La Corporación Boliviana de Fomento: Sus orígenes, organización y actividad* (La Paz: n.p., 1943), 14–15 (hereafter "La Corporación" with appropriate page numbers).

The Bohan Report stressed that economic development projects needed to ultimately create foreign exchange for Bolivia's economy. After all, the projects were to be funded by U.S. loans that Bolivia would eventually have to repay; therefore, the projects sponsored by any development plan had to generate dollars. For example, petroleum was a key sector—oil exports would bring in foreign exchange. The conclusion of the report noted that although there were a number of projects that would benefit Bolivia, these should not be funded by the CBF. The U.S. assistance money should only fund projects that could directly produce foreign exchange. In other words, the CBF would not fund industrial projects producing goods that could not compete in world markets. The upshot was that Bolivia should, therefore, focus on agricultural exports, with a lower terms of trade than industrial exports.[34]

The U.S. ambassador to Bolivia stated that the "success or failure [of the CBF] . . . is one of the most important factors affecting . . . future relations between the United States and Bolivia, and it accordingly behooves the United States to assist the Corporation in every way possible."[35] The CBF's projects—funded by U.S. assistance—all had to be approved by top U.S. officials. Although the Bolivian government had the power to choose half of the directorate that ran the CBF, Bolivia's control over CBF was minimal because of the requirement for U.S. approval—through the Export-Import Bank—of its projects.[36]

The CBF focused on road building, oil production, agricultural production, and health and sanitation projects. The CBF failed for two reasons. First, it was never very large; it "operat[ed] with exceedingly small capital," in the words of the U.S. ambassador, never growing very much beyond the $25 million it had at the beginning of its existence.[37] Second, U.S. money went into only two of its many projects—the construction of the Cochabamba–Santa Cruz highway and the development of the petroleum sector. The highway consumed two-fifths of the CBF's initial budget. The highway was necessary, according to U.S. officials, for the future diversification of the Bolivian economy away from metals toward increased production and export of agricultural products. The highway would open up

---

34. Ibid., 28.
35. Ambassador Walter Thurston to Bolivia to the Secretary of State, May 10, 1945, Decimal File 824.50/5-1045, Record Group (hereafter RG) 59, Department of State Central Files, Records of the Department of State (hereafter DOS Central Files), National Archives and Records Administration (hereafter NA).
36. La Corporación, 25–27.
37. Ambassador Robert Flack to Secretary of State, January 17, 1948, *FRUS, 1947*, vol. 8, *American Republics*, 343.

the fertile agricultural lands of the Oriente to increased private foreign investment in that region.[38] In addition, the State Department used the control it obtained through funding the oil sector to attempt to open up oilfields to private sector exploitation. This would necessarily reduce the power of the national oil monopoly, the Yacimientos Petrolíferos Fiscales Bolivianos (YPFB), itself a form of economic nationalism. The Bolivians had nationalized the oil industry to increase the benefit the nation obtained from its oil reserves. After the initial loan in 1943 to the YPFB, the State Department decided that future loans would be contingent on "tangible evidence of their willingness to allow private enterprise to assist in the development of their petroleum resources."[39]

The CBF never fulfilled its promise of promoting Bolivian development. The agricultural component, funded only by Bolivian government resources, suffered greatly because of disputes between U.S. and Bolivian officials. Regarding agriculture, the CBF favored projects to increase sugar, rice, and wheat production.[40] In general, U.S. priorities lay in sectors that would simultaneously provide raw materials for its economy and foreign exchange for Bolivia's coffers—mining and oil. In addition, U.S. officials stated that before experimental stations to promote agriculture were set up in the countryside to dispense technical assistance to farmers, Bolivia needed to repeal laws that prohibited the export of wild rubber clones (buds or cuttings). According to a State Department memo, the repeal was a "prerequisite to economic collaboration on the part of the United States and the Corporation."[41] Indeed, in 1942, an agreement was reached in which the Bolivian government would sell to the U.S. government's Rubber Reserve its *entire production,* except for what was needed domestically.[42]

Gualberto Villarroel and U.S.-Bolivian Relations

U.S. leaders might have used the CBF not only to develop the Bolivian economy, but also to build political and diplomatic capital as well. The

38. Ambassador Walter Thurston to DOS, "Setting up of Bolivian Development Corporation," February 19, 1945, Decimal File 824.5012-1945, RG 59, DOS Central Files, NA.
39. Acting Secretary of State to Embassy in Bolivia, November 9, 1948, FRUS, 1948, vol. 9, American Republics, 335–36.
40. La Corporación, 17–19.
41. Ambassador Walter Thurston to Department of State, "Setting up of Bolivian Development Corporation," February 19, 1945, Decimal File 824.5012-1945, RG 59, DOS Central Files, NA.
42. U.S. Office of Inter-American Affairs, *Activities of the Coordinator of Inter-American Affairs in Bolivia* (Washington, D.C.: U.S. Government Printing Office, 1943), 5. Not only was

political capital could have proven useful in future crises, which soon racked U.S.-Bolivian relations. In December 1943 a military junta, headed by General Gualberto Villarroel, took power. The junta was backed by a nationalist revolutionary civilian coalition, the Movimiento Nacionalista Revolucionario (Revolutionary Nationalist Movement, MNR). The MNR was started by urban middle- and upper-middle-class intellectuals who argued that Bolivia was not reaping sufficient benefit from its tin mines. The MNR was anti-oligarchy and pro-labor. It aimed to increase the income earned through tin exports by restricting supply in order to raise the price of the metal.[43] MNR members held three leadership positions in the new government.[44]

Historians differ on why Washington was concerned about the new regime. One historian, Cole Blasier, argues that fears of Nazism or, in general, of the Bolivian regime's supposed pro-Axis stance caused Washington to withhold recognition of the Villarroel regime.[45] Another, David Green, agrees that U.S. and British leaders attempted to brand the MNR as Nazi, but the real concern of U.S. officials was the specter of simultaneously fewer and more expensive tin exports.[46] The carefully constructed British plot, which included a forged letter sent to a top Bolivian official, to brand the MNR as Nazi was quite successful in mobilizing world opinion against the new government; however, careful research by R. A. Humphreys has revealed that the United States did know that the British letter was false and knew the MNR's contacts with the Axis were minimal or nonexistent.[47] Even as Secretary of State Cordell Hull believed that Nazi influence in the new Bolivia regime was significant, the majority of top Latin American experts in the U.S. government disagreed.[48] The U.S. concern with the new regime was therefore most likely based on fears of economic nationalism and a fear of limited access to tin supplies.

---

the rubber useful for the U.S. war effort, it would keep the critical material out of the hands of the Axis. The Coordinator of the Office of Inter-American Affairs noted, "It has been reported that large quantities of rubber are going from Bolivia into Argentina and thence to Germany" (ibid., 6).

43. James M. Malloy, "Revolutionary Politics," in *Beyond the Revolution: Bolivia Since 1952*, ed. James M. Malloy and Richard S. Thorn (Pittsburgh: University of Pittsburgh Press, 1971), 115.

44. Klein, *Bolivia*, 218.

45. Blasier, *Hovering Giant*, 48–49.

46. Green, *Containment of Latin America*, 149–50.

47. R. A. Humphreys, *Latin America and the Second World War*, vol. 1, 1939–1942 (London: Athlone Press, 1981), 132.

48. Max Paul Friedman, *Nazis and Good Neighbors: The United States Campaign Against the Germans of Latin America During World War II* (New York: Cambridge University Press, 2003), 127–34.

Washington refused to recognize the new regime until the members of the MNR in the new government were removed—and because of Hull's paranoia about Nazis in Latin America, the eighty-one Axis nationals in Bolivia were expelled.[49] The Bolivian government conceded, and Washington extended recognition in June 1944. A short-term victory for the United States in its relations with Bolivia soured Washington's relationship with the rest of the hemisphere. In 1930, President Herbert Hoover, as part of an attempt to improve United States relations with Latin America, had disavowed the U.S. use of nonrecognition to force concessions from Latin American nations. (Hoover's decision represented an important origin of the much-touted Good Neighbor Policy, Franklin Roosevelt's set of initiatives to improve U.S.–Latin American relations.) The significance of reviving nonrecognition as a form of Yankee intervention was not lost on the Latin Americans.[50]

This worsening of U.S.-Bolivian relations exacerbated Bolivian frustrations with the CBF. The CBF was plagued by fundamental differences with the United States about policy, such as the restriction on raw rubber exports already mentioned. Moreover, its effectiveness was reduced by the reluctance of the Export-Import Bank to approve projects proposed by the Bolivians. To make matters worse, the U.S. Embassy and CBF officials differed over CBF policy. Moreover, a number of the managers were accused of incompetence—in the words of one U.S. Embassy official, the CBF was "a receptacle for political hacks and has-beens."[51] The CBF had pretty much ceased to function effectively by the time of the 1952 revolution.

Although the CBF experiment was not successful, it was reflective of a broader U.S. goal—a goal shared by Bolivia's leaders and many if not most of its elites. Bolivian and U.S. policymakers aimed to prevent radicalism from mushrooming in Bolivia by coming up with policies that would enhance economic growth, such as the CBF. However, an examination of the profound social roots of revolution in Bolivia reveals that even if the CBF had successfully stimulated significant economic growth, the resulting prosperity would not have blunted the rise of radicalism in the late 1940s and early 1950s.

---

49. Siekmeier, *Aid, Nationalism, and Inter-American Relations*, 66–67; Friedman, *Nazis and Good Neighbors*, 130–31. There were fifty-two Germans expelled, and twenty Japanese.

50. Friedman, *Nazis and Good Neighbors*, 128–29, 134.

51. Quoted in Kenneth Duane Lehman, "U.S. Foreign Aid and Revolutionary Nationalism in Bolivia, 1952–1964: The Pragmatics of a Patron-Client Relationship" (Ph.D. diss., University of Texas, 1992), 239.

Nonelite Political Actors: *Campesinos* and Labor

The Bohan Report analyzed a number of economic problems faced by Bolivia's nonelite majority. During the 1930s and 1940s, this nonelite majority began to make demands for improved material well-being. As a result, Bolivia experienced years of rapid social change leading up to the 1952 revolution. During those decades, Bolivia was sparsely populated, and native peoples were in the majority. According to the 1940 census, only 3.5 million people lived in South America's fifth-largest nation in terms of land area. Of them, 54 percent were of native extraction, 32 percent were *mestizos*, or mixed-blood persons, with the remaining 14 percent being white or of other races.[52] Although most views of the Bolivian revolution focus on its leaders, I focus on the actions of the nonelite majority—the *campesinos* and other subaltern classes.[53]

From the 1940s through the 1950s, the views of Bolivian workers and *campesinos* of the state passed through several stages. Before the 1952 revolution, the working classes continuously struggled against the central government, generally seeing it as an oppressive sovereign. During the first four years of the revolution, however, between 1952 and 1956, the subaltern classes dramatically shifted their attitudes and actions toward their erstwhile oppressor. This was because the revolutionary government, the Movimiento Nacionalista Revolucionario (MNR), supported their class interests in some ways, which caused labor, in particular, and peasant groups, to a lesser extent, to support the MNR. The MNR was happy to include labor and the peasantry in its fold—it would give the MNR leadership a degree of control over these groups.

The best way to understand the relationship between the subaltern and the state is to examine how at times the nonelite classes have resisted the state and how, at other times, these groups have negotiated with the power structure to pursue a more robust application of civil rights and achieve improvements in their economic well-being.[54] In the example of Bolivia,

---

52. U.S. Office of Inter-American Affairs, *Activities of the Coordinator of Inter-American Affairs in Bolivia*, iv.

53. Malloy, *Bolivia: The Uncompleted Revolution;* Frontaura Argandoña, *La revolución nacional.* For the intellectual roots of the revolution, see Charles Arnade, "The United States and the Ultimate Roots of the Bolivian Revolution," *Historia: Publicación Bianual del Capítulo Beta Delta de la Sociedad Nacional Honoria de Historia, Phi Alpha Theta* 1, no. 1 (January 1962): 35–49.

54. See Gilbert M. Joseph and Daniel Nugent, eds., *Revolution and the Negotiation of Rule in Modern Mexico* (Durham: Duke University Press, 1999). Another example of a Mexican analysis is Jennie Purnell, *Popular Movements and State Formation in Revolutionary Mex-*

the popular sectors forcefully pressured the state when it seemed unresponsive to their entreaties, yet cooperated with the state when they saw an opening and thought it would be receptive to their demands.[55]

To more fully understand the crucial turns in the relations between the subaltern classes and the central government in the 1940s and 1950s, it is necessary to review events of the Depression years. Although there was significant peasant unrest in the first decades of the twentieth century, a starting point is the previously mentioned Chaco War.[56] To say that the war killed approximately 2 percent of the collective population of its antagonists, Bolivia and Paraguay, dues not begin to scratch the surface of the social and political earthquake it provoked in Bolivia.[57] Bolivia's disastrous loss to Paraguay created significant reverberations throughout the country. Of special importance, the assignment of young and middle-aged men to the battlefront meant that there were fewer people in the villages to protect the large landholders' interests. As a consequence, poor *campesinos* began to express—at the village and state levels—long-repressed grievances regarding their living and working conditions. Following the war, many Bolivians across the nation concluded that the government that had taken them into the bloody conflict needed to be democratized, and some talked of social revolution.[58]

From the perspective of a critical group of middle-class Bolivians, middle-class officers during the war began to sense a feeling of nationalism. For the first time Bolivians from different regions of the nation met each other and began to consider a new type of Bolivia—without authoritarian, military governments that often did the bidding of the largest mining companies.[59]

---

ico: *The Agraristas and Cristeros of Michoacán* (Durham: Duke University Press, 1999). For an argument that subaltern classes living in some of the outlying regions of Peru had a critical role in forming the idea of the state in modern Peru, see David Nugent, *Modernity at the Edge of Empire: State, Individual, and Nation in the Northern Peruvian Andes, 1885–1935* (Stanford: Stanford University Press, 1997), and Florencia Mallon, *Peasant and Nation: The Making of Postcolonial Mexico and Peru* (Berkeley and Los Angeles: University of California Press, 1995).

55. Andrew Boeger, "Struggling for Emancipation: Tungsten Miners and the Bolivian Revolution," in *Workers' Control in Latin America, 1930–1979*, ed. Jonathan Brown (Chapel Hill: University of North Carolina Press, 1997), investigates an example of miners' attempts to work with the MNR in 1940s and 1950s Bolivia.

56. Laura Gotkowitz, *A Revolution for Our Rights: Indigenous Struggles for Land and Justice in Bolivia, 1880–1952* (Durham: Duke University Press, 2007), 132; see also Erick D. Langer, "Andean Rituals of Revolt: The Chayanta Rebellion of 1927," *Ethnohistory* 37 (1990): 235.

57. Farcau, *Chaco War*, ix, gives the figures on the war dead.

58. Antezana Ergueta, *La Clase Media y La Clase Obrera*, 8–10; Irma Torinia, *El nacionalismo en Bolivia de la pre y posguerra del Chaco, 1910–1945* (La Paz: Plural Editores, 2006).

59. Lehman, "U.S. Foreign Aid," 44.

But the most significant social change—which later erupted into revolution—occurred within the popular sectors. Many Indians and workers actively opposed the Bolivian government, which they viewed as working with the exploitative elites, or *rosca* (in Spanish, "spring," or "coil"). *Campesinos* and urban workers, who provided the bulk of the war's cannon fodder, not surprisingly had the strongest incentive to demand a deep restructuring of state and society.

Important developments in labor organization occurred in the 1930s and 1940s. During the 1930s a substantial union movement developed, and in some areas it had a profound impact on local politics. Unionists then launched a drive to influence national politics.[60] It is uncertain how much consensus existed between *campesinos* and urban workers. Some observers see their oppositional stance toward the state as reinforcing an already existing common culture of the dispossessed—and indeed, socialist parties in Bolivia tried to organize both groups.[61] Other scholars emphasize differences between the groups.[62] Although the outcome of this debate is unclear, given the large number of economic and political crises in the 1930s and 1940s, the situation was one in which the two groups had a strong incentive to work together on some level, to promote deep, even revolutionary change. Indeed, we must understand both groups if we are to understand the causes of the 1952 revolution and the course that upheaval took.

For *campesinos*, because the government was preoccupied with fighting the Chaco War, the war represented a great opportunity to advance an already existing peasant movement.[63] In 1934, radical Indians in the Department of La Paz set up what they called the "Sociedad República de Kollasuyo," an organization of Indian peasants that demanded the return of lands that *hacendados* (hacienda owners) in years past had connived or

---

60. Juan H. Jáuregui, "Pucarani: Apuntes para una historia regional," *Historia: Revista de la Carrera de Historia* 23 (1998): 114–15.

61. Guillermo Lora, *A History of the Bolivian Labour Movement, 1848–1971*, ed. Laurence Whitehead, trans. Christine Whitehead (Cambridge: Cambridge University Press, 1977), 103–4, 144.

62. Gustavo Rodríguez Ostria, *El Socavón y el sindicato: Ensayos históricos sobre los trabajadores mineros, siglos XIX–XX* (La Paz: Instituto Latinoamericano de Investigaciones Sociales [ILDIS], 1991), 145.

63. René Danilo Arze Z., *Guerra y conflictos sociales: El caso rural boliviano durante la campaña del Chaco* (La Paz: Centro de Estudios de la Realidad Económica y Social, ediciones CERES, 1987), 132; Jorge Dandler and Juan Torrico A., "From the National Indigenous Congress to the Ayopaya Rebellion: Bolivia, 1945–1947," in *Resistance, Rebellion, and Consciousness in the Andean Peasant World, 18th to 20th Centuries*, ed. Steve J. Stern (Madison: University of Wisconsin Press, 1987), 339–40.

simply appropriated from the Indians. What did the Indians expect from the Chaco War years? José M. Ajacopa, an Indian leader, summed it up nicely: "Our rights as citizens of Bolivia dictate that now more than ever we deserve access to our land, just as sons deserve inheritance from their parents."[64]

A tangential, yet ultimately significant development in the Indians' newfound confidence was the oligarchy's changed view of the *campesinos*. Interestingly, the elites held divided perceptions of the Indian population in this period. On the one hand, Indian movements understandably frightened them. Yet in part because indigenous peoples provided the majority of the foot soldiers in the Chaco, some of Bolivia's well-to-do had a new appreciation for them. In addition, after the disaster in the Chaco, elites concluded that unless the living conditions of the Indians were significantly improved, Bolivia would never advance as a nation.[65] Now, as the wealthy looked at Bolivian history, they saw the relevance of the nation's pre-European past—a heritage, they argued, that made Bolivia distinctive.

Given general discontent among *campesinos*, the growth of a movement to regain lost lands, and a certain sympathy among elements of the upper class, post–Chaco War *campesinos* increased their denunciations of the government. One such critic was Israel Pillericol, who complained to the *prefecto* of the La Paz Department (*prefectura de La Paz*) in an *otrosí* (petition) that military men stationed in his village had committed "outrageous acts of barbarism" on his personal property and requested that they be removed and replaced with military personnel of "good moral background." Petitions to the *prefecto* from other Indians followed; such grievances displayed an increased willingness on the part of Indians to stand up and demand decent treatment. (Although petitioning government officials was common going back to colonial times, in the mid-twentieth century the increase in the number of such petitions calling for redress is

---

64. "La libertad consagrada en la Carta Política de la Nación sobre la necesidad que ahora más que nunca . . . sean los derechos de propiedad respectados como la herencia de padres e hijos. "Liberty expressly stated in the Constitution—above all the rights of the Indians to the properties confiscated from them. The right to these properties needs to be respected to the same degree that one's inheritance is guaranteed." Arze Z., *Guerra y conflictos sociales*, 36.

65. Murdo J. MacLeod, "The Bolivian Novel, the Chaco War, and the Revolution," in *Beyond the Revolution: Bolivia Since 1952*, ed. James M. Malloy and Richard S. Thorn (Pittsburgh: University of Pittsburgh Press, 1971), 343, 349. In "The Problem of National Unity: From the Chaco War to the 1938 Constitutional Convention" (in *Revolution for Our Rights*, 101–30), Laura Gotkowitz discusses how political leaders and campesinos pushed for a more inclusive status and better standard of living for the campesinos.

significant.) Indian Apolinario Condori asked the *prefecto* for justice after locally powerful *mestizos* forced him to bring them water, dispossessed him of a portion of his land, and tried to extort payments from him "as if I were their tenant." Still another aggrieved Indian, Pedro Paredes, claimed the *corregidor* (political leader) of his hometown of Viacha had, at the behest of one "Mercedes N.," broken into the Indians' houses, taken money and goods, and stolen from them bulls and a mule. He realized of course that he could not get fair or even civil treatment at the local level, and he thus appealed to higher authorities: the Indian race ("raza indigena"), he asserted, deserved justice and dignity instead of continued mistreatment.[66]

By 1945, indigenous people in Bolivia had called a conference for the purpose of informing the government that they wanted significant social change—most notably, the abolition of free labor services on large estates and legal limitations on the services that estate owners could ask of their employees.[67] It was one of the first conferences of indigenous persons to address such issues in the entire continent.[68] Although the Bolivian government, remarkably, decreed that some of the peasants' demands be recognized, the directives were not enforced.[69] By July 1946, with a return to right-wing military rule in Bolivia, the peasantry saw little hope of working with the government to obtain redress for their grievances. However, it is important to note that after the Chaco War a new generation of Indian and *campesino* leaders arose—and, critically, began forging tentative alliances with some populist urban-based movements and political parties.[70] This leadership was one reason for the sustained level of rural protest all the way up through the 1952 Bolivian revolution—not only against landlords but also against the state—to pressure it to ensure civil rights for Indians.[71]

Indeed, some *campesinos* worked with a new political group, the Movimiento Nacionalista Revolucionario (MNR), which was formed in 1939 and had some influence in the Villarroel government (1943–46). Significantly,

66. Isreal Pillericol to Señor Prefecto, April 23, 1940; Apolinario Condori to Prefecto, June 26, 1940; and Pedro Paredes to Señor Prefecto de Departamento, Box 407, Prefecturales Expedientes, Archivo de La Paz, La Paz, Bolivia.
67. Silvia Rivera Cusicanqui, *"Oppressed but Not Defeated": Peasant Struggles Among the Aymara and Qhechwa in Bolivia, 1900–1980* (Geneva: U.N. Research Institute for Social Development, 1987), 53; Dandler and Torrico A., "National Indigenous Congress," 345–46.
68. Gotkowitz, *Revolution for Our Rights*, 2.
69. Dandler and Torrico A., "National Indigenous Congress," 370.
70. Gotkowitz, *Revolution for Our Rights*, 15.
71. Ibid., 234–35, 262, 267.

however, the MNR by the late 1940s was not calling upon the *hacendados* to redistribute their land among the poor Indians. Instead, it called for modernization in the countryside: this approach involved wholesale markets, better rural education, and an improved legal system in the *campo*. Simultaneously, the MNR asked for further study of land reform.[72]

Before the 1952 revolution, *campesinos*, in particular those who did not own land and worked on the large haciendas at a subsistence level, defined their sense of citizenship, and ultimately self-respect, by the term *lucha*, or struggle—the sustained quest for their former lands, and the fight against the *patrón*, church, and oligarchy. Many Indians saw their struggle for land and justice stretching back to the colonial era. Yet they continued to press on with their demands.[73] They believed that only through this sustained engagement would they ever gain their rights as citizens. Only then would they be treated with the dignity befitting human beings, and only then would they have justice.[74] The *campesinos'* ability to come together to press their demands was enhanced by their ethnic cohesion and deep collective memory.[75]

The other dissatisfied group before the revolution was the workers, in particular the miners, who like the *campesinos* saw the state as an entity to be opposed. The miners wanted emancipation from poverty and second-class citizen status. Collectively, they had become a considerable force in society during the 1940s when they had organized nationwide into labor unions.

Some introductory comments on the labor movement are in order. Although unionism stretched back to the years 1919–20, when the railroad workers launched union drives, the decade of the 1940s proved pivotal.[76] The two primary causes behind union (*sindicato*) activism included the Catavi massacre of December 1942, in which the Bolivian military helped

72. Rivera Cusicanqui, *"Oppressed but Not Defeated,"* 59.
73. Manuel Yapiticona, Manuel Ramos, and others, quoted in Gotkowitz, *Revolution for Our Rights*, 88. In petitioning the government, peasants would collectively write the petition.
74. Arze Z., *Guerra y conflictos sociales*, x. For an analysis of the 1940s, see Dandler and Torrico A., "National Indigenous Congress," 351–75. For a good overview of the literature on indigenous people and their quest for justice after Bolivia's independence up through the 1952 revolution, see Nancy Grey Postero, *Now We Are Citizens: Indigenous Politics in Postmulticultural Bolivia* (Stanford: Stanford University Press, 2007), 31–36.
75. Rivera Cusicanqui, *"Oppressed but Not Defeated,"* 11–70; Laura Gotkowitz, "'Under the Dominion of the Indian': Rural Mobilization, the Law, and Revolutionary Nationalism in Bolivia in the 1940s," in *Political Cultures in the Andes, 1750–1950*, ed. Nils Jacobsen and Cristóbal Aljovín de Losada (Durham: Duke University Press, 2005), 137–58.
76. Lora, *Bolivian Labour Movement*, 112–16.

suppress labor unrest, killing at least thirty-five striking miners and their supporters, and, more generally, poor economic conditions (especially after World War II). It was during the 1940s that miners began to join unions in large numbers for the first time.[77]

However, their anger at poor conditions and brutal, even deadly, treatment on the part of the mine owners did not automatically cause a powerful union movement to coalesce. The small size of the Bolivian working class in the 1940s limited labor's political clout. The 1950 census, the first for the country in the twentieth century, recorded only about 43,000 full-time miners, or about 3.2 percent of the population.[78] Further limiting the movement's clout at the national level were structural impediments. Bolivia's very difficult terrain makes it cumbersome and expensive to transport bulky and heavy minerals. When it comes to the actual process of mining, Bolivia's valuable ores tend to be mixed in the rock hauled out of the ground. Therefore, often complicated and labor-intensive extractive processes have to be used to separate out the lucrative minerals.[79] To be competitive in world markets, mine owners need to relentlessly search for savings in the price of inputs to production, most notably in wages.

Interestingly, union leaders found that the small size of the mining workforce made it easier to organize the rank and file.[80] In addition, the nature of work in the mines helped to create strong solidarity among miners: because the work was dangerous, and workers toiled in close quarters, they quickly realized the importance of mutual reliance, which often lead to a strong sense of unity.[81] Another factor which increased miners' clout was their growing realization of their power as the producers of Bolivia's only major source of foreign exchange, and more generally, the most vibrant part of Bolivia's economy.

77. J. M. Balcázar, the minister of labor, health, and welfare, wrote to Tomás Manuel Elío, the minister of foreign affairs, in 1943, describing the Bolivian working class as suffering from "poor nutrition and sanitation and sickness" and "low salaries." Ministerio de Trabajo, Salud y Previsión Social, *Ministerio de Trabajo, Salud, y Previsión Social, 1943*, Archivo de Relaciones Exteriores, La Paz, Bolivia (hereafter ARE).
78. República de Bolivia, Ministerio de Hacienda y Estadística, Dirección General de Estadística y Censos, *Censo Demografico, 1950* (La Paz: Dirección General de Estadística y Censos, 1955), 140, 142.
79. Sinforoso Cabrera, labor leader from the 1950s and 1960s, interview, August 4, 1999, La Paz. Unless otherwise indicated, all interviews cited were conducted by the author.
80. Lora, *Bolivian Labour Movement*, vii–ix.
81. Steve Volk, "Tin and Imperialism," *NACLA's Latin America and Empire Report* 8, no. 2 (February 1974): 14.

Bolivia, the United States, and the Roots of Revolution

In the late 1930s and early 1940s, workers managed to hash out a tacit accord with the "military socialist" governments of Germán Busch, José David Toro, and Gualberto Villarroel. These reformist governments introduced social legislation that, though sporadically implemented, benefited workers.[82] Villarroel's government even went so far as to pass a law protecting union leaders from forced dismissal or transfer.[83] These regimes aimed to create progressive state labor policy while endeavoring to control the existing labor movement by creating governmental institutions to link state power to labor groups.[84] But by the mid-1940s, it is important to note, many workers were making demands independent of the state.[85] Workers at the Chojlla mine, for example, by 1944 were calling for a general strike to destroy *rosca*-style capitalism, which benefited only a tiny number of wealthy Bolivians.[86] To increase their influence at the national level, miners formed the Federación Sindical de Trabajadores Mineros de Bolivia (FSTMB), the Miner's Federation of Bolivia, in 1944. The FSTMB emerged as a dynamic and powerful segment of the labor movement, even working to organize *campesinos* in the countryside.[87] It acted as a force struggling against the military governments of the *sexenio* (1946–52) and proved key to the MNR's triumph in 1952.[88] The oft-quoted Thesis of Pulacayo (authored by the Trotskyite Partido Obrero Revolucionario) expressed the desire on the part of the FSTMB to set up a totally different type of state: "Conflicts should be resolved under the direction of the workers, and by them alone."[89] The Thesis of Pulacayo united the miners under one banner and presented a persuasive argument that the now-united miners needed to strongly oppose, violently if necessary, the state.[90]

82. Ponencias del II Congreso nacional de trabajadores mineros de Bolivia efectuando en la villa imperial de "Potosí," 1–8 de junio 1945, "Congresos FSTMB 4.1," Sistema de Documentación e Información Dirección General de Estadística y Censos n Sindical, La Paz, Bolivia (hereafter SIDIS). During Toro's brief tenure (1936–37), he actually required, in corporatist fashion, the unionization of worker, professional, and managerial groups. Rotchin, *Clientelist State*, 47.
83. Gotkowitz, *Revolution for Our Rights*, 175.
84. Ibid., 112–13.
85. Ibid., 113.
86. FSTMB de Chojlla a Dr. Federico Álvares Plata, 7 junio de 1944, Chojlla, 1944–1956, 4406072, SIDIS.
87. Lora, *Bolivian Labour Movement*, 280.
88. Lehman, "U.S. Foreign Aid," 119.
89. "Rights guaranteed by the Constitution." Tesis de Pulcayo, quoted in Lora, *Bolivian Labour Movement*, 247.
90. Rodríguez Ostria, *El Socavón y el sindicato*, 130.

In general, the state used force to support the mining companies in their efforts to control the miners. A good example is the Catavi massacre of December 1942, where troops fired on striking miners, killing at least thirty-five. One important outcome of the Catavi massacre was that the FSTMB began to work more closely with the MNR.[91]

However, there were also times in which the management thought it important to treat the miners well. Elías Villamil V., the *procurador* (a top official) of the Compañía Estañifera de Cerro Grande, in the department of Oruro, for example, ordered that a boss inclined to mistreat his workers had to be immediately removed. On September 9, 1942, four months before the Catavi massacre, for instance, Villamil petitioned the minister of government in La Paz to implement "las garantías consagradas por la constitución política del Estado" [the guarantees granted by the constitution]. He was probably referring to the Mining Code, which called for decent treatment of workers, though the Code was never rigorously enforced.

Significantly, in this case, Villamil appealed to the politicians to enforce the Code for a particular reason: the abusive boss had caused an exodus of workers at a time—World War II—when Bolivia needed to produce a great deal of tin for the war effort. Villamil, in his petition, itemized the negative consequences of low tin production: the government treasury would suffer and Bolivia would not be able to fulfill the terms of the contracts it had signed with the United States.[92] World War II, then, offered opportunities for the miners in Bolivia to garner higher wages and increase their ranks.

By the mid-1940s unions had begun working with the MNR.[93] Starting out as a social movement in 1939, the multiclass (but urban-based) MNR became a political party in the 1940s, participating in the Villarroel regime, which came to power late in 1943. After Villarroel's assassination in 1946, many miners (as well as other Bolivians) became more radicalized, calling for a thorough reorganization of society.[94]

The tragic end to Villarroel's regime paralleled a period of increasing reform and democratization in Latin America from the mid- to late 1940s. In part because of the ideological nature of World War II and the Allies'

91. Dunkerley, *Rebellion in the Veins*, 15–16.
92. Elias Villamil V. to the Minister of Government, September 9, 1942, Number 2, Papers of Col. Ballivan Saracho, Box 33, Archivo de La Paz, La Paz, Bolivia.
93. Boeger, "Struggling for Emancipation," 223–26.
94. Lora, *Bolivian Labor Movement*, 276. In 1948, the FSTMB proclaimed that the future of Bolivia rested on the FSTMB reaching its goals, and that its successes would help to build a new social order. "Inauguracion Oficial del V Congreso de Trabadores Mineros," 11 junio de 1948, Congresos FSTMB 4.1, SIDIS.

victory over the Axis powers, the 1944 to 1948 period represented an opening for Latin American leaders and political parties that advocated representative government and social and economic reforms that would benefit the popular sectors. However, a series of military coups in Latin America, starting in 1946 with Villarroel's ouster, represented a right-wing reaction to the flowering of reform in the mid-1940s. For Bolivia, however, Villarroel's ouster represented the beginning of a period of tumultuous revolutionary change, ending with the outbreak of the 1952 revolution.[95]

During the critically important *sexenio*, from 1946 to 1952, when the MNR was not in power, the government at times violently repressed the miners' expressions of their grievances. The miners implemented a two-pronged strategy. To survive, they built stronger organizations. Also, as I have noted, they began to work with the MNR. During the *sexenio*, they further developed their sense of unity and self-confidence. Indeed, for the first time they thought they could influence political events at the national level and change society to make it more egalitarian.[96]

The increased mobilization of *campesinos* proved especially important in laying the groundwork for the Bolivian revolution.[97] Simultaneous with the increase in social discontent among the popular sectors in the mid- to late 1940s, two other events shook Bolivian history. First, as the MNR increased its labor-organizing activities in Bolivia—in particular working with the FSTMB—the Bolivian political party system began to disintegrate.[98] Second, relations between the United States and Bolivia deteriorated. Notably, even Bolivian elites began to criticize U.S. policy. After World War II, the Bolivian foreign minister was asked what the United States had left behind. He stated, "Empty tin cans, . . . broken-down Frigidaires, rural air strips from which their airplanes took off with their household goods, their office employees, and their blondes. In the tin and wolfram mines, cavities in the ground and cavities among the democratic workers who left their lungs behind in the tunnels in order to save democracy."[99] Víctor Andrade, who served as ambassador to the United States

---

95. Leslie Bethell and Ian Roxborough, eds., *Latin America Between the Second World War and the Cold War, 1944–1948* (Cambridge: Cambridge University Press, 1992), 1–32; 327–34.

96. Rodríguez Ostria, *El Socavón y el sindicato*, 143.

97. On the role of the miners in the coming of the revolution, see Alexander, *Bolivian National Revolution*, xviii–xvi and 278–79, and Malloy, "Revolutionary Politics," 117. On the role of the mobilized campesinos, see Gotkowitz, *Revolution for Our Rights*, 275, 285.

98. Herbert S. Klein, *Parties and Political Change in Bolivia, 1880–1952* (New York: Cambridge University Press, 1969), 375, 389.

99. Donald M. Dozer, *Are We Good Neighbors? Three Decades of Inter-American Relations, 1930–1960* (Gainesville: University of Florida Press, 1959), 200–201.

from 1944 to 1946, 1952 to 1958, and 1960 to 1962, expressed a widely held sentiment that Bolivia had made significant sacrifices for the Allied war effort during the war by selling strategic minerals, in particular tin, to the United States for below-market prices. Consequently, Bolivia deserved a long-term tin contract and economic development assistance after the war.[100]

A long-term tin contract was key for Bolivia. From Bolivia's point of view, a long-term contract from the United States was imperative because the only place where the low-grade Bolivian tin could be refined was in Texas City, Texas. However, in the immediate postwar period, U.S. producers did not offer such a contract to Bolivian mine owners.[101] Indeed, in the late 1940s and 1950s, as revolutionary sentiment seethed just below the surface, U.S. and Bolivian officials could not agree on a price. U.S. officials clung to their "final offer" of $1.03 per pound of tin ore, while at the same time Bolivia demanded more. Negotiations finally resumed in early 1952 but were cut off by the Bolivian revolution in April of that year.[102]

Bolivian leaders, seeing proceeds from tin sales dropping after World War II, vigorously pursued the continuation of economic assistance from the United States—which began during World War II—and the Andean nation did receive some needed aid.[103] It was not enough to compensate for the lack of a lucrative export contract with the United States; yet, significantly, on a per-capita basis, Bolivia received more assistance than any other Latin American country. U.S. assistance has been central to U.S.-Bolivian relations from the 1940s to the present. In one sense, U.S. assistance represented an alliance between the more cautious elements of the MNR and the United States and was, thus, another manifestation of the traditional patron-client relationship. But such assistance did not cause Bolivian leaders to abandon an important theme in recent Bolivian history—economic nationalism. Despite a temporary convergence of interests in the early 1950s, economic nationalism would continue to have a major influence on U.S.-Bolivian relations.

100. Víctor Andrade Uzquiano, *My Missions for Revolutionary Bolivia, 1944–1962* (Pittsburgh: University of Pittsburgh Press, 1976), 54–74.
101. In *My Missions for Revolutionary Bolivia* Andrade details his attempts to convince the U.S. government to offer a long-term tin contract to Bolivia.
102. Lehman, *Bolivia and the United States*, 97–98.
103. According to the "Greenbook" of the U.S. Agency for International Development (USAID), Bolivia received an average of $400,000 per year from 1946 to 1949, and an average of $500,000 per year from 1950 to 1951. Bolivia's allocation of assistance increased during this period despite a sharp cut in U.S. aid to Latin America, from $29.6 million in 1946 to 17.4 in 1951. See U.S. Agency for International Development, *U.S. Overseas Loans and Grants*, http://qesdb.usaid.gov/cgi-bin/broker.exe (accessed October 16, 2007).

THE BOLIVIAN REVOLUTION AND THE UNITED STATES

Why Bolivia?

In a December 1992 interview with Bolivian president Jaime Paz Zamora, newsman Peter Jennings asked him if Washington had enough influence—because of U.S. government economic assistance to the nonindustrialized nation—to get the Bolivian president to change his chosen cabinet appointees. Paz Zamora said yes. The implication was that U.S. government economic assistance gave the United States significant leverage over Bolivian policy. Many accepted at face value Paz Zamora's concession and concluded that Bolivia was so dependent on U.S. aid that Washington policymakers could virtually call the shots in that nonindustrialized Andean nation.[1]

However, the infamous interview brings up some questions: How did Bolivia come to receive large amounts of U.S. assistance? And what was the effect of such assistance on Bolivian policy? This chapter argues that although Bolivia, as early as the 1950s, was a major recipient of U.S. assistance, the Andean nation was its own actor (or at least more beholden to internal actors than to external ones). Although some scholars argue otherwise, the Bolivians, despite U.S. efforts to tame the revolution and internal dissent among the revolutionaries, managed to chart their own course during the tumultuous 1950s.[2] Certainly U.S. assistance gave the

---

1. Walter Goodman, "ABC on the Trail of Cocaine Traffickers in Bolivia," *New York Times*, December 28, 1992, C16.
2. Works that argue that the United States used its influence to tame the Bolivian revolution include Whitehead, *The United States and Bolivia*, and Zunes, "Decisions on Intervention."

northern giant some leverage; but U.S. officials did not control the Bolivian polity in the 1950s.

The 1952 Bolivian revolution transformed the polity and the nation's relations with the outside world. Previous interpretations of U.S.-Bolivian relations from 1952 to 1956 have stressed U.S. security concerns. Washington officials, the authors of these interpretations argue, wanted to prevent a Soviet-backed communist regime from taking power in Bolivia.[3] Six months after the revolution, U.S. diplomats in La Paz, however, privately told their British counterparts that they did not see a Moscow-led communist party coming to power.[4] The threats Washington *did* see were economic stagnation and political chaos on the one hand and Bolivian economic nationalism on the other. U.S. policymakers thought the Bolivian government's statist capitalism would exacerbate the Andean nation's already existing economic and political difficulties.

As was the case for most of Latin America, although Bolivia had not been part of a formal, political empire since 1825, most scholars have viewed the Bolivian economy and society as part of the European–North American sphere of influence after the nation's independence from Spain.[5] Social and economic elites attempted to impose a Western-oriented social and economic system on the majority-Indian nation because the elites saw this system as reflecting their own self-interest.[6] The 1952 upheaval in Bolivia fits into the broader pattern of postwar Third World

---

3. Blasier, *Hovering Giant*, 135; Rabe, *Eisenhower and Latin America*, 77–82; Lehman, *Bolivia and the United States*, 91–146. Blasier states that "the MNR's vaguely leftist program, including proposals for the nationalization of the tin mines, disturbed conservative circles in Washington aroused by the anti-Communist campaigns of Senator Joseph McCarthy" (129–30). Rabe and Lehman discuss both anticommunist and anti-economic nationalism motives. Rabe states that U.S. aid to Bolivia, which would reach about $200 million during the course of the 1950s, was used "to keep Bolivia non-Communist and to force the MNR to adopt free trade and investment policies" (78). However, he emphasizes the anticommunist motive: "Dr. [Milton] Eisenhower [the president's younger brother and adviser on Latin American affairs] successfully urged the president to assist the Bolivian as a humanitarian gesture and as a way of preventing communism" (82).

4. J. Garnett Lomax, British ambassador in La Paz, to J. H. A. Watson Esq., British Embassy, Washington, D.C., October 11, 1952, AX 1016/7, FO/97707, Foreign Office (hereafter FO) 371, Public Record Office, Kew Garden, United Kingdom (hereafter PRO); J. H. A. Watson to R. Cecil, Esq., American Department, FO, October 5, 1952, AX 1016/5, FO/97707, FO 371, PRO. An internal State Department memorandum makes the same argument. See Carlos Navia Ribera, *Los Estados Unidos y la revolución nacional*, 115.

5. Benjamin Keen and Keith Haynes, *A History of Latin America*, 6th ed. (Boston: Houghton Mifflin, 2000), 179–80.

6. Kevin Healy, *Llamas, Weavings, and Organic Chocolate: Multicultural Grassroots Development in the Andes and Amazon of Bolivia* (Notre Dame: University of Notre Dame Press, 2001), 1–16. See also Marsh, *Bankers in Bolivia*.

decolonization.⁷ With the revolution, nonelite Bolivians strove for and, in some ways, achieved influence for the first time.⁸ The revolutionaries of the emerging Third World nations, who were throwing off the yoke of European colonialism at this time, shared a number of goals—in particular, political autonomy and economic development. The disintegration of the European empires in the developing world proves important because, of course, it occurred in the context of the intensifying cold war of the 1950s. Western leaders feared the newly emerging nations of the developing world would gravitate toward the Soviet bloc. Not surprisingly, seeing an opportunity offered by the cold war competition between the United States and the communist bloc, Bolivian leaders attempted (as other developing-world nations did) to play the Soviet Union off against the West in order to receive more U.S. assistance.⁹

Within the context of U.S.–Latin American relations, Bolivia both reflects this history, but at the same time stands out in key respects. Certainly during the cold war, U.S. officials wanted Latin America (including Bolivia) to remain noncommunist.¹⁰ Further, given expanding U.S. commitments in other parts of the globe, Washington leaders wanted a hemispheric policy on the cheap. Often, "communism" was a catchall term for

 7. Gabriel Kolko, *Confronting the Third World: United States Foreign Policy, 1945–1980* (New York: Pantheon Books, 1988), 17–23; H. W. Brands, *The Specter of Neutralism: The United States and the Emergence of the Third World, 1947–1960* (New York: Columbia University Press, 1989), 1–10. For a more recent interpretation that focuses on Africa, see Thomas Borstelmann, *The Cold War and the Color Line: American Race Relations in the Global Arena* (Cambridge: Harvard University Press, 2001), 95–97. Also, on the Bandung Conference of 1955, which included a number of recently independent nations, see Jason Parker, "Small Victory, Missed Chances: The Eisenhower Administration, the Bandung Conference, and the Turning of the Cold War," in *The Eisenhower Administration, the Third World, and the Globalization of the Cold War*, ed. Kathryn C. Statler and Andrew L. Johns (Lanham, Md.: Rowman and Littlefield, 2006), 153–74.

 8. Carlos Montenegro, *Nacionalismo y coloniaje, su expresión histórica en la prensa de Bolivia* (La Paz: Ediciones Autonomía, 1943).

 9. For information on the intensifying Soviet-U.S. competition in the developing world, see Robert J. McMahon, *The Limits of Empire: The United States and Southeast Asia Since World War II* (New York: Columbia University Press, 1999), 69–75. For Latin America, see Cole Blasier, *The Giant's Rival: The USSR and Latin America* (Pittsburgh: University of Pittsburgh Press, 1983).

 10. Key works on this topic include Wood, *The Dismantling of the Good Neighbor Policy*; Kyle Longley, *In the Eagle's Shadow: The United States and Latin America* (Wheeling, Ill.: Harland Davidson, 2002), 193–235; and Rabe, *Eisenhower and Latin America*. For excellent essays on the changing historiography of U.S.–Latin American relations, see Stephen G. Rabe, "Marching Ahead (Slowly): The Historiography of Inter-American Relations," *Diplomatic History* 13 (Summer 1989): 297–316; Mark T. Gilderhus, "An Emerging Synthesis? U.S.–Latin American Relations Since the Second World War," *Diplomatic History* 16 (Summer 1992): 429–52; and Max Paul Friedman, "Retiring the Puppets, Bringing Latin America

many of Washington's fears, including left-wing nationalism. Indeed, U.S. officials feared that communists would co-opt Latin American nationalism. Consequently, Washington wanted to go beyond simply eliminating communism to promote a U.S.-centered, capitalist economic system in the hemisphere. It wanted to quash economic nationalism in the region.[11]

However, the Bolivian case was different from the rest of the region. During the 1950s Washington attempted to intervene more directly in Bolivia than in the rest of the region.[12] Although normally U.S. officials avoided giving economic assistance to Latin America nations, Washington officials made an exception with Bolivia, fearing that without such assistance the Bolivian polity could collapse. In addition, Washington leaders went further in their attempt to eliminate economic nationalism compared to other nations in the region, because relatively small quantities of U.S. assistance to the poor nation of Bolivia gave Washington leaders significant leverage over Bolivia to achieve U.S. goals.[13]

Consequently, the best way to understand the conflicts between the United States and Bolivia during this period is to look at Bolivia's nationalistic policies, in particular its economic nationalism—which flowed directly out of the nation's revolution—and the U.S. response to these policies. Washington used aid to attempt to limit, or even eliminate, economic nationalism. The view from Washington was that Bolivia had to provide a friendly environment for foreign private sector investment that they thought would spur growth, which was necessary for pro-U.S. political stability.[14] To promote economic growth, *norteamericano* officials believed, the United States had no choice but to support the revolutionary government with economic assistance. Bolivia was a test of Washington's ability to nation-build in the developing world by using U.S.-sponsored modernization theory—that Western-style free-market capitalism (open to foreign trade and investment) could produce benefits for middle-class and working-class Bolivians.

Back In: Recent Scholarship on United States–Latin American Relations," *Diplomatic History* 27, no. 5 (November 2003): 621–36.

11. See Siekmeier, *Aid, Nationalism, and Inter-American Relations*.

12. Matthew Loayza, "An 'Aladdin's Lamp' for Free Enterprise: Eisenhower, Fiscal Conservatism, and Latin American Nationalism, 1953–61," *Diplomacy and Statecraft* 14 (September 2003): 83–105; Siekmeier, *Aid, Nationalism, and Inter-American Relations*.

13. Whitehead, *The United States and Bolivia*.

14. William F. Gray to Department of State, May 7, 1959, Decimal File 824.00 TA [Technical Assistance]/5–0759, RG 59, DOS Central Files, NA; Henry Dearborn to Henry F. Holland, June 8, 1955, Decimal File 720.5-MSP/6–855, RG 59, DOS Central Files, NA.

Washington used its economic support to pursue its own goals—of a hemisphere open to foreign trade and investment. Washington's goals did not always coincide with Bolivia's vision of economic self-strengthening—in particular, developing its agricultural potential and diversifying its economy, and using state control of sectors of the economy to ensure that resources considered "national patrimony" (oil and gas) would directly benefit the Bolivian nation. In this way, U.S. policy hindered the Bolivian government in its quest to fulfill its new, revolutionary goals. But despite Bolivia's dependence on the U.S. tin market, the nation's increasing reliance on U.S. government assistance, and U.S. efforts to turn back portions of the revolution, the MNR managed to keep in place many aspects of its momentous revolutionary transformation.

The Bolivian Revolution and the United States: The Early Years

In 1952, Bolivia erupted in one of the few truly social revolutions in recent Latin American history.[15] The urban middle class wanted to eviscerate the *rosca*'s control of Bolivia's economy, society, and political system.[16] Moreover, new social actors emerged, such as an organized *campesino* (peasant) movement.[17] The Movimiento Nacionalista Revolucionario (MNR), which came to power with the upheaval, advocated economic nationalism to alleviate Bolivia's social and economic problems.[18] That is, the MNR wanted to strengthen Bolivia's economy by enacting land reform, nationalizing the three largest mining companies, and (for the more conservative members of the MNR) diversifying the economy.[19] Interestingly, a significant

---

15. Erick D. Langer, *Economic Change and Rural Resistance in Southern Bolivia* (Stanford: Stanford University Press, 1989), 200. An excellent introduction to the Bolivian revolution is Malloy, *Bolivia: The Uncompleted Revolution*. A recent, Bolivian view is in Franco Gamboa Rocabado, *Itinerario de la esperanza y el desconcierto: Ensayos sobre política, sociedad y democracia en Bolivia* (La Paz: Muela del Diablo Editores, 2001), 15–95.
16. Economic Commission for Latin America (hereafter ECLA), "Economic Policy of Bolivia in 1952–64," *Economic Bulletin for Latin America* 12 (October 1967): 64.
17. José M. Gordillo, *Arrando en la historia: la experiencia política campesina en Cochabamba* (La Paz: Universidad Mayor de San Simón, Plural Editores Centro de Estudio de la Realidad Económica y Social, 1998), 11.
18. For a definition of economic nationalism in the Latin American context, see Shoshana B. Tancer, *Economic Nationalism in Latin America: The Quest for Economic Independence* (New York: Praeger, 1976), 12.
19. ECLA, "Economic Policy of Bolivia," 63.

portion of the MNR's platform reflected the recommendations of the Bohan Report, discussed in chapter 1.[20]

In 1951, Bolivian voters elected MNR candidate Víctor Paz Estenssoro to the presidency, but a military coup prevented his inauguration. In response, on April 12, 1952, the MNR took power through force, winning a short series of battles against a discredited Bolivian army. Militias made up of mine workers proved crucial in the victory.[21] Although after 1956 the MNR began to fragment into various different factions, from 1952 to 1956, it was possible to talk about two general tendencies, leftist and cautiously moderate.[22] In terms of sheer numbers, the Left had a clear majority; but the leadership of the movement was almost entirely from the moderate faction. Bolivia's first two post-1952 presidents, Paz Estenssoro and Hernán Siles Suazo, were moderates. Two broad goals united the MNR: diversification of the economy and improvement of the Bolivian infrastructure, in particular roads, water, schools, and electricity.[23] Three more specific goals were shared by nearly all the revolutionaries: universal suffrage for women and Indians, land reform, and nationalization of the tin mines.

The strength of the powerful Left lay in the strong, well-organized labor unions. The preeminence of the tin miners' unions was enhanced by their militias, which collectively were more powerful than the small Bolivian army. The flamboyant and charismatic leader of the major Bolivian workers' organization, the Central Obrera Boliviana (COB), Juan Lechín

---

20. Richard S. Thorn, "The Economic Transformation," in *Beyond the Revolution: Bolivia Since 1952*, ed. James M. Malloy and Richard S. Thorn (Pittsburgh: University of Pittsburgh Press, 1971), 165; U.N. Economic and Social Council, ECLA, *Development of Agriculture in Bolivia*, E/CN-12/218/Add.2 (New York: United Nations, 1951), 7–8.

21. Whitehead, *The United States and Bolivia*, 6–7.

22. After 1956 the MNR began to factionalize. In 1956 Walter Guevara Arze openly broke with the party. In 1960 he started his Movimiento Revolucionario Autentico. His was a right-wing movement: the reason for breaking away from the MNR was that it had not adhered to the dictum, "la democracia fundadad en conceptos occidentales de los valores humanos" (democracy based on Western conception of human values). He also espoused the principle "la iniciativa privadad es beneficios apara la colectividad" (private initiative benefits all). See José Gamarra Zorrilla, *Liberalismo y neoliberalismo: Breve interpretación de la historia política de Bolivia (1879–1993)* (La Paz: Editorial Los Amigos del Libro, 1993), 173. See also Malloy, *Bolivia: The Uncompleted Revolution*, 241.

23. Malloy, *Bolivia: The Uncompleted Revolution*, 217, 222, 300, identifies Paz Estenssoro and Siles Suazo as part of a "pragmatic nationalistic center," but I think the evidence shows them to be rightward-leaning. On the definition of infrastructure, see James V. Kohl, "National Revolution to Revolution of Restoration: Arms and Factional Politics in Bolivia," *Inter-American Economic Affairs* 39, no. 1 (Summer 1985): 5.

Oquendo, became minister of mines in the new revolutionary government.[24] The Left wanted the state to nationalize all the mines, railways, and *latifundia* (large plantations) and for the workers to run these institutions. Indeed, the COB called for workers to occupy the factories.[25] Finally, the Left feared that U.S. assistance would reinforce Bolivian dependency on the United States.[26]

The more cautious moderates in the MNR, on the other hand, advocated private sector investment, in particular foreign private investment. They were very interested in oil production.[27] Oil sales could provide the country with a source of foreign exchange and, some of the moderates argued, dramatically increase the pace of Bolivian development. Unlike the Left, the moderate members did not fear that U.S. dominance would come with its aid; they argued that the United States simply wanted to promote growth in Bolivia that was beneficial to both the Bolivians and the *norteamericanos*.[28] The moderates also wanted to promote diversification by shifting labor from the nationalized tin mines to agricultural pursuits. One of the cautious moderates, Walter Guevara Arze, the MNR's first foreign minister, realized the powerful labor leaders would see this shift as a threat to their power; he admonished the MNR to move cautiously in this regard in order to maintain harmony in the ruling coalition.[29]

The rightist members of the MNR advocated a political economy similar to that of Acción Democrática (AD) in Venezuela (although the MNR platform called for more state control of the economy). Darlene Rivas, in a recent essay, nicely sums up AD's program: "liberal democracy with a modern diversified economy . . . [with] a nonexploitative,

---

24. Juan Lechín Oquendo, interview, February 20, 1997, La Paz.

25. Central Obrero Boliviano (COB), *Programa ideológico y estatuos de la C.O.B. aprobados por el Congreso Nacional de Trabajadores* (La Paz: COB, October 31, 1954), 32, Bolivian Pamphlets Collection at the University of Pittsburgh Library (hereafter Pittsburgh Pamphlets); Lora, *Bolivian Labour Movement*, 282.

26. Mario Torres Calleja, *Ayuda americana: Una experiencia frustrada* (La Paz: Federacio'n Sindical de Trabajadores Mineros de Bolivia, 1962), 66.

27. Carlos Dujovne, *Trabajo y salarios en la revolución nacional* (La Paz: Subsecretaria de Prensa, Informaciones y Cultura, 1955), 37, Pittsburgh Pamphlets; Walter Guevera Arze, *Plan inmediato de política económica del gobierno de la revolución nacional* (La Paz: Ministerio de Relaciones Exteriores, 1955), 70; James W. Wilkie, *Bolivian Foreign Trade: Historical Problems and MNR Revolutionary Policy, 1952–64* (Buffalo: Council on International Studies, State University of New York at Buffalo, 1971), 2.

28. Speech of Paz Estenssoro, February 24, 1954, Decimal File 824.062/2-2454, RG 59, DOS Central Files, NA.

29. Guevara Arze, *Plan inmediato*, 45.

reformed capitalism."[30] It is important to note that before the revolution Paz Estenssoro had spent six years in exile in Buenos Aires working for Juan Perón's government, and many comparisons have been made between the MNR and the Peronists. Yet in reality the right-wing leadership of the MNR advocated an economic polity that lay, in political terms, somewhere between the liberal political economy of Venezuela's AD and the firm state control of Perón.

Early on, it became clear that harmony between the MNR's factions was impossible.[31] Rightists saw developing the private sector, and ties to the United States, as important. Leftists were wary of the private sector, especially foreign private capital; it could be a dangerous source of power that could be used to control and exploit working-class Bolivians, and foreign enterprises, the leftists feared, might simply sell off Bolivia's resources, leaving little gain for the nation.[32] This disagreement widened as the 1950s progressed and by the end of the decade had severely weakened the MNR.[33]

Put simply, U.S. officials wanted the Left subservient to the moderate wing of the party.[34] A tacit alliance was formed between the moderate MNR leadership and U.S. leaders when they gave economic assistance to Bolivia. Washington wanted to keep the cautious moderates in control of the Bolivian revolution.[35] In a recent essay, Robert McMahon noted that often Third World leaders reached out to the United States to bolster their leadership positions at home.[36] In this light, it is important to note that Paz Estenssoro made it clear to Washington leaders that support for the MNR—in particular, for his faction of the MNR—would ensure pro-U.S.

30. Darlene Rivas, "Like Boxing with Joe Louis: Nelson Rockefeller in Venezuela, 1945–1948," in *Empire and Revolution: The United States and the Third World Since 1945*, ed. Peter Hahn and Mary Ann Heiss (Columbus: Ohio State University Press, 2001), 220.

31. American Embassy in La Paz to the Department of State, September 15, 1952, Decimal File 824.06/9–1552, RG 59, DOS Central Files, NA.

32. Alfredo Franco Guachalla, *Acotaciones para la doctrina del partido* (La Paz: Editorial "Casegural," 1961), 9, 12, Pittsburgh Pamphlets.

33. "Uncordial Relations Between Ambassador Andrade and Minister of Mines Lechín," memorandum of conversation, April 14, 1954, Decimal File 824.25/4–1454, RG 59, DOS Central Files, NA.

34. Lehman, "U.S. Foreign Aid," 280, 325; Lehman, "Revolutions and Attributions," 198.

35. Lehman, *Bolivia and the United States*, 113.

36. Robert McMahon, "Introduction," in *Empire and Revolution: The United States and the Third World Since 1945*, ed. Peter Hahn and Mary Ann Heiss (Columbus: Ohio State University Press, 2001), 9. An important example of a Latin American leader exerting some control over U.S. policy was José Figueres in Costa Rica. See Longley, *The Sparrow and the Hawk.*

stability in the nation. U.S. leaders were relieved: they feared that a breakup of the MNR might lead to chaos and that the left-wing segment of the MNR might emerge victorious.

Despite intragovernmental conflict, the revolution achieved a number of goals, one of the most important being land reform. Government leaders implemented a historic decree establishing a land reform on August 2, 1953. They did this for moral, economic, and pragmatic political reasons. Many argued that the feudal-like agricultural system exploited the peasantry and should be demolished. Land reform was a prerequisite, top MNR officials stated, for modernizing agriculture and increasing output.[37] In addition, the urban-based MNR was forced to implement land reform quickly because of increasing unrest in the countryside. Some landless peasants were taking over parts of haciendas.[38] The reform stated that land distributed by means of the reform must be "developed," and there were limits to how much land a single person could own. The revolutionaries tried to soften the blow to large landholders by stipulating that indemnities were to be paid to those whose land was expropriated.[39]

Despite the significance of the agrarian reform, first on the agenda for the MNR was the expropriation of the three largest mining companies, all of which were foreign owned. And this issue proved to be more contentious with respect to U.S.-Bolivian relations. Indeed, the issue of U.S. recognition of the regime was complicated by the MNR's nationalization of the three largest mining companies. On October 31, 1952, the MNR set up the Corporación Minera de Bolivia, or COMIBOL, formed from the companies of the three "tin barons." Historically, the MNR claimed, the profits of the mining industry had not been invested in Bolivia. Therefore, the MNR thought nationalization could provide the revenue it needed to reach its goals. The nationalization, of course, eliminated the power of the tin barons, whom the MNR feared.[40]

The Bolivians proved to be cautious revolutionaries, however. The new government, in particular its ambassador to the United States, Víctor Andrade Uzquiano, assured the *norteamericano* officials that the MNR was

37. Public Relations Office, Office of the Ministry of Foreign Affairs, *Bolivia's Struggle* (La Paz: Public Relations Office, Office of the Ministry of Foreign Affairs, 1956), 13, Pittsburgh Pamphlets.
38. Langer, *Southern Bolivia*, 200.
39. Public Relations Office, *Bolivia's Struggle*, 26.
40. Contreras C., *Bolivian Tin Mining Industry*, 9; Andrade, *My Missions for Revolutionary Bolivia*, 159.

not anti–private property, anti-American, or pro-Soviet.[41] Specifically regarding land reform, Paz Estenssoro emphasized that the Bolivian government would not touch "large properties which are worked on a 'capitalistic' basis."[42] The MNR was not communist; it shunned the pro-Moscow Bolivian Communist Party because the communists had allied with the anti-MNR authoritarian regimes in the 1940s.[43] Some of the members of the MNR's left wing—most notably some of the leaders of the powerful mine workers' union—were Trotskyites and thus not connected in any way with Moscow.[44] Moreover, the MNR went out of its way not to publicly criticize U.S. policy in the hemisphere—in particular Washington's move to oust the revolutionary regime of Jacobo Arbenz Guzmán in Guatemala in the early 1950s. In fact, in private, nearly all the MNR leadership thought that the party should support the Guatemalan revolutionaries. But in the end—because Bolivia needed U.S. diplomatic recognition and economic assistance—the MNR quietly accepted the idea of U.S. hegemony in the Western Hemisphere.[45]

The MNR's cautious centrism laid the groundwork for U.S. recognition of Paz Estenssoro's government on June 2, 1952.[46] Washington informed Bolivian leaders that recognition and future U.S. assistance would be held up until Bolivia promised to compensate the former mine owners.[47] U.S. assistance was key for right-wing members of the MNR in their bid to remain dominant in the coalition with their left-wing partners. Indeed, right-wing Bolivian officials saw U.S. economic assistance as a means of preserving their hard-won revolutionary gains.

For their part, the Bolivians agreed to compensate foreign investors who had holdings in the three largest mining companies.[48] However, the

---

41. Report of Bolivian Foreign Ministry on the Policy of the Government of Bolivia in the Negotiations of the Sale of Bolivian Tin, April 11, 1953, Decimal File 724.00/4–1153, RG 59, DOS Central Files, NA. U.S. stockholders owned at most 25 percent of only one of the largest three mining companies, Patiño Mines and Enterprises, Consolidated. Blasier, *Hovering Giant*, 87–88.

42. Memorandum of conversation, July 7, 1953, "Fiscal 1954–General 1955," Box 149, Geographical File, RG 469, Records of the Agency for International Development and Predecessor Agencies, NA.

43. Walter Guevara Arze, *Planteamientos de la revolución nacional en la décima conferencia inter-americana* (La Paz: Ministerio de Relaciones Exteriores y Culto, Departamento de Prensa y Publicaciones, 1954), 20, Pittsburgh Pamphlets.

44. Lora, *Bolivian Labour Movement*, 282.

45. Lehman, *Bolivia and the United States*, 116–17.

46. Blasier, *Hovering Giant*, 88, 131.

47. Zunes, "The United States and Bolivia," 38.

48. Andrade to Guevara Arze, August 9, 1954, *Embajada boliviana en Washington, julio–diciembre 1954*, ARE. Bolivia agreed in 1953 to compensate the former mine owners $21.7

Bolivian government did not think it was obligated to indemnify those who invested after the revolution (and before the nationalization became official on October 31, 1952). These investors, the MNR maintained, might have invested to capitalize on the probability that Washington would attempt to coerce Bolivia to reimburse U.S. investors after the nationalization took place.[49]

The United States ended up dispensing about $200 million of aid to Bolivia during the 1950s, a period when Washington officials did not want to disperse large amounts of foreign aid.[50] Even the famous U.S. aid package to Greece and Turkey in 1947 that launched the Truman Doctrine, was only $400 million.[51] In context, this number is very large: it was significantly more than any other Latin American government received during this decade. Why was Bolivia the exception? One important reason was that there was a history of U.S. economic assistance to Bolivia that dated back to 1942 and thus Bolivian officials understood how one went about getting foreign aid. Second, Ambassador Andrade knew how to cajole aid from the North American giant—he thoroughly understood how Washington worked and used this knowledge to influence U.S. policy.[52]

A new era in public-sector assistance to Latin America began with Bolivia. In a response to a letter sent to President Eisenhower on October 1, 1953, by Bolivian president Paz Estenssoro that requested emergency assistance (in particular food), Eisenhower stated that the United States would allocate the requested help "to assist Bolivia in this emergency and to help accelerate the economic diversification of your country."[53] However, U.S. assistance quickly grew beyond food aid to direct U.S. government grants.

---

million in installments. George M. Ingram, *Expropriation of U.S. Property in South America: Nationalization of Oil and Copper Companies in Peru, Bolivia, and Chile* (New York: Praeger, 1974), 132. By 1962, the MNR had paid US$20,236,663. George Jackson Eder, *Inflation and Development in Latin America: A Case History of Inflation and Stabilization in Bolivia* (Ann Arbor: Graduate School of Business Administration, University of Michigan, 1968), 549.

49. Report of Bolivian Foreign Ministry on the Policy of the Government of Bolivia in the Negotiations of the Sale of Bolivian Tin, April 11, 1953, Decimal File 724.00/4–1153, RG 59, DOS Central Files, NA.

50. Wilkie, *Bolivian Revolution and U.S. Aid*, 48; Statistics and Reports Division, *U.S. Overseas Loans and Grants*, 41.

51. Bolivia received 4.5 percent of all economic assistance given to Latin America during Eisenhower's tenure in office. Francis Adams, *Dollar Diplomacy: United States Economic Assistance to Latin America* (Aldershot, England: Ashgate, 2000), 129; Lawrence S. Wittner, *American Intervention in Greece, 1943–1947* (New York: Columbia University Press, 1982), 80.

52. Siekmeier, "Trailblazer Diplomat."

53. Dwight David Eisenhower, *Public Papers of the Presidents of the United States: Dwight David Eisenhower, 1953* (Washington, D.C.: U.S. Government Printing Office, 1954), 659.

A top Washington official who helped pave the way for U.S. assistance to Bolivia was Dr. Milton Eisenhower, the president's younger brother and Latin American adviser. He reflected the consensus view among U.S. Latin American policymakers: without assistance, the MNR would collapse and a virulently anti-American regime might come to power.[54] Fear, however, was not the only driving force behind Washington's policy. The "Outline Plan of Operations with Respect to Bolivia" maintained that "under the impact of United States aid and assistance, the regime has become increasingly inclined to accept United States viewpoints."[55] Most prominently, these "viewpoints" were admonitions that Bolivia keep its economy open to trade and foster a good investment climate. More specifically, this meant keeping the conservative wing of the MNR ascendant.[56] Finally, Bolivia became a laboratory in which officials could apply their hemispheric policy.[57]

Somewhat surprisingly, given the early cold war context, in 1953 fears of communism did not prominently figure into U.S. policymakers' considerations. Dr. Eisenhower believed the MNR's assurances that it was not communist; nor did he think a communist government would come to power in Bolivia if the MNR fell. Regarding the agrarian reform, Dr. Eisenhower noted that, "certainly the land reform movement was not 'Communist.' . . . Feudalism is far closer to Communism than the system of owner-operated farms installed by the Paz Estenssoro Government."[58] He stated in a letter to the president: "Should the present government fall, it seems probable that it will not be succeeded by a communist government nor by a fascist one."[59] U.S. policymakers, instead, feared a chaotic situation if the

---

For a fuller exploration of the Eisenhower administration's Bolivian aid policy, see Kenneth Lehman, "Braked but Not Broken: Mexico and Bolivia: Factoring the United States into the Revolutionary Equation," in *Proclaiming Revolution: Bolivia in Comparative Perspective*, ed. Merilee S. Grindle and Pilar Domingo (Cambridge: David Rockefeller Center of Latin American Studies, Harvard University Press, 2003).

54. Milton Eisenhower to Dwight David Eisenhower (hereafter DDE), January 11, 1954, "Eisenhower, Milton—South American Report 1953 (1)," Box 13, Name Series, Dwight David Eisenhower (DDE), Papers as President of the United States (hereafter Papers as President), Eisenhower Presidential Library, Abilene, Kans. (hereafter EL); Alexander, *Bolivian National Revolution*, 260–61.

55. Miron Burgin to John L. Topping, March 21, 1956, Decimal File 611.24/3–2156, RG 59, DOS Central Files, NA.

56. Lehman, "U.S. Foreign Aid," 489; G. Earl Sanders, "The Quiet Experiment in U.S Foreign Policy," *The Americas* 33 (Spring 1976): 25–49.

57. An excellent survey of U.S.-Bolivian relations in the 1950s, which touches on U.S.-Latin American relations in those years, is Francisco Roque Bacarreza, *Los años del cóndor*.

58. Eisenhower, *The Wine Is Bitter*, 68.

59. Milton Eisenhower to DDE, July 24, 1953, "Eisenhower, Milton, South American Report 1953 (5)," Box 13, Name Series, DDE: Papers as President, EL. Milton Eisenhower emphasizes this point in *The Wine Is Bitter*, 67–68.

MNR fell—in which radical leftists might fill the void and implement statist controls on the economy. Washington wanted to avoid a disintegration of the Bolivian government—an occurrence that could lead to a hostile regime coming to power in La Paz. (Since the MNR had virtually destroyed the Bolivian army, the United States did not have the option of supporting the military against the MNR.)

The Different Facets of U.S. Aid

During its first term, the Eisenhower administration provided two types of aid, monetary grants in 1953 and food grants in 1954. This represented a historic change; these types of aid had not previously been given to Latin American nations. In addition, the context in which the aid was given was significant. In 1953, Dr. Eisenhower visited Bolivia as part of a trip through South America. Citing food shortages and an imminent drop in the price of tin (the Korean War was winding down, and demand would slacken), Bolivian officials pressed the influential younger Eisenhower for U.S. aid.[60] The Bolivians were well aware that divisions within the MNR could hurt their efforts to receive assistance from the United States.[61] If the Bolivians appeared divided, the United States might withhold aid for fear the MNR coalition might disintegrate or take advantage of a divided Bolivia to weaken it further. Either way, the Bolivians realized the importance of presenting a united front.

One area in which Washington successfully opened up the Bolivian economy was the petroleum industry. Many in the U.S. petroleum industry believed that Bolivia had rich, unexploited oil fields.[62] The State Department wanted to funnel private sector investment toward Bolivia, and rightist MNR leaders thought that foreign investment would spur oil production. Initially, however, the prospects for exploiting Bolivia's oil looked poor for *norteamericano* oil companies. After all, the Bolivian government had nationalized Standard Oil in 1937—an action that inspired the leaders of the incipient MNR. And more ominous for U.S. leaders, late in 1952,

---

60. Speech of Paz Estenssoro, quoted in memorandum of conversation, February 24, 1954, Decimal File 824.062/2-2454, RG 59, DOS Central Files, NA. See also Eisenhower, *The Wine Is Bitter*, 194.

61. Foreign Minister to Bolivian Embassy in Washington, September 5, 1953, *Embajada boliviana en Washington, 1952–1956*, 264, ARE.

62. Whitehead, *The United States and Bolivia*, appendix 2, 28.

Bolivia and Iran established a "verbal agreement" to exchange information and establish "mutual cooperation" regarding the nationalization of the oil industries in those two nations.[63]

Instead, U.S. assistance led to a partial privatization of the oil industry. Bolivia received much-needed foreign investment—but at a high cost: it lost a good deal of control over its oil industry to foreign entities. In 1955 Bolivia revamped its Petroleum Code and opened the oil industry to foreign investment. This was in part because *norteamericano* lawyers helped write the Code. Washington ensured enactment of the Code by threatening to cut assistance if the law was not passed.[64] Under the Code foreign private sector companies fared well; the Bolivian state-owned oil company, the Yacimientos Petrolíferos Fiscales Bolivianos (YPFB), received only 11 percent of the total oil field concessions. All oil fields were open for current exploitation; the Bolivian code was the only Latin American oil code that did not cordon off some oil fields for future private exploitation. Other provisions gave the private sector oil companies first choice over which lands to exploit. Finally, the Code gave the private oil companies the right to market their products in Bolivia, a grant that severely hurt the YPFB's efforts in this area.[65] From the point of view of the U.S. and other foreign oil companies, the new Code was one of the most generous in all of Latin America.

Oil policy was not the only significant change in U.S.-Bolivian relations in the years 1954–55. In 1954 *norteamericano* officials began providing food aid. This not only alleviated hunger in Bolivia, but helped to reduce the storage costs of foodstuffs incurred by the U.S. government. In an effort to assist *norteamericano* farmers, a powerful constituency, Washington had stockpiled domestic agricultural products to raise their prices.[66] Public Law (PL) 480 aid began to flow to Bolivia in 1954.

63. Foreign Ministry in Bolivia to the Bolivian Embassy in the United States, December 2, 1952, *Embajada boliviana en Washington, 1952–1956*, 31, ARE.
64. Eder, *Inflation and Development in Latin America*, 60; Thomas Mann to Raymond G. Leddy, September 17, 1954, Country File Guatemala, 9, Holland Papers, Lot File (hereafter Lot) 57D295, Box 3, NA.
65. Whitehead, *The United States and Bolivia*, 29–33; ECLA, "Economic Policy of Bolivia," 80–81; Lois Deicke Martin, "Bolivia in 1956: An Analysis of Political and Economic Events," *Hispanic American Report: An Analysis of Developments in Spain, Portugal, and Latin America* 11, no. 1 (1958): 20–21.
66. Silberstein to Williams, May 23, 1957, Miscellaneous Material, Lot 63D87, Box 4, Office of Inter-American Regional Economic Affairs, RG 59, NA; Russell Edgerton, *Sub-Cabinet Politics and Policy Commitment: The Birth of the Development Loan Fund* (Syracuse, N.Y.: Inter-University Case Program, 1970), 27; "Proposed Instructions with Respect to Programs to Raise Consumption Levels and Accelerate Economic Development," June 18, 1956,

Unfortunately for Bolivia, Washington's food aid partially thwarted one of the goals of the revolution, diversification of the economy. Much of U.S. aid to Bolivia was given in the form of surplus foodstuffs. Between Fiscal Year (FY) 1954 and FY 1961, 15.9 percent of the aid was given in the form of foodstuffs. In FY 1955, the food-aid program was at its height: 47.8 percent of Washington's economic assistance was in the form of food aid—this high proportion of food assistance is understandable given Bolivia's traditional difficulty in feeding itself and the disruptions that flowed from the revolution and land reform.[67] Once in Bolivia, the surplus agricultural goods were sold and the funds put in special accounts to fund economic development projects. An important part of PL 480 aid to Bolivia was wheat flour, which had a predictable, and disastrous, effect on the Bolivian milling industry. Flour imports shot up, increasing from $1.6 million in 1953 to $9.2 million in 1961. This rise was particularly damaging because the Bolivians wanted to reduce the country's dependency on food imports. Bolivia's production of wheat and wheat flour plummeted. Wheat flour production dropped from 58.7 million kilos in 1953 to 6.1 million kilos in 1960.[68]

U.S.-Bolivian Relations Reach a Crossroads by 1956

Aid policy, however, did not comprise the sum total of U.S.-Bolivian relations in these years. The United States had been the main purchaser of Bolivian tin since World War I; during World War II Bolivian tin was very important to the U.S. war effort.[69] Washington's tin policy in the 1950s turned out to be a big disappointment for Bolivia. In March 1953, just over four months after the nationalization of the mines, the U.S. government-run Reconstruction Finance Corporation (RFC) announced it would not

---

PL 480 Loan Policy, Lot 63D87, Box 1, Office of Inter-American Regional Economic Affairs, RG 59, NA.

67. Bolivia received 4.3 percent of the total PL 480 aid given to Latin America during the Eisenhower administration. U.S. AID, Statistics and Reports Division, *U.S. Foreign Assistance*, 28, 30. This includes U.S. donations to international organizations.

68. República de Bolivia, Ministerio de Hacienda, Dirección General de Estadística y Censos, *Boletín Estadístico* 89 (1964): 109, 64. For an excellent analysis of the wheat-milling industry in Bolivia, and on the effect that U.S. policies had on it, see Laura Scobari de Querejazu, *Historia de la industria molinera boliviana* (La Paz: Asociación de Industriales Molineros, 1987), 104–21, and Melvin Burke, "Does 'Food for Peace' Assistance Damage the Bolivian Economy?" *Inter-American Economic Affairs* 25, no. 1 (Summer 1971): 3–21.

69. Contreras, *Bolivian Tin Mining Industry*, 6, 18.

purchase any more tin for its "buffer stock." Ambassador Andrade was angered by the decision.

> For my part . . . I expressed my profound disagreement [with the RFC's policy] because they were treating inter-American affairs with great indifference and without taking into effect the political aspects of inter-American relations. . . . I reminded them [U.S. officials] that Bolivia supported the United States during its moment of truth [during World War II] and did not benefit from the War, nor did it try to use its fortunate situation [i.e., as a tin producer during the War] for self-benefit. . . . At the same time I told them that Bolivia had always tried to help out the *norteamericanos* in its international relations. During the Cold War the Bolivians had remained loyal to the United States. In light of this, I told them it seemed contradictory—they desired Bolivian tin for strategic reasons they said, but then announced their lack of interest in buying it. They did not respond to my pointing out of the contradiction.[70]

Throughout the decade, Andrade pushed for a long-term contract for the sale of tin to the RFC, a key goal as tin revenues were to provide financial resources for the revolution. However, it was politically impossible for the U.S. government to stockpile more tin—U.S. officials could simply not defend granting long-term contracts to Bolivia to build up the tin stockpile, especially while world supplies were increasing and prices were falling. Washington leaders put their own bottom line (saving money by minimizing the tin stockpile) above Bolivia's interests. But because Bolivia made a convincing case that it needed assistance, Washington found aid to be the political path of least resistance.[71]

The RFC did reverse its policy of not buying Bolivian tin, but all it offered was a one-year contract in July 1953.[72] And indeed, this proved a hollow victory for Bolivia. The RFC soon reverted back to a policy that seemed to threaten Bolivia's economic interests. In 1955 Washington announced it would close a government-run smelter in Texas City in mid-1956, a facility

---

70. Andrade to Guevara Arze, "Negociaciones de venta del estaño," March 13, 1955, *Embajada boliviana en Washington, enero–junio 1953*, ARE.
71. Lehman, "Braked but Not Broken," 102; Blasier, *Hovering Giant*, 133–38.
72. Andrade to Guevara Arze, January 11, 1954, *Embajada boliviana en Washington, enero–junio 1954*, ARE; Andrade to Guevara Arze, June 27, 1953, *Embajada boliviana en Washington, enero–junio 1953*, ARE; Lehman, "U.S. Foreign Aid," 458–59.

specially equipped to handle low-grade Bolivian ores.[73] Government funding for the smelter represented, in effect, a form of assistance for Bolivia. Although there were different views in the first Eisenhower administration (1953–57) on the necessity of giving U.S. foreign assistance, fiscal conservatives, more often than not, won the debate. In particular the secretary of the treasury, George Humphrey, saw the U.S. government's subsidy of the Texas City smelter as wasteful federal government spending that needed to be stopped immediately. Not only did these fiscal conservatives want to curtail the U.S. federal government budget, they had a deep faith in the free-market system for allocating resources and rewarding efficient producers while punishing less efficient ones.[74]

Although the MNR could claim that it promoted economic, social, and political progress, there was still a long way to go. All in all, U.S. policy did not help the revolutionaries reach their goals. In January 1955, Ambassador Andrade sent a letter to General Glen E. Edgerton, chairman of the U.S. Export-Import Bank, outlining three "primary objectives" of the MNR. These objectives were not news to Edgerton, since the revolutionaries had stressed the importance of these objectives since their triumph in 1952. Andrade succinctly summarized them as follows: "1) to diminish the cost of the production of our minerals; 2) to accelerate the production of a dollar-producing commodity like oil, and 3) to diversify the domestic economy by increasing production of foodstuffs and other essential commodities that today are imported."[75] The large amount of U.S. assistance did little to help Bolivia achieve these goals—indeed, U.S. food assistance hindered Bolivia in its quest for economic diversification and self-sufficiency in critically important products.

By 1956, U.S.-Bolivian relations were at a crossroads. U.S. aid policy toward Bolivia had grown from a stopgap, emergency program to a program that aimed to prove that Washington could promote development in a poor nation—it aimed to show that inter-American economic relations could better the lives of average Bolivians, and by extension, all Latin Americans.[76] Although the idea of "modernization theory"—that the

---

73. Rabe, *Eisenhower and Latin America*, 82.

74. For more information on the debate within the Eisenhower administration over whether to give foreign assistance, and George Humphrey's anti-assistance position, see Siekmeier, *Aid, Nationalism, and Inter-American Relations*, 173–76.

75. Andrade to Glen E. Edgerton, January 24, 1955, *Embajada boliviana en Washington, enero–junio 1955*, ARE.

76. Andrade to Guevara Arze, January 10, 1956, *Embajada boliviana en Washington, enero–junio 1956*, ARE. Andrade also mentioned that the "ideological struggle" between the

United States, with a well-constructed assistance policy, could promote a capitalist economic development open to private sector investment and trade in the developing world—was still in its infancy in the 1950s, U.S. leaders used the principles of the theory in coming up with their Bolivia policy.[77] Andrade nicely summarized Bolivia's new importance to the United States: "The case of Bolivia is a 'test case' of economic cooperation and technical assistance which can help to assemble the present factors towards a successful conclusion: a major crisis, potential riches to develop, and a government and people willing to develop them. If technical assistance and aid do not work in Bolivia, they will not work in the rest of Latin America."[78] Indeed, the destinies of Bolivia and the United States were now closely linked. Andrade was correct to point out that "the occurrences of 1953 were a turning point in U.S. history."[79] If Bolivia collapsed, U.S. prestige would be damaged.[80]

The Role of Ambassador Víctor Andrade

Víctor Andrade played an important role in U.S.-Bolivian relations during the 1952 Bolivian revolution. One of Bolivia's top diplomats of the twentieth century, Andrade served as Bolivian ambassador to the United States from 1944 to 1946; from 1952 to 1958; and from 1960 to 1962, crucial years in the run-up to the 1952 Bolivian revolution and during the revolution itself. He was one of the first ambassadors from the nonindustrialized world to be able to influence his nation's relationship with the United States. His understanding of U.S. culture proved key to "selling" the Bolivian revolution to U.S. officials.[81]

Soviet Union and the United States was taking place in the developing world (including Bolivia): each wanted to prove itself the better friend to developing nations.

77. For an excellent description of the power of modernization theory over the minds of U.S. officials with regard to Third World policy, see Latham, *Modernization as Ideology*. In his impressive *Latin American Underdevelopment: A History of Perspectives in the United States, 1970–1965* (Baton Rouge: Louisiana State University Press, 1995), James William Park defines modernization theory as an attempt "to order and formalize increasingly complex explanations for underdevelopment and to propose remedies consonant with U.S. historical experience" (167).

78. Andrade to Guevara Arze, January 10, 1956, No. 5, "Memorandum—Recopilación de antecedentes sobre asistencia económica y técnica de los EE.UU. a Bolivia," *Embajada boliviana en Washington, enero–junio 1956*, 9–17, ARE.

79. Ibid.

80. Philip W. Bonsal to Roy R. Rubottom, December 4, 1958, Decimal File 824.00 TA/ 12-0458, RG 59, DOS Central Files, NA.

81. Andrade, *My Missions for Revolutionary Bolivia*, 136–37.

Given the long history of U.S. hostility toward Latin American revolutionaries, it is remarkable that Washington gave a significant amount of assistance to the MNR.[82] Most explanations focus on internal Washington politics and how U.S. policymakers framed their Latin American policy.[83] However, scholars have not fully investigated Andrade's part in the shaping of the U.S.-Bolivian relationship during Bolivia's crucial prerevolutionary and revolutionary years.[84]

Andrade skillfully used his abilities as a public speaker and as someone who could make and maintain contacts with important people in a deliberate, systematic way to attempt to influence U.S. policy. More specifically, Andrade used his position to try to propel one group of revolutionaries, the cautious moderates of the MNR, to power. Although his actions reinforced already existing tendencies among Washington officialdom, Andrade proved to be an important trailblazer for future Bolivian leaders in their attempts to influence U.S. policy.

There is a small, but growing literature on attempts by developing-world leaders to influence Washington policymakers during the 1950s.[85] Recent studies of Taiwan and Tibet have focused on how leaders in the developing world have exerted some influence on Washington's actions in Asia.[86] There is a growing body of literature that emphasizes the importance of individuals in the making of U.S.–Latin American relations in the

---

82. According to U.S. Agency for International Development, Statistics and Reports Division, Office of Programs and Policy Coordination, Agency for Development, *U.S. Overseas Loans and Grants: Obligations and Loan Authorizations* (Washington, D.C.: U.S. Government Printing Office, 1985), 41, the amount was $192.5 million for 1953–61. For a detailed quantitative analysis of the Bolivia aid program that focuses on U.S. economic aid's impact on the Bolivian national budget, see Wilkie, *Bolivian Revolution and U.S. Aid*, 48. Wilkie, using a variety of U.S. Agency for International Development sources, says that the total aid given during this period was $198.2 million.

83. In addition to works by Blasier and Rabe, see also Zunes, "The United States and Bolivia."

84. Andrade began his career as a diplomat when he became Bolivia's ambassador to the United States from 1944 to 1946. In addition, in 1958 he became Bolivia's foreign minister, but then returned to the ambassadorship in 1960, a post he held until 1962. Willaim H. Brubeck, Executive Secretary, to McGeorge Bundy, February 13, 1962, Folder "Bol-Gen 8/62–12/62," Box 10, Country File: Bolivia, National Security File (hereafter NSF), John F. Kennedy Library, Boston, Mass. (hereafter JFK Library).

85. For a review of the literature, see Zachary Karabell, *Architects of Intervention: The United States, the Third World, and the Cold War, 1946–1962* (Baton Rouge: Louisana State University Press, 1999), 7n16.

86. Nick Cullather, "'Fuel for the Good Dragon': The United States and Industrial Policy in Taiwan, 1950–1965," in *Empire and Revolution: The United States and the Third World Since 1945*, ed. Peter Hahn and Mary Ann Heiss (Columbus: Ohio State University Press,

1950s.[87] More recent works have discussed how Latin American leaders subtly yet persistently attempted (at times successfully) to influence Washington's policy in the Americas.[88]

Previous historical studies of individuals' efforts in shaping U.S.–Latin American relations have, in general, centered on white individuals, or nonwhites from the United States.[89] What is lacking is a study of nonwhite Latin American officials. Andrade, who was of Indian background, proved to be an important early example of a nonwhite developing-world leader who managed to influence U.S. policy.

Andrade's race is an important part of his story. A key context for Andrade's work in Washington is the changing nature of race relations both in the United States and the wider world. Starting in the 1940s, nonwhites around the world began to systematically challenge the white-dominated racial hierarchy.[90] The Bandung Conference of 1955, a meeting of developing-world leaders mainly from Asia and Africa, was a good example of this new spirit.[91] The response of European and U.S. officials (while understanding the potential power of populations of the nonindustrialized world) was to maintain their racist attitudes. The 1952 Bolivian revolution, because it gave all Indians the right to vote for the first time in Bolivian history, represented, like Bandung, an effort on the part of nonwhites to increase their influence. Moreover, Andrade, as an Aymara Indian, in a

---

2001), 242–68; Guoqiang Zheng, "The Invisible Hand: The United States and the Aftermath of the Tibetan Revolt, 1959–1960," *American Review of China Studies: Journal of the Association of Chinese Professors of Social Sciences in the U.S.* 4 (Spring 2003): 49–64.

87. Two works on this topic include Charles D. Ameringer, *The Democratic Left in Exile: The Antidictatorial Struggle in the Caribbean, 1945–1949* (Coral Gables: University of Miami Press, 1974), and C. Neale Ronning and Albert P. Vannucci, *Ambassadors in Foreign Policy: The Influence of Individuals on U.S.–Latin American Policy* (New York: Praeger, 1987).

88. Rivas, "Like Boxing with Joe Louis"; Longley, *The Sparrow and the Hawk*.

89. Brenda Gayle Plummer, *Rising Wind: Black Americans and U.S. Foreign Affairs, 1935–1960* (Chapel Hill: University of North Carolina Press, 1996) and *Window on Freedom: Race, Civil Rights, and Foreign Affairs, 1945–1988* (Chapel Hill: University of North Carolina Press, 2003), and Michael Krenn, *Black Diplomacy: African Americans in the State Department, 1945–1966* (Armonk, N.Y.: M. E. Sharpe), are recent examples of works that look at African American diplomats from the United States.

90. Plummer, *Rising Wind*, 167–328; Borstelmann, *The Cold War and the Color Line*, 85–134; Mary L. Dudziak, *Cold War Civil Rights: Race and the Image of American Democracy* (Princeton: Princeton University Press, 2000), 79–114.

91. For recent works on the Bandung Conference that center on race, see Parker, "Small Victory, Missed Chance"; Penny M. Von Eschen, *Race Against Empire: Black Americans and Anticolonialism, 1937–1957* (Ithaca: Cornell University Press, 1997); and Cary Fraser, "An American Dilemma: Race and Realpolitik in the American Response to the Bandung Conference, 1955," in *Window on Freedom: Race, Civil Rights, and Foreign Affairs, 1945–1988*, ed. Brenda Gayle Plummer (Chapel Hill: University of North Carolina Press, 2003), 115–40.

sense represented an increase in influence for Bolivians of indigenous heritage. He was the first Bolivian ambassador of indigenous heritage.[92] And indeed, he had to face racism in his relationship with Washington's representatives in Latin America.[93]

Andrade was born in 1905 in Chulumani, a town in the semitropical Yungas region of Bolivia, approximately eighty miles northeast of the nation's capital.[94] Most Indians in the Yungas were and are Aymara. Although the majority of Indians had very modest means, Andrade came from a family of landowners. He enrolled in the Colegio Metodista (also known as the American Institute) in La Paz, run by Methodist missionaries from the United States. There he acquired proficiency in the English language at a time when few Bolivians spoke it.[95] But he learned far more than English. Andrade claimed in his memoirs that "the democratic idea of the American teachers [at the Institute] had great influence on the intellectuals" who would agitate for revolutionary change in Bolivia—including himself. Andrade concluded, "[The Institute's teachers] . . . put the Bolivian first—his problems, his needs, and his aspirations. They tried to lift him up and incorporate him into contemporary civilized life without his losing his personality or his culture."[96]

He also learned about the United States and about the technological revolution unfolding in the industrialized world at that time. He wanted to help bring this kind of modernization to his native country. In many respects, he proved representative of a new, postwar middle class that emerged in Latin America partly as the result of increased industrialization. During the Great Depression and World War II, Latin American nations could no longer rely on imports of capital goods from abroad and found it necessary to at least begin to industrialize.[97]

Andrade so distinguished himself as a student that the Colegio Metodista offered him a teaching position immediately after his graduation.[98]

Like many of the leaders who formed the nucleus of the early MNR, Andrade served in the Chaco War against Paraguay (1932–35). The war, a

92. Julio Sanjines Goitia, *148 años de las relaciones diplomáticas Bolivia–Estados Unidos* (La Paz: Centro Boliviano Americano, 1996), 81–86.
93. When Andrade came to the home of a U.S. official, the official called to his wife that a "savage" was at the door. Lehman, *Bolivia and the United States*, 130.
94. The Aymara, who have lived in Bolivia for centuries, live in the greater La Paz–Lake Titicaca region.
95. Andrade, *My Missions for Revolutionary Bolivia*, 3–4.
96. Ibid., 4.
97. Ameringer, *Democratic Left in Exile*, 19.
98. Lupe Andrade Salmón, interview, April 15, 1997, La Paz.

devastating defeat for Bolivia, raised questions for many Bolivian citizens about Bolivia's very unequal, even backward social, economic, and political systems. In large part, the Indians had been the cannon fodder. They, however, were not the only ones who were angry. The younger officers severely criticized the poor decisions of the generals. All in all, the war offered a unique opportunity for critics of Bolivia's government and society from various parts of the nation to meet each other and compare notes.[99]

In the mid-1940s, Andrade and other MNR members served in the reformist government of Gualberto Villarroel, an administration that foreshadowed the revolution in some respects. The reformist Villarroel attempted during his tenure to improve life for Bolivia's middle class and its workers. As Villarroel's minister of labor, health, and social services, Andrade attempted to mitigate the problems faced by those of meager means.

As an official representative of Bolivia, Andrade attended a World Labor Conference in the United States in April 1944; the meeting was convened by the International Labor Office. This trip was his first visit to North America. The first hurdle he faced was the fact that the United States had refused to recognize the Villarroel regime on the grounds that it was fascist. Andrade, who very much appreciated the importance of U.S. recognition, emphasized in conversations with U.S. officials that Villarroel in no way favored fascism, that in fact he represented a grassroots desire on the part of many Bolivians for social change. A month after the conference, the United States granted recognition.[100]

The World Labor Conference proved to be a turning point in Andrade's career. There, he forged ties to important U.S. journalists. More important, he made contact with some prominent labor leaders from the United States.[101] These union officials, in particular well-connected organizers

99. Herbert S. Klein, *Bolivia*, 187; Klein, *Orígenes de la revolución nacional boliviana: La crisis de la generación del Chaco*, trans. Rodolfo Medrano (La Paz: Editorial Juventud, 1968), 221–22, 321–33. An important history of the Chaco War is Roberto Querejazu Calvo, *Historia de la Guerra del Chaco* (La Paz: Librería Editorial "Juventud," 1990). This is an updated version of his highly regarded *Masamaclay: Historia política, diplomática y militar de la Guerra del Chaco* (La Paz: Editorial Los Amigos del Libro, 1975), which went through four editions.

100. Andrade helped this process along by writing to Laurence Duggan, assistant secretary of state for Inter-American Affairs, describing Bolivia's attempts at this time to solve its social problems, in particular the problem of poor working conditions. Andrade to Laurence Duggan, May 18, 1949, Box 3, Andrade Papers, La Paz. U.S. recognition, however, came at a price. The MNR members of the cabinet were forced to resign. Andrade, *My Missions for Revolutionary Bolivia*, 28.

101. Victor Andrade Uzquiano, *La revolución boliviana y los Estados Unidos, 1944–1962* (La Paz: Editorial Gisbert, 1979), 47.

from the Congress of Industrial Organizations (CIO), proved to be very important to Andrade when he was appointed ambassador to the United States from 1944 to 1946, and later on in the 1950s.[102] In the latter period, these unionists helped him get access to top members of Congress and other important Washington leaders.

Further, the conference gave him confidence to fight for Bolivia's interests in the world arena. In 1946 a *golpe de estado* (coup d'état) toppled Villarroel's government and forced Andrade into exile. However, before his abrupt departure from his ambassadorship, he successfully prevailed upon U.S. officials to lift a restriction that they had placed on Bolivia preventing it from selling its tin to third parties. Andrade carried out his goal by threatening to appeal to the new United Nations (where Andrade had served as Bolivia's representative) and argued that the U.S. rule was an unfair trade restriction.[103]

At a very early stage of his career, Andrade learned two things. First, he recognized his ability to influence U.S. policy. Second, he concluded that Villarroel's ouster meant that deeper social change would be necessary to prevent the toppling of future reformist governments.

At the same time, Andrade came to believe that building a strong relationship with the United States was imperative. His traumatic experiences in the Chaco War had taught him that Bolivia needed to deepen its ties to its giant neighbor to the north. Andrade believed (a view not held by all observers) that friendly U.S.-Bolivian relations might have deterred Paraguay and Argentina from allying against Bolivia.[104] Also, he believed that in the postwar era the United States would amass a great degree of control over Latin America.[105] Finally, Andrade and other members of the middle-class segment of the MNR, most notably Walter Guevara Arze, firmly believed that U.S. economic aid was needed for Bolivia to accomplish vital goals—most notably diversification of the economy.[106]

102. Although at first the Latin American representative of the American Federation of Labor (AFL), Serafino Romualdi, was very critical of the MNR, he later reversed his position. Romualdi to Andrade, April 14, 1949, Box 3, AP; Ernesto Galarza, CIO official, to Romualdi, June 8, 1949, Box 3, AP; Blasier, *Hovering Giant*, 130. The Congress of Industrial Organizations (CIO), however, proved to be a much better friend than the AFL for the MNR.
103. Blasier, *Hovering Giant*, 51.
104. Lupe Andrade Salmón, interview, April 15, 1997, La Paz.
105. Andrade to President Gualberto Villarroel, July 4, 1946, Box 1, AP.
106. Andrade, "Jura al Gabinete—Palacio de Gobierno, Día Martes 18 de Agosto, 1958, hrs 12:00," Box 1, AP. See also Guevara Arze, *Plan inmediato*.

The Ambassador Arrives in Washington

From the moment he arrived in Washington in 1952, Andrade anticipated his job would be difficult. He recognized that a sea change had transpired in U.S. foreign policy toward Latin America beginning in the mid-1940s. In memos to his superiors in La Paz he observed that those Roosevelt administration officials who had once supported the Good Neighbor Policy had been replaced by supporters of big business. The Good Neighbor Policy was moribund, he argued; Washington officials were now primarily concerned with creating a climate conducive for U.S. exports to the region. As he put it in a letter to Bolivia's foreign minister, U.S. policy toward its neighbors to the south was to be "more focused on commerce" and "less inclined to consider friendly inter-American political relations as important."[107] However, Andrade also knew that U.S. officials, especially as fears of the spreading influence of communism mounted, wanted a stable, pro-*norteamericano* Latin America. For that reason, Andrade had some hope that U.S. officials would extend aid to Bolivia.

Andrade was correct—his job would be difficult, and the difficulty was even exacerbated by his government's own actions. As mentioned previously, only a few months after his arrival in 1952, the MNR nationalized the holdings of the tin barons.[108] There was a broad consensus in Bolivia,

---

107. The quotation is from Andrade to Foreign Minister, December 20, 1944, Box 2, AP. (All translations from the Spanish are mine.) Andrade particularly bemoaned the rise to prominence in the Roosevelt administration in 1944–45 of Edward Stettinius, William Clayton, and Nelson Rockefeller, whom he described as "business magnates," although he and Rockefeller later became good friends. Andrade to President Gualberto Villarroel, late 1944, Box 2, AP. In addition, Andrade feared the policy changed signaled by the appointments of Jesse Jones, who he said was "of known reactionary leanings," and Leo Crowley of the Foreign Economic Administration, whom he termed "a Wall Street shark." As evidence of these new conservative leanings, in late 1944 Andrade noted his difficulty, and ultimate failure, in getting the U.S. government to continue to accept a "labor clause" in contracts signed between U.S. companies operating in Bolivia and Bolivian entities. The "labor clause," which U.S. officials agreed to in 1942, forced the U.S. companies to adhere to Bolivia's laws regarding working conditions and pay, which meant that a specific portion of the returns on sales of metals to the United States went to the workers. Andrade, *La revolución boliviana*, 60–62, 97; Andrade to Foreign Minister D. Gustavo Chacón, December 28, 1944, Box 2, AP. Later, in 1948, Andrade argued that William Clayton had a great deal of control over U.S. economic policy toward Latin America, and he wanted to use this power to ensure open markets for U.S. businessmen. Andrade to Corporación Fomento de Venezuela, November 20, 1948, Box 3, AP.

108. In addition to the nationalization of the tin barons' holdings, all private sector mines that exported minerals had to sell them to the Banco Minero de Bolivia, and all mineral exporters' foreign exchange earnings had to be converted into bolivianos (the Bolivian cur-

with which Andrade concurred, that the tin barons' Bolivian holdings needed to be nationalized; only this bold move would, once and for all, eviscerate their political power.

In the wake of the nationalization, Andrade took immediate steps to combat anti-MNR propaganda by the former tin barons. Andrade's attempted preemptive strike did not deter the tin barons from launching a counteroffensive in Washington to undermine the revolution. They aimed, first, to put the MNR on the defensive by forcing the Bolivian government to concede significant indemnification. Second, they wished to thwart the MNR government's goals and even drive it from power.[109] To these ends, the once-powerful tin barons hired a public relations firm to convince Washington officials of the Bolivian revolution's communist orientation. While this firm dispatched anti-MNR material to U.S. officials, the former tin barons themselves engaged in efforts to get the U.S. press to publish anti-MNR articles. In addition, the mining moguls helped to finance the translation and distribution of an anti-MNR book entitled *The Tragedy of Bolivia: A People Crucified*, which tarred the MNR as having had fascist-totalitarian, communist, and Peronist tendencies during different phases of its history.[110] Much of Andrade's efforts in the early 1950s went toward countering the tin barons' lobbying campaign.[111]

But his message went beyond simply responding to the tin barons' attacks on the MNR. Andrade never tired of expounding on two very important needs. First, he explained that the Bolivian government desired U.S. aid as investment capital to lower the production cost of Bolivian minerals,

---

rency) at the Central Bank at the official rate of exchange. Thorn, "Economic Transformation," 160; Dunkerley, *Rebellion in the Veins*, 58.

109. Roque, *Los años del cóndor*, 185. Andrade thought that the tin barons wanted "to convince the [U.S.] Congress to eliminate the aid program, causing hunger which would produce chaos," discrediting the MNR. Andrade to Antenor Patiño R. (the son of Simón I. Patiño, one of the original tin barons), June 15, 1958, Box 3, AP.

110. Andrade, *My Missions for Revolutionary Bolivia*, 136; Alberto Ostria Gutierrez, *The Tragedy of Bolivia: A People Crucified* (New York: Devin Adair, 1958), 4–14, 95, 111, 221–24, 134–37, 191–204. Interestingly, the book taps into the strong current of Bolivian nationalism at that time by concluding that the MNR had reduced itself to "abject pleading" to the United States for aid money (177).

111. A fair fight it was not. At the end of January 1953, *Hanson's Latin American Letter* discussed the "line-up of the fight for the Bolivian properties, law and public relations." For the tin barons' part, they were planning to pay $100,000 (plus expenses) to a public relations firm, and an additional $24,000 and fees "scaled to effectiveness" to former senator Millard Tydings's law firm for "negotiations and any necessary legal actions." For the MNR's part they had hired $4,000 (plus expenses) of services from the public relations firm of Selvage, Lee, and Chase and were planning to pay former senator John Danaher $2,500 up front plus more later if he, "generally speaking," got "results." "Bolivia Hires Ex-Senator Danaher," *Hanson's Latin American Letter*, January 31, 1953, Box 3, AP.

develop the oil industry, and diversify and develop its economy, especially the agricultural sector. Second, he assured U.S. officials that the MNR government was anticommunist, moderate, and pro-American.[112] Andrade made it clear to U.S. officials that it was in their interest to support the MNR, specifically, the cautious, moderate wing of the party.[113] His remarkable success at swinging U.S. government support toward the faction of the MNR of which he was a member is an excellent example of how the relatively weak can influence the relatively powerful.[114]

In reality, as mentioned previously, only the conservative wing of the Bolivian revolution was anticommunist, moderate, and pro-American. Enlisting U.S. support, the ambassador hoped, would lead his wing of the revolution to triumph over the competing, more radical element of the MNR, which was calling for eventual worker management of the means of production and an anti-American stance. Judging from his voluminous correspondence, Andrade's circle of friends and associates was from the moderate wing of the party. The diplomatic notes exchanged between the Bolivian embassy in Washington and La Paz, and the correspondence between Andrade and the middle-class leadership of the revolution, show that Andrade firmly believed in, and tried to implement, the politically moderate, economically capitalist, and diplomatically pro-American views of his wing of the party.

When discussing the Bolivian revolution with U.S. leaders, Andrade emphasized that the United States "needs to understand . . . that whatever government succeeds ours would be *unfavorable* to its [U.S.] foreign policy" (emphasis added). Andrade understood both the U.S. fear that the

---

112. Víctor Andrade to Glen E. Edgerton, January 24, 1955, *Embajada boliviana en Washington, enero–junio 1955*, ARE; "Comentarios hechos en el departamento de estado sobre los sucesos de la séptima convención nacional del M.N.R.," January 27, 1956, Box 3, AP. When speaking to the cabinet of the Bolivian government, Andrade was more forceful: U.S. aid could provide a means by which Bolivia could achieve "true economic independence." Andrade, "Jura al Gabinete—Palacio de Gobierno, Día Martes 18 de Agosto, 1958, hrs 12:00," Box 1, AP.

113. Andrade outlined the differences between Lechín's faction and the more moderate MNR membership in a meeting with the U.S. ambassador to Bolivia Edward Sparks. Andrade saw Lechín as the leader of a minority faction of radicals in the MNR and Paz Estenssoro as representing the majority of the Bolivian people. Memorandum of conversation, April 14, 1954, Decimal File 824.25/4–1454, RG 59, DOS Central Files, NA.

114. One author who has examined how the relatively poor have argued to the wealthy that it is in the interests of the wealthy to aid them is Scott, *Weapons of the Weak*, 308–12. For more citations on this theme, see John J. Dwyer, "Diplomatic Weapons of the Weak: Mexican Policymaking During the U.S.-Mexican Agrarian Dispute, 1934–1941," *Diplomatic History* 26, no. 3 (Summer 2002): 375–95, especially notes 2 and 3.

revolution might take an economic nationalist turn and the acute anticommunism of 1950s Washington—which, of course, included congressmen who voted for foreign aid bills. He emphasized that treating Bolivia well would provide the most "significant propaganda against communism" in Bolivia.[115] The vast majority of U.S. officials agreed.

Andrade's efforts to garner U.S. support for the moderate segment of the revolution were helped by President Paz Estenssoro's assurances to U.S. officials that Bolivia would not support other Latin American revolutions. In addition, Paz also assured U.S. leaders that agrarian reform would enhance Bolivian capitalism and that the nationalization of the three largest mining companies would not spread to other parts of the Bolivia economy.[116]

Andrade's Techniques: An Analysis

Andrade's considerable skill as a diplomat emanated not only from his thorough knowledge of U.S. political culture, but also from his systematic and persistent quest to promote the Bolivian revolution in the United States. Andrade used three main strategies to get his message across. First, he developed friendships to gain access to powerful people in Washington.[117] For example, he realized the labor leaders he met during his 1944 visit to the United States could help him make contact with top Washington leaders. In this regard, Gardner Jackson of the Congress of Industrial Organizations (CIO) was instrumental when he introduced Andrade to Dr. Milton Eisenhower.[118] Andrade seized the chance to befriend the younger

---

115. Lehman, "Revolutions and Attributions," 198; Andrade to President Víctor Paz Estenssoro, February 21, 1953, Box 3, AP.

116. Lehman, *Bolivia and the United States*, 116–17; Blasier, *Hovering Giant*, 88, 131. Paz told top U.S. officials that large properties run on a "capitalistic" basis would not be touched. Memorandum of conversation, July 7, 1953, "Fiscal 1954–General 1955," Box 149, Geographical File, RG 469, Records of the Agency for International Development and Predecessor Agencies, NA.

117. Andrade outlined the importance of attempting to influence U.S. policy in a memorandum to the Foreign Ministry. Andrade to Foreign Minister, "Memorandum—Recopilación de antecedentes sobre asistencia económica y técnica de los EE.UU a Bolivia," January 10, 1956, No. 6, *Embajada boliviana en Washington, enero–junio 1956*, 12–13, ARE.

118. Andrade, *My Missions for Revolutionary Bolivia*, 171. During Andrade's tenure as ambassador, Jackson emphasized that the MNR represented the only hope for a pro-U.S. stability in Bolivia, and a crumbling of the MNR would be "a real blow" to U.S. prestige in Latin America. He also mentioned the importance of Bolivian tin. Jackson to M. Eisenhower,

Eisenhower and was the only Latin American representative to brief him before his 1953 trip to South America.[119]

Why did the CIO take an interest in Bolivia? First, the CIO felt a sense of solidarity with the Bolivian workers, who experienced very poor working and living conditions. These conditions were dramatically exposed to CIO leaders when they traveled to Bolivia in 1942 to investigate the Catavi massacre.[120] However, the CIO had a more narrow, institutional reason for supporting the Bolivian revolution: the U.S. government in the early 1950s contemplated shutting down its smelter in Texas City, the only one in the United States that could refine low-grade Bolivian ore. The revolutionaries pleaded with U.S. leaders to keep it open because tin sales to the North Americans could provide much-needed foreign exchange. CIO leaders also wanted the Texas City plant to continue processing ore because the union represented the workers in the facility.[121]

When Milton Eisenhower returned from Latin America, he reported that Latin America was in need of more development aid.[122] Eisenhower

---

November 28, 1956, Box 1, AP. Jackson was not the only CIO official concerned with Bolivia. Ernesto Galarza, another top CIO officer, was supportive of Andrade's efforts in Washington. Galarza's interest in Bolivia stretched back at least until 1931, when he wrote an article on Bolivia's economic and political problems in the 1920s and early 1930s. His article highlighted the poor working conditions in Bolivia and the country's large national debt. Galarza, "Debts, Dictatorship, and Revolution in Bolivia and Peru," *Foreign Policy Reports*, May 13, 1931, 101–18.

119. Andrade was the only South American ambassador to have briefed Milton Eisenhower before his trip. Andrade's connections in Washington help to explain this. U.S. Senator Ralph Flanders from Vermont wrote to Milton Eisenhower, urging him to meet with Andrade before leaving for South America. Flanders to M. Eisenhower, May 21, 1953, Box 3, AP. Flanders also spoke of Bolivia's difficulty in producing food to feed itself, despite large tracts of arable land. Sam B. Bledsoe, a top official at Selvage, Lee, and Chase, the public relations firm Andrade briefly hired, also wrote to Milton Eisenhower, saying that Andrade "probably could give you more and better information about Latin America than almost anyone else in Washington." Bledsoe to M. Eisenhower, May 5, 1953, Box 3, AP. Andrade knew that U.S. leaders often knew little about Latin America, and Andrade skillfully used his position as the main educator of Eisenhower and other officials to attempt to influence U.S. policy.

120. John Moors Cabot, Assistant Secretary of State for Inter-American Affairs, to Jacob Potofsky of the CIO, June [?] 1953, Box 1, AP. A 1954 CIO convention resolution stated, "Our [U.S.] foreign policy . . . must be based on the decent aspirations of people everywhere—to live in peace, friendship and harmony with those of other lands, working in brotherhood to raise living standards, to promote freedom and to achieve personal security." Quoted in Robert Zieger, *The CIO, 1935–1955* (Chapel Hill: University of North Carolina Press, 1995), 329.

121. Walter P. Reuther, President of CIO, to Arthur S. Flemming, Director, Office of Defense Mobilization, May 9, 1954, Box 1, AP.

122. Milton Eisenhower, *Report to the President: United States–Latin American Relations*, November 18, 1953 (Washington, D.C.: Department of State, 1953), 32–33.

had been impressed with Paz Estenssoro's government, believing it was implementing needed reforms.[123] Andrade's post-1953 efforts to portray the Bolivian revolution in a positive light proved to be a constant reinforcement of Dr. Eisenhower's initial assessment of the revolution.

Another particularly important person whom Andrade befriended was Nelson Rockefeller. Rockefeller served in important positions in President Eisenhower's administration, and he had earlier served as a Latin American expert in Franklin Roosevelt's administration. Rockefeller and Andrade first met in Santiago, Chile, at an international conference in 1942.[124] Early on, the men developed mutual respect. Rockefeller very much appreciated Andrade's work at the United Nations conference in San Francisco in 1945 and generally respected Andrade's intelligence and skill as a diplomat. For Andrade's part, he very much admired Rockefeller and valued him as an extension of an earlier foreign policy posture, the last holdover of the quickly fading Good Neighbor policy.[125] And there were more personal reasons for Andrade's friendship with Rockefeller. While Andrade was in exile in 1948–49, Rockefeller paid his salary as a visiting professor at the New School for Social Research in New York City. Later he worked for Rockefeller's International Basic Economy Corporation in Ecuador.[126]

Andrade cultivated his friendships with powerful people by emphasizing that Bolivian foreign policy had traditionally supported key U.S. interests.[127] In one conversation with State Department officials, for example, he stressed that Bolivia had always been interested in maintaining an open market with the United States. Andrade made this assertion in the context of one of his persistent struggles during the 1950s: his efforts to secure a long-term contract to sell tin to the United States, specifically to the Reconstruction Finance Corporation (RFC), the U.S. government agency that

---

123. Eisenhower, *The Wine Is Bitter*, 67–68.

124. "Notes on Activities with Nelson Rockefeller," Folder 53, Countries Series, Box 9, Nelson A. Rockefeller, Personal, RG 4, Rockefeller Family Archives, Rockefeller Archive Center, Tarrytown, N.Y.

125. Rockefeller to Hubert C. Winans, June 17, 1948, Box 3, AP; Andrade to Nelson Rockefeller, November 28, 1958, Box 3, AP; Andrade to Corporación Fomento de Venezuela, November 20, 1948, Box 3, AP.

126. Bryn J. Hovde, President of the New School for Social Research, to Andrade, March 11, 1949, Box 3, AP.

127. In the past, when successfully "selling" a policy, policymakers have tapped into time-honored, long-standing policies of their nation that have become myths. Eldon Kenworthy explored how U.S. policymakers have successfully "sold" policy toward Latin America to the North American public in his *America/Américas: Myth in the Making of U.S. Policy Toward Latin America* (University Park: Pennsylvania State University Press, 1995), esp. 1–54.

stockpiled critical raw materials. (Andrade was ultimately unsuccessful in his efforts in this area.)[128] If the U.S. government agreed to a long-term contract, he thought, the Bolivian people would be more inclined to accept the idea of a U.S. "Open Door" in Bolivia.[129]

In addition to developing personal friendships in an attempt to influence U.S. policy, Andrade carefully monitored and attempted to shape Bolivia's image in the U.S. press. He kept careful track of what the *norteamericano* media published on Bolivia; in addition, he briefly hired a public relations firm (Selvage, Lee, and Chase) to help him vigilantly and continuously keep abreast of what North American newsmen were printing on Bolivia. Andrade met with influential Washington journalists Marquis Childs, Walter Lippmann, Arthur Krock, and Herbert Matthews, as well as nourishing a rewarding and close friendship with Drew Pearson, a *Washington Post* columnist at the time.[130] Although the *Washington Post* is significant even today in shaping U.S.–Latin American relations, in the 1950s it was the main source of information on Latin America for most lawmakers.[131] Moreover, these reporters wrote the *Post's* society section, covering "cultural events" that the ambassador and his family attended and social events that he organized. These activities provided an important forum for Bolivia to raise its profile on the Washington circuit.[132]

This dimension of Andrade's lobbying efforts was connected to his third technique for influencing U.S. policy—educating the *norteamericanos* about the Bolivian revolution while making himself well known in Washington circles. Andrade frequently gave speeches to universities, fraternal organizations, entrepreneurial groups, and civic clubs throughout the United States, trying to raise the public's consciousness regarding Bolivia.

---

128. The Eisenhower administration at first denied Bolivia's request to sell tin to the Reconstruction Finance Corporation (RFC). In early 1953 the RFC said it would not purchase tin, but in July of that same year it reversed itself and offered Bolivia a one-year contract to buy tin. During the 1950s, the RFC occasionally gave Bolivia one-year contracts. Andrade to Foreign Minister, "Negociaciones de venta del estaño," March 12, 1953, *Embajada boliviana en Washington, enero–junio 1953*, ARE; Andrade, *La revolución boliviana*, 227–28.

129. Andrade to Foreign Minister, "Conversación con Departamento de Estado," January 11, 1954, *Embajada boliviana en Washington, enero–junio 1954*, 4, ARE. Andrade's personal interpretation of U.S. history argued that the Open Door Policy had historically been extremely important to the United States and explains why the United States was the wealthiest country in the world. Andrade, *La revolución boliviana*, 280–82; Andrade, "Speech at the New School," February 25, 1948, Box 1, AP.

130. Andrade, *La revolución boliviana*, 215–16; Lupe Andrade Salmón, interview, April 15, 1997, La Paz.

131. Michael J. Kryzanek, *U.S.–Latin American Relations*, 2nd ed. (Westport, Conn.: Praeger, 1990), 140–41.

132. Lupe Andrade Salmón, interview, April 15, 1997, La Paz.

Andrade was a man of great personal charm, a "man's man" who thrived in the many all-male social settings of 1950s Washington.[133] He played golf very well, often with top officials, including President Eisenhower. (Andrade had met Eisenhower in New York when Eisenhower was president of Columbia University in 1950.)[134] And finally, he would often invite Washington officials and members of the press corps to his residence, at times entertaining them by playing the guitar and singing tunes in his native language of Aymara. Bolivia was a little-known country in 1950s Washington, but Andrade's herculean efforts put it on the map, at least in Washington circles.

In his attempts to influence U.S. policy, Andrade paid particular attention to congressmen, for he knew that they appropriated aid funds.[135] Andrade cultivated friendships with the few pro-MNR congressmen, such as Oregon's Wayne Morse,[136] but he was more intent on "converting," or at least neutralizing, anti-MNR legislators. He recognized that more opposition existed in Congress to increased assistance to Bolivia than did in the executive branch. Consequently, he confronted legislators who opposed increasing economic assistance to Bolivia, trying to get them to see the importance of help for Bolivia. For example, when Senator Frank Lausche of Ohio (Republican) asked Andrade if Bolivia's land reform was communist, he replied that no, breaking up the large *haciendas* and distributing land to the landless actually promoted private ownership and enterprise. Andrade used a personal example with Lausche. He noted that his own parents owned enough land such that under the 1953 Bolivian Agrarian Reform the MNR redistributed their property to the poor landless Indians who worked on it.[137]

These lobbying techniques proved immensely valuable given the nature of the nation Andrade represented. Andrade recognized that the State Department, because of Bolivia's small size and poverty, was not very interested in Bolivia's problems.[138] Therefore, simply appealing to State

---

133. Ibid.
134. Guido Orias Luna et al., eds., *16 personajes paceños* (La Paz: Ediciones Casa de la Cultura, 1988), 35.
135. Andrade to Foreign Minister, "Memorandum—Recopilación de antecedentes sobre asistencia económica y técnica de los EE.UU a Bolivia," January 10, 1956, No. 6, *Embajada boliviana en Washington, enero–junio 1956*, 16, ARE.
136. "Senator Wayne Morse—Suggested Draft," November 23, 1956, Box 1, AP. This was probably written by Andrade.
137. Andrade, *My Missions for Revolutionary Bolivia*, 131–32.
138. Lupe Andrade Salmón, interview, April 15, 1997, La Paz; Julio Sanjines Goitia, interview, March 18, 1997, La Paz.

Department officials would not be effective. From the DOS perspective, the nonindustrialized nation was too far from the principal flashpoints of the cold war. Moreover, *norteamericano* interest in Bolivian tin was diminishing. During World War II, Bolivian tin had been very important to the United States, as it was the Western Hemisphere's only source of the strategic mineral. By the beginning of the 1950s, however, the Reconstruction Finance Corporation had stockpiled a hefty surplus, and U.S. buyers were becoming more interested in higher-grade Indonesian, Malaysian, and Nigerian tin. Andrade's lobbying efforts thus can be seen as a way of compensating for the State Department's lack of interest.[139] Andrade hoped that perhaps Bolivia could somehow capitalize on the traditional affinity U.S. society had for the "underdog."[140]

Although it is impossible to fully measure the effect of Andrade's efforts, it seems clear that U.S. officials responded.[141] From 1953 to 1961, Bolivia secured nearly $200 million of aid. The support came in various forms: foodstuffs, technical assistance, and monetary grants.[142] In the final analysis, Andrade succeeded in acquiring U.S. aid for Bolivia in large part because of his understanding of U.S. motives for giving assistance to Bolivia.

Andrade's Role: An Assessment

In a 1956 report to the Bolivian Foreign Ministry, Andrade argued that Bolivia was a "test case" for the United States: could it prove that its assistance could help a small nation with potential going through a social revolution to emerge as a stable ally? Andrade went on to argue (to his Bolivian

---

139. Gardner Jackson said that the "lower echelons" of the State Department were more concerned with a settlement with the former tin barons than with Bolivia's problems. Gardner Jackson to Milton Eisenhower, November 28, 1956, Box 1, AP.

140. "Diplomacia a la moderna: Un embajador tiene que ser más campechano que coretsano," *Visión: Revista Internacional*, September 27, 1957, 27.

141. It is important to note, however, that Andrade was not the only Latin American leader who successfully wielded influence in Washington at this time. José "Pepe" Figueres, the leader of Costa Rica's 1948 revolution, managed to garner quite a bit of support in Washington through lobbying. He used many of the same techniques as Andrade. See Longley, *The Sparrow and the Hawk*, 68–69, 71, 121–23, 129–30, 144–45, 163. In addition, Rómulo Betancourt of Acción Democrática of Venezuela also cultivated important political and other sorts of leaders in the United States when he was in exile in the late 1940s and 1950s. See Ameringer, *Democratic Left in Exile*, 222–59.

142. By 1958 U.S. aid supplied one-third of the Bolivian government's budget. This economic aid, in addition to providing a needed tonic for the Bolivian economy, also helped to

colleagues and U.S. officials) that the "test" was particularly important since both the United States and the communist bloc sought influence over the developing world. The argument resonated with Washington officials who desired to prove that a "wealthy capitalist country" could successfully assist a poor, nonindustrialized nation.[143] Effective U.S. assistance to Bolivia might prove a model for the rest of Latin America and even an example to the world, thereby benefiting U.S. foreign policy. Here was an example of powerful country successfully helping a weaker one and simultaneously bringing the benefits of capitalism to poorer nations.[144]

U.S. economic assistance proved significant for the stability of the MNR regime during its first four years. For one thing, only ten months after it took office, the Bolivian government was seriously rocked by an abortive coup.[145] The regime maintained stability long enough for elections in 1956; the election was widely considered to be honest even though the MNR did use its position as incumbent to rally its supporters. It was the first plebiscite in a generation. Andrade noted in speeches in the United States that the election represented a victory for U.S. foreign policy, since Washington had been giving aid to the MNR government.[146]

At mid-decade, however, the nation's future looked uncertain because tin, Bolivia's main export and in many ways the mainstay of the economy, dropped in price—rapidly. Bolivia acutely felt the pain that flowed from its long-term integration into the world capitalist system as a producer of raw materials.[147] Historically speaking, since colonial times Bolivia's economy

---

defeat the lobbying efforts of the former tin barons. Once the United States had given its "stamp of approval" to the Bolivian revolution, it was hard for the former tin barons to convince Washington policymakers that the MNR was communist. Andrade, *La revolución boliviana*, 257. However, "the political cost [to Bolivia] of such assistance was naturally very high indeed." Dunkerley, *Rebellion in the Veins*, 82.

143. Andrade to Foreign Minister, "Memorandum—Recopilación de antecedentes sobre asitencia económica y técnica de los EE.UU a Bolivia," January 10, 1956, No. 6, *Embajada boliviana en Washington, enero–junio 1956*, 16, ARE.

144. Víctor Andrade Uzquiano, *Bolivia: Problems and Promise* (Washington, D.C: Embassy of Bolivia, 1956), 35, 52–53.

145. Malloy, "Revolutionary Politics," 126.

146. Ibid., 131. Martin, *Bolivia in 1956*, 5–6.

147. World systems theory is outlined in Immanuel Wallerstein, *The Modern World-System: Capitalist Agriculture and the Origins of the European World-Economy in the Sixteenth Century* (New York: Academic Press, 1976). For an application to the late 1940s and early 1950s, see Bruce Cumings, *Origins of the Korean War* (Ithaca: Cornell University Press, 2004), vol. 2. The sharp fall in the price of tin severely hurt the Bolivian economy. From January 1953 to June 1954 the price dropped from $1.21 per pound to $0.80 per pound. President Paz Estenssoro put it dramatically: "A one cent drop in price represented a 600,000 to 700,000 dollar drop in the annual income of Bolivia." See Thorn, "Economic Transformation," 173–74, and Wilkie, *Bolivian Revolution and U.S. Aid*, 32.

had been dependent on outsiders—it needed the money from the export of its raw materials simply to survive.

As the economy stagnated and declined in the mid-1950s, the Bolivians resorted to a stopgap solution employed by many governments in trouble: printing money. In 1956, when prices rose to their highest level since the inflation index was invented, concerned officials in Washington responded with the Economic Stabilization Plan. It was an austerity scheme, apparently the first of its kind in history targeted for a nonindustrialized country. The Economic Stabilization Plan aimed not only to end inflation but also to spur economic growth by making Bolivia more attractive to foreign investment. In the long run it was to benefit the majority of Bolivians. Furthermore, the *norteamericanos* informed Bolivian officials from the beginning that if they did not accept the directives of the plan, aid would be cut.[148]

Andrade commented on the U.S. strategy in a memo to his superiors at the Foreign Ministry, "It is reasonable to hope that this commission [sent by the International Cooperation Administration, the State Department's main aid-giving agency, to implement the Economic Stabilization Plan] will not produce fundamental changes in the Bolivian political scene."[149] What he could not tell the Foreign Ministry, however, was that he believed the plan would help the right-wing faction of the MNR triumph over the left-wing faction, which is ultimately what happened.

In the end, the Economic Stabilization Plan, discussed in more detail in the next chapter, had a tremendous impact on the Bolivian polity. Certainly it helped the right-wing faction supplant the left, but more generally, the plan soon had the "revolution in retreat," as one scholar put it.[150] Under the terms of the plan, U.S. and International Monetary Fund officials forced the MNR to cut expenditures, which included severely reducing the budget of the state-run mining industry. Strikes flared, many of which turned violent. As the era of *co-gobierno* approached an end, right-wing MNR members celebrated and the left-wing members stewed.

How are Andrade's actions in Washington to be assessed? He did an excellent job making Bolivia's case before Congress and the executive

---

148. Many interpretations of the Stabilization Plan argue it was a qualified success. The U.S. economist who implemented it was George Jackson Eder, who gives his perspective in his *Inflation and Development in Latin America*. Scholars who argue the Plan was a qualified success include Rabe, *Eisenhower and Latin America*, 81–82, and Blasier, *Hovering Giant*, 140.

149. Andrade to Foreign Minister, "Memorandum—Recopilación de antecedentes sobre asistencia económica y técnica de los EE.UU a Bolivia," January 10, 1956, No. 6, *Embajada boliviana en Washington, enero–junio 1956*, 16, ARE.

150. Dunkerley, *Rebellion in the Veins*, 83.

branch. It was clear that Washington officials had listened to his arguments, not the propaganda of the former tin barons. Moreover, because of his efforts, Bolivia, in the eyes of U.S. officials, stood out from the crowd of other nonindustrialized nations. Further, because Andrade's message resonated with U.S. policymakers' desire for a friendly, stable Bolivia, aid from the *norteamericanos* helped Andrade lift the right-wing faction of the MNR to (albeit brief) control in Bolivia—especially after 1956.

Interestingly, Andrade's success as an ambassador reflected his ability to convince Washington leaders that the MNR's program meshed with U.S. interests, while at the same time ensuring that Bolivia did not become overly dependent on the United States. State Department official Thomas Mann noted that Andrade "sometimes furnishes sensitive [U.S.] written material to anti-U.S. elements in La Paz."[151] In this way Andrade signaled U.S. officials that Bolivia would continue to carve out a foreign policy at times independent of U.S. desires.

Yet Andrade's significance is longer term. Andrade provided a foundation for future ambassadors from Bolivia.[152] His successors used his contacts and his techniques; the "Andrade system" became his most important legacy. Subsequent Bolivian ambassadors to the United States used his approach to maintain good relations with Washington policymakers.[153] Indeed, U.S.-Bolivian relations, with some exceptions, remained cordial through the end of the twentieth century.

---

151. Memorandum from Thomas Mann to the Undersecretary, February 14, 1961, Folder Bolivia 1961 (ARA Files), Lots 62D418 and 64D15, Box 2, Bureau of Inter-American Affairs, Subject Files of the Assistant Secretary, 1959–1962, RG 59, NA.

152. Julio Sanjines Goitia, interview, March 18, 1997, La Paz.

153. Andrade's successor, Julio Sanjines Goitia, like Andrade, excelled at lobbying U.S. officials. In a March 29, 1967, telegram to the Department of State U.S. ambassador to Bolivia Douglas Henderson referred to Ambassador Sanjines's "lobbying talents." See Editorial Note, *FRUS, 1964–1968*, vol. 31, *American Republics: Central and South America; Mexico* (hereafter "vol. 31"), 371.

THE SPLINTERING OF THE REVOLUTION

A Collapsing Economy and Growing Distrust

As discussed in chapter 2, in 1956–57 the United States and the MNR agreed to implement a program called the Economic Stabilization Plan to control rampant inflation. The plan included a number of austerity measures that the Bolivian public found painful to accept. Early on in the implementation of the plan, William T. Briggs, the deputy director of the Office of West Coast Affairs, which included Bolivia, wrote a prescient memorandum to his boss, Roy R. Rubottom, assistant secretary of state for Inter-American Affairs. He noted, among other problems, "There are weak spots, some serious enough to pose real threat to the program's continuance." He listed a number of problems: the plan did not impose tax reforms on Bolivian citizens to provide for an increase in government revenue; there was no mechanism to ensure that local currency receipts of sales of U.S. food aid would be deposited in the proper counterpart fund accounts; and there was no specific mechanism to control wage growth at state-run companies. Although expressing his support for the plan, Briggs concluded, "Failure to correct the weak spots in the program could pose serious difficulties even to continuing aid on the present scale."[1]

There is no indication Rubottom responded to Briggs's memorandum. Indeed, Washington officials did not express much interest in the details of the Economic Stabilization Plan or its implications for Bolivia. The impact of the plan on Bolivia, however, was nothing short of immense. During the late 1950s and early 1960s, the revolution retrenched, if

---

1. William T. Briggs to Roy R. Rubottom, May 9, 1957, Economic, Box 1, Roy R. Rubottom Papers, Lot 59D573, RG 59, NA.

temporarily.[2] A combination of internal and external factors—those beyond the control of Bolivia—put the brakes on the revolution. Nonetheless, many of the revolutionary reforms of the 1952–56 era remained in place through the late 1950s, into the 1960s, and beyond.[3]

If one wants to point to a single international factor to explain the problems the Bolivians faced in the late 1950s, it would be the rapid fall of the world price of tin, which began in the mid-1950s. *Norteamericano* officials realized the problems that the falling price of tin inflicted on Bolivia. Tin sales were down because of reduced post–Korean War demand and the declining ore content of Bolivia's easily exploitable veins.[4] The price of tin plummeted from $1.21 per pound in January 1953 to $0.80 in June 1954, while the cost of production remained around $1.03 per pound. As a result, COMIBOL ran deficits—deficits that were covered by drafts from the Central Bank. As the money supply increased, Bolivian inflation shot up.[5] The cost of living in La Paz rose 124 percent in 1954, 80 percent in 1955, and a record 179 percent in 1956.[6] The value of tin exports, caused by falling prices and declining production, dropped from $60.1 million in 1954, to $36.4 million in 1958.[7]

At the center of Bolivia's problems were COMIBOL's financial difficulties. These were exacerbated by a system of multiple exchange rates that forced the tin-mining giant to sell its foreign exchange earnings to the Central Bank at the low official exchange rate, in effect siphoning off resources from the mining company. Between 1952 and 1956, the gap between the

---

2. Dunkerley sums up this phenomenon in "Revolution in Retreat, 1956–1964," in *Rebellion in the Veins*, 83–119. In 1964, the military threw out the MNR leadership, which had ruled since the 1952 revolution. One can argue the revolution had nearly disintegrated because its leaders had failed to institutionalize it. Revolutionary policies—most particularly land reform, universal suffrage, and the nationalization of the three largest mining companies—did linger on after the 1964 *golpe*, however. Susan Eckstein, *Impact of Revolution: A Comparative Analysis of Mexico and Bolivia* (London: Sage Publications, 1976), 35.

3. "Bolivia," *Hispanic American Report: An Analysis of Developments in Spain, Portugal, and Latin America* 11, no. 1 (1958): 40–41.

4. Eder, *Inflation and Development in Latin America*, 53.

5. Franklin Antezana Paz, *La política monetaria de Bolivia* (La Paz: Banco Central de Bolivia, 1954), 7, 48, Pittsburgh Pamphlets.

6. Republica de Bolivia, Dirección General de Estadística y Censos, *Boletín Estadístico* 89 (1964): 38. The 1956 rate was the highest since Bolivia began keeping records on price levels in 1931.

7. James W. Wilkie, "U.S. Foreign Policy and Economic Assistance in Bolivia, 1948–1976," in *Modern Day Bolivia*, ed. Jerry Ladman (Tempe: University of Arizona Press, 1982), 101. By 1957–58, the real price of tin, calculated in 1970 dollars, had fallen to its lowest level during the 1950–85 period. See Wilkie, "Bolivia: Ironies in the National Revolutionary Process, 1952–86," *Statistical Abstract of Latin America (SALA)* 25, ed. James W. Wilkie and David Lorey (1987): 922–23.

official and free-market rates grew enormously, and COMIBOL's problems grew along with it.[8]

Moreover, overvalued exchange rates hurt the Bolivian economy in other, predictable ways. The high, official exchange rate discouraged indigenous production and encouraged imports. Shortages of key goods, including food, occurred when foreign exchange earnings ran low. Smuggling became a serious problem.[9]

Washington officials feared a collapse of the Bolivian economy and government. It was to prevent this, and to help promote a friendlier climate for foreign investment, that U.S. officials designed and implemented the Economic Stabilization Plan for Bolivia. Bolivia, as Ambassador Andrade noted (discussed in the previous chapter), was a "test case." This plan was the first of its kind to be implemented in the nonindustrialized world. The Bolivians accepted the plan because they had been given an ultimatum: no plan—no aid.[10]

Laurence Whitehead has argued that the plan amounted to "neo-colonial" control of Bolivia.[11] Indeed, U.S. assistance was very important to Bolivia. As tin prices sank, and with it the Bolivian economy, U.S. assistance became more and more important. Consequently, both sectors of the MNR, the centrists and the Left, agreed that Bolivia had to make the painful reforms called for in the plan.

Some members of the cautious moderate wing of the MNR saw the plan as a way of containing the power of the Left. In essence, the moderate *movimientistas* were making a tacit alliance with the United States to contain the Left in Bolivia. The shared goal of the Bolivian moderates and U.S. officials was to contain the power of the Left without driving it out of the government. Although if the Left exited the coalition it would significantly weaken the MNR, Ambassador Andrade did not fear that the MNR would fall from power.[12]

Even as the Left warily supported the plan, top Bolivian officials on the Left, in particular labor leader and government official Juan Lechín, feared the U.S. intervention that the plan represented. As it turned out, the plan

---

8. Thorn, "Economic Transformation," 173–74, 376.
9. Ibid., 179.
10. George Jackson Eder, the head of the U.S. economic team that imposed the U.S. and IMF austerity/stabilization plan on Bolivia, tells his side of the story in his *Inflation and Development in Latin America*, 141–242.
11. Whitehead, *The United States and Bolivia*, 22.
12. Memorandum of conversation, April 14, 1954, Decimal File 824.25/4–1454, RG 59, DOS Central Files, NA.

had a very significant effect on the Bolivian economy and, ultimately, the political scene. To begin, it called for COMIBOL to cut wages and reduce the number of workers who worked in the company's mines, which provoked violent strikes.[13] Washington's goals, however, went further. It hoped to help create a friendly climate for international trade and foreign private investment. Exchange rates were to float freely, limiting the ability of the government to maintain the value of its currency and ward off an influx of inexpensive foreign goods. More significantly, Bolivia had to reign in some of its revolutionary policies—for example, the land reform was temporarily halted. Moreover, the Bolivian government was forced to cut its budget for some economic diversification projects, including some hydroelectric plants and government-subsidized sugar refineries.[14] Rapid curtailment of the money supply and a balanced budget proved to be the draconian context within which these reforms were implemented.[15]

The austerity dictated by the plan caused the economy to severely contract. How the state allocated scarcer resources quickly became an intractable political problem. Next, and most significant, the fragile moderate-leftist MNR coalition split. Workers, in particular the miners, suffered the most under the U.S. and IMF austerity/stabilization plan. Budget cuts hit workers, the core of the left-wing faction of the MNR, in numerous ways. First, government subsidies to COMIBOL's stores that supplied the miners, called *pulperías,* were cut, causing price increases for many goods.[16] More seriously, curtailing COMIBOL's budget meant that unproductive mines were closed, which forced large layoffs. The miners went on strike, and protests turned violent.[17] Some U.S. officials feared the worst: Ambassador Philip Bonsal informed the State Department that the Bolivian government was facing a "serious test of strength." He concluded, "Anything you can do to help could well be [a] critical factor in [the] success [of] this enterprise in which the U.S. Government has invested so much prestige and money."[18]

Although there were significant inherent tensions within the MNR independent of the plan and U.S. policy overall, Washington's actions had a

13. Lora, *Bolivian Labour Movement,* 312, 319–20, 327.
14. Eder, *Inflation and Development in Latin America,* 77–78; Torres Calleja, *Ayuda americana,* 66.
15. Winston Moore Casanovas, "Capital Accumulation and Revolutionary Nationalism in Bolivia, 1952–1985," in *The State and Capital Accumulation in Latin America,* ed. Chrisian Anglade and Carlos Fortin, vol. 2 (Pittsburgh: University of Pittsburgh Press, 1990), 36.
16. Rotchin, *Clientelist State,* 75.
17. Lora, *Bolivian Labour Movement,* 312, 319–20, 327.
18. Bonsal to Roy R. Rubottom, December 4, 1958, Decimal File 824.00 TA/12-0458, RG 59, DOS Central Files, NA.

major impact on the MNR. The coup de grace of the MNR was that the Left had to bear the majority of the costs imposed by the plan.[19] As leftists began to lose interest in the national project of the MNR, it teetered on the edge of collapse. The plan so weakened the MNR that it relied more and more on the military—which, since 1958, had been aided and even reorganized with U.S. help.[20] U.S. leaders realized that with the breakup of the MNR having influence over a more powerful military was critically important.

As economic problems worsened, the Bolivian government became more dependent on aid. Consequently, the Bolivian government was careful in these years to maintain good relations with the United States and to put the best face possible on what was happening.[21] This was ironic, because the plan was intended to *reduce* Bolivia's dependence on outside assistance.

Dependence bred distrust. Despite Bolivia's attempt to maintain harmonious relations with its powerful North American "neighbor," the strain in U.S.-Bolivian relations could be seen by early 1959. Bolivian frustrations with the Economic Stabilization Plan bubbled just below the surface. Tension in Bolivia reached the breaking point. An offhand remark supposedly made by a U.S. official, subsequently published in *Time* magazine, caused an uproar. Rumors swept La Paz that a U.S. official said that Bolivia should be partitioned by its neighbors because it was doing such a poor job of governing itself. Anti-American demonstrations broke out, resulting in two deaths, several wounded, and $70,000 of property damage.[22] Relations between the two nations reached their nadir.[23] Interestingly, Andrade (who had left his ambassadorial post to briefly serve as foreign minister) publicly criticized the supposed remarks to maintain his

---

19. Lora, *Bolivian Labour Movement*, 327; Juan Lechín Oquendo, interview, February 20, 1997, La Paz.

20. Dunkerley, *Rebellion in the Veins*, 92–93. For an overview of U.S.-Bolivian relations from 1956 to 1960 and the decline of the MNR, see Siekmeier, "'[T]he most generous assistance,'" 33–37. For information on the reorganizing and building up of the Bolivian military in these years, see Raúl Barrios Morón, *Ejército y revolución en Bolivia, 1952–1960*, Investigación inédita realizada con el apoyo de CLACSO y FLACSO-Bolivia, Parte IV (La Paz: CLACSO y FLACSO-Bolivia, 1986); Gary Prado Salmón, *Poder y fuerzas armadas, 1949–1982* (La Paz: Los Amigos del Libro, 1987); and Kohl, "National Revolution," 22–23.

21. Ministerio de Relaciones Exteriores a Embajador Andrade, 16 de enero 1958, *Colección Enviados Reservados, 1958*, ARE ("reservados" are classified documents); Ministerio de Relaciones Exteriores a Ministerio de Estado en el Despacho de Hacienda y Estadística, 29 de mayo 1958, *Colección Enviados Reservados, 1958*, ARE.

22. Lehman, *Bolivia and the United States*, 114–15.

23. Ministerio de Relaciones Exteriores a Fernando Baptista Gumucio, Encargado de Necogios a.i. de Bolivia, Caracas, Venezuela, 4 de abril 1959, *Colección Enviados Reservados, 1959*, ARE.

Bolivian nationalist credentials while quietly informing U.S. citizens, including a newsman, that Bolivia was not anti-American and that a continued flow of U.S. economic assistance was very important to the nation.[24]

The Slow Unraveling of the MNR

The political ramifications of the Economic Stabilization Plan proved to be most significant. As early as 1956, high-level officials in the Foreign Ministry (Ministerio de Relaciones Exteriores) predicted that the plan would provoke serious problems, specifically "political and social crises." In other words, until the economic problems were mitigated, the political and social problems would remain. Curtailing the money supply would not promote an immediate, steady inflow of the dollars the Andean nation needed, Bolivian officials maintained, to purchase needed imports.[25]

Indeed, the plan forced the moderate MNR leadership to make a crucial decision: it decided to undercut the Left's power base. No longer would the centrists attempt to walk a fine line between maintaining support from the Left and keeping U.S. leaders happy. There were two key turning points in the effort of the moderates to undercut the Left. First, the left-wing base of the MNR split. The more radical faction, under the leadership of Juan Lechín Oquendo, minister of mines from 1952 to 1956 and vice president from 1956 to 1960, and supported principally by the Federación Sindical de Trabajos y Mineros de Bolivia, drifted further and further away from the MNR. The more moderate Bloque Reestructuradora del COB (Bloc for Restructuring the COB), under the leadership of President Hernán Siles Suazo, remained closely tied to the MNR.[26]

The *campesinos* splintered along with the MNR leadership. Inspired by the 1959 Cuban revolution (a revolution that had begun in the countryside), some *campesinos*, those on the left, envisioning someday perhaps taking power through armed revolution, drifted away from all the various factions of the MNR.[27] The MNR responded by reaching out to the *campesinos* who would participate in the party. One example came in 1959, when the MNR leadership offered radical José Rosa Guevara a position as head

24. Siekmeier, "Trailblazer Diplomat," 405n96.
25. "Memorandum," 6 de junio 1956, *Colección Enviados Reservados, 1956*, ARE.
26. Rotchin, *Clientelist State*, 76.
27. José M. Gordillo, *Campesinos revolucionarios en Bolivia: Identidad, territorio y sexualidad en el Valle Alto de Cochabamba, 1952–1964* (La Paz: Promec, 1999), 115–46.

of the MNR peasant organization in the Potosí area. Previously Rosa Guevara had organized peasants outside the MNR system. U.S. officials noted that appointing Guevara was "somewhat of a master stroke by [President] Siles." Not only had the MNR co-opted a radical leader during a time when the party was splintering, the support of Guevara's group "gave the GOB [Bolivian government] the support of this powerful *campesino* faction against the striking miners."[28] This move on the part of the MNR would presage the efforts of 1960s Bolivian military leaders to build a coalition of the military and the *campesinos*.

A second important event occurred in 1960 when the moderates of the MNR denied Lechín's ascendency to the head of the party and a shot at running for the presidency. The leadership of the unified MNR leadership had agreed that Lechín would be the presidential candidate in 1960. However, the post-plan MNR had turned to the right and reversed the party's decision to nominate Lechín. Instead, Paz Estenssoro, a middle-class MNR leader, the leader of the 1952 revolution and president from 1952 to 1956, assumed the party's candidacy in 1960 and won the presidency that same year to begin his second term as president of Bolivia.[29]

Looking for Friends in the East Bloc and the Military Trump Card

As the MNR fragmented, it expanded its attempts to look abroad for support to somehow halt the decline of the revolution. Bolivia began to exert more control over its relations with the United States. An important turn came when the previously solidly pro-U.S. MNR began seeking aid from the Eastern bloc (communist) nations. As early as 1958, Víctor Paz Estenssoro thought that Bolivia could leverage more assistance from the *norteamericanos* by appealing to the Eastern bloc for aid. Bolivia proved to be a trailblazer in this regard; only Mexico, Argentina, and Uruguay had relations with the Soviet Union at this point. The Latin American nations were expected to support the United States in the United Nations.[30] The MNR's initial feelers toward the Soviet Union went against the grain of U.S.–Latin American relations, and of course were not appreciated in Washington.

---

28. Ernest Siracusa to Assistant Secretary of State Roy Rubottom, April 13, 1959, Bolivia, 1959, Lot 64D24, Box 1, Bureau of Inter-American Affairs, Records of the Special Assistant on Communism, 1958–1961, RG 59, NA.

29. Klein, *Bolivia*, 241, 244.

30. Joseph Smith, *The United States and Latin America: A History of American Diplomacy, 1776–2000* (New York: Routledge, 2005), 117; see also Blasier, *Giant's Rival*, 16.

The Bolivian attempt to reach out to the Soviets faltered at first. The Soviet Union dumped tin on the world market, sending the Bolivian economy into further turmoil. Naturally, Bolivian-Soviet relations were very strained.[31] But playing off the East against the West proved too useful a strategy to abandon. Indeed, it represented an inexpensive way for small, nonindustrialized Bolivia to increase its benefits from working within the patron-client system. Risking ire from the leader of the "free world," Bolivian leaders again thought of looking to the communist nations for aid. There were a variety of reasons for this. First, the leaders of Bolivia wanted to chart a neutralist course—between the great blocs fighting the cold war. In addition, the MNR desperately needed friends from somewhere—anywhere—to maintain itself in power. By toying with accepting East bloc aid, the MNR could shore up sorely needed support from the Bolivian Left, which the MNR had recently forsaken.[32] Most important, however, Bolivian leaders wanted to force themselves onto the radar screen of the United States. Castro's 1959 surge to power in Cuba signaled to the MNR that "playing the Soviet card" might force the United States to give Bolivia more assistance to keep it in the "Western camp."

Washington leaders disliked Bolivia's attempt to play the East off against the West. In a memo from Acting Secretary of State Clarence Dillon to the embassy in La Paz, Dillon emphasized that "under no circumstances" should the Bolivians permit "the establishment of a Soviet diplomatic mission in La Paz since it would be used primarily in an effort to subvert Bolivia and to replace Paz by someone amenable to Soviet direction."[33] The Bolivians did, however, establish relations with the Soviet Union (although not until 1969). Even though the U.S. ambassador at one point lectured President Paz Estensorro about getting too close to the Soviet Union, Paz Estensorro refused to promise to comply with U.S. wishes.[34] It could be argued that the Bolivian tactic of reaching out the Soviets in order to get the attention of the United States succeeded.

Despite this success, however, Bolivia paid a steep price for the increased assistance it received from the United States—the very stability of the nation itself. The stipulations attached to U.S assistance alienated the

---

31. Ministerio de Relaciones Exteriores a Embajador Andrade, 18 de julio 1958, *Colección Enviados Reservados, 1958,* ARE.

32. Lehman, *Bolivia and the United States,* 133–34.

33. Dillon to the embassy in Bolivia, November 7, 1960, Decimal File 724.00/10–2660, RG 59, Central Files, NA.

34. Telegram from the embassy in La Paz to the Department of State, August 2, 1962, Decimal File 724.5-MSP/8–260, RG 59, DOS Central Files, NA.

Left, facilitating their exit from the MNR government; the middle-class portion of the MNR concluded that the weakening of the government that resulted was worth it. Only U.S. assistance, these Bolivians concluded, could pave the way for a diversified economy in the long run.[35] Moreover, the middle class concluded (ultimately incorrectly) that only U.S. assistance could provide the necessary funds to keep the MNR knitted together with the centrist MNR leadership in charge. Indeed, in the 1950s the assistance had provided the MNR with valuable political space in which to consolidate its power during the chaotic period after their 1952 triumph. In the 1950s Bolivia accepted U.S. aid not out of desperation but as a calculated move to maximize the gains that could be gotten as the client in a patron-client relationship. By the 1960s, however, U.S. assistance was actually helping to pull the nation apart.

U.S. assistance policy took an important turn in 1960. Although the United States had given a small amount of materiel to the Bolivian military in 1958, and the centrist MNR leaders had requested military assistance from the United States as early as 1956, in 1960 Paz asked for a significant increase in military assistance, in part to prop up his increasingly shaky regime. He asked for a $1 million grant of military aid, and received it.[36] The origins of the U.S. military assistance program reveal key aspects of U.S. policy toward Bolivia. In 1956, conceding that strengthening the military might threaten democracy in Bolivia, State Department official Maurice Bernbaum, in a letter to Assistant Secretary of State for Inter-American Affairs Henry Holland, summed up the U.S. government's reasoning: "Our purpose should be to see the formal military so strengthened that there would be some responsible body from which leadership might emerge should the Bolivian government fall or become seriously weakened through a split in the MNR or should leftist elements eventually take over responsibility." Bernbaum noted that Bolivia's democratic tradition was weak in any regard, and the worst-case scenario from Washington's perspective was a power vacuum leading to uncertainty or, worse, chaos. Bernbaum noted that military aid offered "insurance" against such an eventuality.[37]

35. Lehman, "U.S. Foreign Aid," 398–99.
36. Ernest Siracusa to Assistant Secretary of State Henry Holland, March 30, 1956, Bolivian Equipment, Box 1, Lot 61D374, Office of Inter-American Regional Political Affairs, Country and Subject Files, 1950–1953, RG 59, NA. See also Lehman, *Bolivia and the United States*, 148–49.
37. Bernbaum to Assistant Secretary of State Henry Holland, March 6, 1956, Bolivian Equipment, Box 1, Lot 61D374, Office of Inter-American Regional Political Affairs, Country and Subject Files, 1950–1953, RG 59, NA.

The military assistance came in a number of different forms. First, some of the aid came in the form of counterinsurgency instructors trained in antiguerrilla, anticommunist, and internal security techniques. Other aid came in the form of tear gas canisters and grenades—perhaps because it appeared that the MNR was crumbling and, further, that Bolivian society was unraveling.[38] Some assistance aided the MNR in putting down what top State Department officials saw as "anti-government, Communist-led and inspired groups" in Bolivia. According to Thomas Mann, a top State Department official, the Bolivian army, in putting down an uprising in Cliza, outside Cochabamba, had "run out of ammunition and requested immediate U.S. assistance." Washington officials complied, sending the requested materiel.[39]

A particular type of U.S. military assistance proved especially significant for future U.S.-Bolivian relations. Some U.S. military assistance was funneled into "civic action" programs. Although Bolivia was not the first Latin American nation to implement such programs, because of the small size of the Bolivian military the programs had a disproportionally large impact on Bolivian society. Shortly after the 1952 revolution, the Bolivian military had implemented a program of *ejército productora* (producing army), following the Brazilian model.[40] Under this doctrine, the military was to be used to carry out infrastructure projects in the countryside as a means of promoting economic development. Because Washington heartily approved of the military engaging in economic development activities—the "producing army" program meshed with Washington's economic goals for Latin America and the developing world while keeping the military too distracted to foment a coup—a good portion of U.S. military assistance flowed into civic action programs. By the end of 1963, one-fifth of the Bolivian military's man-hours were devoted to civic action programs.[41]

For its part, the Bolivian military, aided by the United States, began to see the political possibilities of building a coalition with some of the more

38. Ministerio de Relaciones Exteriores a Mario Díez de Medina, Ministro de Estado en el Despacho de Defensa Nacional, 22 de febrero 1960, *Colección Enviados Reservados, 1960*, ARE.
39. Thomas Mann to the Secretary of State, November 18, 1960, Bolivia 1960, Box 1, Lots 62D18 and 64D15, Bureau of Inter-American Affairs, Subject Files of the Assistant Secretary, 1959–1962, RG 59 (ARA Files), NA.
40. Rotchin, *Clientelist State*, 80–81.
41. Ibid., 83; William H. Brill, *Military Intervention in Bolivia: The Overthrow of Paz Estenssoro and the MNR* (Washington, D.C.: Institute for the Comparative Study of Political Systems, 1967), 3.

conservative *campesino* groups.⁴² When General René Barrientos Ortuño came to power by means of a coup in 1964, he would build upon the links between the military and the *campesinos* that had been forged during the implementation of the civic action programs.

Bolivia as a "Test Case"

A key part of the story of U.S.-Bolivian relations in the late 1950s and early 1960s is how the MNR's middle-class leadership quietly but skillfully stoked Washington's fear of a breakup or collapse of the MNR. Washington's fears of the possibility of post-MNR chaos in Bolivia kept U.S. assistance flowing. Not surprisingly, it is important to note that all the different types of aid were specifically tailored to help the Bolivian middle-class centrists—they doled it out to their supporters. They advocated and got a privatized petroleum industry. And through the Economic Stabilization Plan they broke the power of the Left.

All in all, U.S. economic assistance had a big impact on Bolivia during the 1950s. Bolivia, at least in the short run, benefited economically (even though U.S. assistance exacerbated preexisting political divisions in the MNR coalition). From the beginning of its relationship with the United States, Bolivia had learned to maximize the benefits as a client in a patron-client relationship. In the 1950s it was no different—except that the U.S. government was dispensing large amounts of assistance to Bolivia, and Bolivia wanted to increase that flow of funds. Another way of putting it is that Bolivia, for centuries, had been trading one form of dependency for another—in the 1950s it simply traded dependency on tin for dependency on U.S. assistance. Ambassador Andrade (as discussed in chapter 2) played a crucial role in this historic transformation that—as became clear later—had a tremendous impact on the Bolivian economy and its foreign policy.

Although U.S.-Bolivian relations were unique in some ways, Washington's policy toward Bolivia fit nicely into Eisenhower's "New Look" foreign policy. Eisenhower wanted to avoid using conventional military forces whenever possible.⁴³ (Using U.S. force in Bolivia would have been a logistical nightmare.) Since U.S. leaders did not fear an imminent communist

---

42. Gordillo, *Campesinos Revolucionarios en Bolivia*, 116.
43. An important part of Eisenhower's strategy for fighting communism was economic assistance, especially the Mutual Security Program (MSP). See Thomas G. Paterson, J. Garry

threat in the Andean nation, the administration never contemplated the overt use of U.S. force or even covert paramilitary action. The Bolivian case dramatically contrasts with the administration's use of covert paramilitary action in Guatemala during the same period.[44] Eisenhower rested his hopes in Bolivia in a relatively new policy technique: relatively large amounts of assistance to a Third World nation despite the objections of some of his top advisers (at least in his first term) who opposed large foreign assistance programs.[45]

But the most significant aspect of U.S.-Bolivian relations in the 1950s, and beyond—from Washington's viewpoint—was Bolivia's role as a test case for how economic assistance could prove an important tool of U.S. diplomacy in the hemisphere. Indeed, by the end of the 1950s, U.S. policy-makers were explicit about Bolivia's pioneering role in U.S. assistance policy. In 1959, a State Department report noted that U.S. assistance policy in the Andean nation "sought to demonstrate that people in social revolution can make effective gains through cooperation with the U.S." The authors concluded that a perceived failure of U.S. policy in the nation "might well affect the receptivity to U.S. collaboration of underdeveloped nations in the hemisphere and elsewhere, with a corresponding increased willingness on their part to consider Soviet offers of assistance."[46] Interestingly, despite the problems in U.S. assistance policy toward Bolivia, by the late 1950s U.S. leaders expanded the Bolivian aid policy to the rest of the region. If Washington officials had thought through the lessons of the Bolivian experience in the 1950s more carefully, Bolivia's example could have perhaps helped U.S. officials avoid the pitfalls of future U.S. assistance initiatives—but Washington leaders chose not to reflect on how the Economic Stabilization Plan had divided the MNR.

Clifford, and Kenneth J. Hagan, *American Foreign Relations: A History Since 1895*, 5th ed., vol. 2 (Boston: Houghton Mifflin, 2000), 279–80; Robert R. Bowie and Richard H. Immerman, *Waging Peace: How Eisenhower Shaped an Enduring Cold War Strategy* (New York: Oxford University Press, 1998), 90, 101, 159, 163; and Blance Wiesen Cook, *The Declassified Eisenhower: A Divided Legacy* (Garden City, N.Y.: Doubleday, 1981), 210, 309, 334, 339, 340. A good overall history of the MSP and other Eisenhower aid initiatives is in Burton I. Kaufman, *Trade Not Aid: Eisenhower's Foreign Economic Policy* (Baltimore: Johns Hopkins University Press, 1982).

44. Martha L. Cottam, *Images and Intervention: U.S. Policies in Latin America* (Pittsburgh: University of Pittsburgh Press, 1994), 51–53. See also Lehman, "Revolutions and Attributions."

45. Siekmeier, *Aid, Nationalism, and Inter-American Relations*, 279–91.

46. "Bolivia Policy Review," n.d., Summary and Policy Review of Bolivia (Political) 1959, Box 27, RG 59, Lot 62D249, Subject Files Relating to Bolivia, 1958–1960, Records of the Bureau of Inter-American Affairs, General Records of the Department of State, NA.

The lack of study of the Bolivian experiment in economic assistance hurt U.S. interests in the long run. A study of the impact of U.S. assistance to Bolivia in the 1950s would have shown that it was mainly Bolivian elites who benefited from foreign aid.[47] Bolivia proved to be a trailblazer for the Alliance for Progress (the Alliance), and the problems the United States experienced with its aid program toward Bolivia are reflected in the problems Washington experienced with the Alliance. The huge assistance program simultaneously raised expectations for a better life for the region's poor, yet the benefits of U.S. assistance were heavily skewed toward the wealthy.[48] It is clear the Alliance for Progress did not lay the groundwork for a pro-U.S. stability in Latin America.

Even as the economic crisis caused by the Economic Stabilization Plan hampered the MNR from continuing to pursue its revolutionary goals, key elements of the revolution lived on. In particular, COMIBOL still existed, and the land reform continued. In the words of Laurence Whitehead, the MNR had accomplished a "remarkably revolutionary transformation"— the powerful rural elite lost a great deal of its power and *campesino* unions spread throughout the countryside. Moreover, as the Bolivian state gained power in the countryside, it could more effectively promote state-sponsored education.[49] The political participation spurred by the revolution had dramatically changed the political culture.[50]

Two key points are important here. First, a historic change occurred in U.S.-Bolivian relations in the 1950s—the two countries forged a very close relationship based on Bolivia's perceived need for U.S. assistance. Second, the MNR became severely split in the 1950s, and that split was exacerbated by the U.S.-sponsored Economic Stabilization Plan. Nevertheless, the MNR's revolution proved to be the most significant turning point in recent Bolivian history.[51] Despite the hurdles the nation faced in the 1950s, despite the control that the United States exerted through its assistance, despite the division in the MNR and the political polarization of late 1950s

---

47. Healy, *Llamas, Weavings, and Organic Chocolate*, 17–38.

48. Walter LaFeber, *Inevitable Revolutions: The United States in Central America*, 2nd ed. (New York: W. W. Norton, 1993), 161, 194.

49. Laurence Whitehead, "The Bolivian National Revolution: A Twenty-first Century Perspective," in *Proclaiming Revolution: Bolivia in Comparative Perspective*, ed. Merilee S. Grindle and Pilar Domingo (Cambridge: David Rockefeller Center for Latin American Studies, Harvard University Press, 2003), 49–50.

50. Bolivia's electorate rose from 6.6 percent of the population in 1951 to 33.8 percent. Ibid., 32.

51. For three recent analyses on the Bolivian revolution in comparative perspective, see Merilee S. Grindle, "1952 and All That: The Bolivian Revolution in Comparative Perspective";

and early 1960s, and despite the democratically elected MNR's ouster in 1964 by General René Barrientos Ortuño, the revolution survived. Indeed, the revolution would cast its long shadow over the history of Bolivia even as the military regimes of the 1960s and 1970s consolidated their power.

Bolivia and the Alliance for Progress, 1961–1964

The Alliance for Progress represented the biggest economic assistance program for the developing world ever devised by the United States—or any other nation. The Alliance was set apart from earlier aid programs by more than just its size. It was the first U.S. assistance program to collect and allocate not just U.S. funds, but monies from the recipient countries.[52] In early 1961, President John F. Kennedy (JFK) pledged $20 billion of U.S. assistance to Latin America and called upon the nations of that region to pledge $80 billion as their contribution to the Alliance.

Although the Alliance had a military assistance component, its economic-assistance goal was, in one sense, a more interesting, fundamental, even remarkable break with the previous history of inter-American relations.[53] Until 1961, U.S. (and many Latin American) leaders had viewed U.S.–Latin American relations in terms of continental military security. Now, at the highest levels of government, there was frank acknowledgment and discussion of the assumed fundamental link between economic development and mutual self-protection.[54] With the Alliance, and forever

---

Whitehead, "Bolivian National Revolution"; and James Dunkerley, "The Origins of the Bolivian Revolution in the Twentieth Century: Some Reflections," all in *Proclaiming Revolution: Bolivia in Comparative Perspective*, ed. Merilee S. Grindle and Pilar Domingo (Cambridge: David Rockefeller Center for Latin American Studies, Harvard University Press, 2003).

52. U.S. leaders astutely recognized that historically many Latin Americans have seen Washington's actions—including economic assistance—as imperialistic. U.S. officials calling on the Latin Americans to contribute to the Alliance would (in a preemptive fashion) blunt such criticism.

53. A significant portion of the increased U.S. military assistance went toward counterinsurgency efforts. U.S. military personnel stepped up the training of their Latin American counterparts at the Southern Command in the Panama Canal Zone. In addition, the United States set up the Inter-American Policy Academy in the Zone in 1962 to train Latin American police and security officers. See Clara Nieto, *Masters of War: Latin America and United States Aggression from the Cuban Revolution Through the Clinton Years*, trans. Chris Brandt (New York: Seven Stories Press, 2003), 154–55, and Walter LaFeber, "The Alliances for Progress," in *Bordering on Trouble: Resources and Politics in Latin America*, ed. Andrew Maguire and Janet Welsh Brown (Bethesda, Md.: Adler and Adler, 1986), 338–40.

54. On the importance of economic development to the Alliance, see Jack Heller and Miguel S. Wionczek, "The Assumptions of the Alliance," in *The Alliance for Progress: A Retrospective*, ed. L. Ronald Scheman (New York: Praeger, 1988), 131–32.

after, "collective security" would not be just a military issue but a developmental one as well.

Kennedy made the Alliance an early centerpiece of his foreign policy, which as a whole placed new emphasis on U.S. relations with the developing world. He was responding to Soviet premier Nikita Khrushchev's assertion that the Soviets would be the only superpower to benefit from the wars of national liberation occurring in the Third World in the late 1950s and early 1960s. The young president was also responding to Fidel Castro's challenge to Washington's dominance of inter-American relations.[55]

In the early 1960s, U.S. officials were particularly concerned about preventing the communist powers from gaining allies in the developing world. The Alliance symbolized a key strategy in this endeavor; but it was only one such foreign policy technique. For example, Kennedy reached out to noncommunist Asian and African leaders also, supporting them more strongly than Eisenhower had.[56]

The rhetoric of the Alliance for Progress called for the United States and the countries to its south to confront basic structural problems in Latin America together.[57] JFK's words during the unveiling of the Alliance addressed problems of deficiencies of "homes, work and land, health and schools." Improvements in these areas would make democracy more real for the region's poor.[58] Moreover, Kennedy and top U.S. officials proposed tax and administrative reforms. The administration proposed two main techniques for achieving these ambitious goals: long-term planning and, of course, foreign capital on concessional terms.[59] From Washington's vantage point, more stable—and most important, pro-U.S.—democracies in a land prone to military coups would provide insurance against future communist aggression.[60]

---

55. LaFeber, *Inevitable Revolutions*, 150–53.

56. Thomas Borstelmann, "'Hedging Our Bets and Buying Time': John Kennedy and Racial Revolutions in the American South and Southern Africa," *Diplomatic History* 24, no. 3 (Summer 2000): 438.

57. Stephen Rabe, *The Most Dangerous Area in the World: John F. Kennedy Confronts Communist Revolution in Latin America* (Chapel Hill: University of North Carolina Press, 1999), 148–52; Rabe, "Controlling Revolutions: Latin America, the Alliance for Progress, and Cold War Anti-communism," in *Kennedy's Quest for Victory: American Foreign Policy, 1961–1963*, ed. Thomas Paterson (New York: Oxford University Press, 1989), 105–22.

58. John Fitzgerald Kennedy, *Public Papers of the Presidents of the United States: John Fitzgerald Kennedy, 1961* (Washington, D.C.: U.S. Government Printing Office, 1962), 174–75.

59. Enrique Lerdau, "The Alliance for Progress: The Learning Experience," in *The Alliance for Progress: A Retrospective*, ed. L. Ronald Scheman (New York: Praeger, 1988), 167.

60. Washington foreign policymakers feared that corrupt, repressive regimes like Cuba's Batista government would lead to more Castros in Latin America. See Rabe, "Controlling Revolutions."

Despite this initial idealism, the Alliance never confronted the basic economic and social problems afflicting Latin America. Instead, it raised expectations for a better life among the nonelite in the region while their situation remained the same or even deteriorated. Latin American politicians correctly viewed the Alliance's funds as a source of capital that would not have to be raised internally for infrastructure projects. Alliance money could be used to get these nations out of a bind. Few Latin American nations had the resources to provide for the immediate—and increasing—needs and wants of their people on the one hand, and to invest capital for long-term industrialization on the other.[61] When it came to the tough choices that had to be made in societies with limited resources, Alliance money meant that economic development projects, most desired by the middle class, could proceed without the elite having to make significant sacrifices.

Yet because of the sheer magnitude of Latin American social and economic problems, Alliance funds did not even partially meet the goals of the program. Taxing the elite could provide such monies, but historically this had never happened. Further, politicians (except for left-wing leaders) feared raising the subjects of land reform and democracy. In general, Latin American politicians saw themselves sitting atop a potentially violent volcano: the wealthy in the region controlled the vast majority of the wealth, and the nonelites increasingly wanted a bigger slice of the pie. The leadership, the elites, and a good portion of the middle class did not want to do or say anything that might spark a social revolution.

Why did the Alliance fail?[62] Although scholars have discussed many reasons, I will focus on only two.[63] One school of thought maintains that the Alliance's assumptions were basically sound—that economic aid, fairly distributed within the Latin American societies, would lead directly to economic growth. With the resultant economic development, a newly

---

61. Guillermo O'Donnell, "Towards an Alternative Conceptualization of South American Politics," in *Promise of Development: Theories of Change in Latin America*, ed. Peter F. Klarén and Thomas J. Bossert (Boulder, Colo.: Westview Press, 1987), 239–75.

62. Abraham Lowenthal, "'Liberal,' 'Radical' and 'Bureaucratic' Perspectives on U.S. Latin American Policy: The Case of the Alliance for Progress," in *Latin America and the United States: The Changing Political Realities*, ed. Julio Cotler and Richard Fagen (Stanford: Stanford University Press, 1974), 212–35.

63. A prominent left-wing critic describes the Alliance as reinforcing Latin American dependency on the United States. See Samuel L. Baily, *The United States and the Development of South America, 1945–1975* (New York: New Viewpoints, 1976). A more conservative critic states that Latin American underdevelopment had nothing to do with the failure of the Alliance; such underdevelopment results from a deeper phenomenon, specifically, Latin American culture. See Lawrence Harrison, *Underdevelopment Is a State of Mind: The Case of Latin America* (Cambridge: Harvard University Press, 1985).

strengthened Latin American middle class would provide the vanguard for democracy. Because the Alliance's assumptions were essentially correct, the only explanation for the failure of the assistance program was faulty implementation, or simply that it needed more time to work.[64]

A second "consensus" school of thought argues the opposite. These scholars maintain that the Alliance rested on *faulty* assumptions. U.S. officials thought that an aid program modeled after the Marshall Plan and the U.S. assistance package to Japan in the 1950s could prove useful for Latin America. *Norteamericano* officials assumed that infrastructure projects, modest industrial growth, economic, social, and political reform, and the expansion of government services would solve significant social problems in Latin America. Robert A. Packenham and other authors of this latter school argue that faulty assumptions on the part of U.S. leaders, especially regarding the stimulation of Latin American development, doomed the Alliance from the beginning. Simply put, Washington leaders held two incorrect preconceptions: that economic growth in the poorer nations of the world would be relatively smooth, easy, and fast, and that this development would occur along the course that industrialization took in the United States and Western Europe (not a smooth, easy, or fast process at all; industrialization anywhere in the world required centuries of preparation).[65]

Whatever the nature of the academic debate, the Alliance for Progress focused on maintaining friendly (pro-U.S.), stable, noncommunist regimes south of the Rio Grande. Despite the Kennedy administration's rhetoric emphasizing the humanitarian side of Alliance assistance, U.S. leaders never systematically confronted the structural problems of the region.[66]

How did Bolivia and U.S.-Bolivian relations fare during the Alliance years? To answer this question, a little bit of background is necessary. It is

---

64. One book that argues that faulty implementation doomed the Alliance is Jerome Levinson and Juan de Onís, *The Alliance That Lost Its Way* (Chicago: Quadrangle, 1970). A book that argues that the Alliance was on the right track but needed more time to effect change is Edwin McCammon Martin, *Kennedy and Latin America* (Lanham, Md.: University Press of America, 1994), 458–61.

65. Packenham, *Liberal America and the Third World;* Howard J. Wiarda, "Did the Alliance 'Lose Its Way,' or Were Its Assumptions All Wrong from the Beginning and Are Those Assumptions Still with Us?" in *The Alliance for Progress: A Retrospective,* ed. L. Ronald Scheman (New York: Praeger, 1988), 95–118; Enrique Lerdau, "Alliance for Progress," ibid., 179; Peter T. Klarén, "Lost Promise: Explaining Latin American Development," in *Promise of Development: Theories of Change in Latin America,* ed. Peter F. Klarén and Thomas J. Bossert (Boulder, Colo.: Westview Press, 1987), 3–31.

66. Wiarda, "Did the Alliance 'Lose Its Way?'"

important to consider how much influence the United States exerted over Bolivia in the 1960s. Previous interpretations of U.S.-Bolivian relations have stressed U.S control over Bolivian affairs.[67] However, these interpretations overstate the power the United States had over Bolivian affairs. Indeed, Bolivia enjoyed a degree of control over its relationship with its giant North American counterpart.

Bolivian Economic Development and U.S. Anticommunism

When it came to understanding the problems of Bolivian economic development, U.S. officials were at a loss. Indeed, their lack of understanding stretched beyond Bolivia. U.S. leaders never really understood why Latin American economic development had proceeded in a very different fashion than development in the United States, or why wealth accumulation in the region had not benefited the majority of the population or fueled the growth of a large middle class as it had in the United States. In the case of Bolivia, *norteamericano* leaders swung from one extreme view to another. On the one hand, they assumed that U.S. economic and military power could control the nation and thus quickly solve its problems. On the other, Washington officials often considered all efforts on the part of any outsider who wanted to promote economic growth in Bolivia as futile. This loss of interest in Bolivia helps to explain why by the end of the 1960s, the United States quietly dropped the Alliance for Progress.[68]

Interestingly, for its part, Bolivia had begun laying the groundwork, many thought, for a stable, pro-U.S. polity. Bolivia had come through its 1952 revolution remarkably well. The primary reason the nation experienced stability in the 1950s was that the revolution quickly addressed two of the main problems of prerevolutionary Bolivia. First, the nationalization of the three largest mining enterprises, all foreign owned, ended the concentration of economic and political power in the hands of a small number of businessmen who often invested the profits of Bolivia's mines overseas. Next, land reform terminated a manorial agrarian system, empowering rural Indians to a degree unthinkable before the revolution.

---

67. Whitehead, *The United States and Bolivia;* Navia Ribera, *Los Estados Unidos y la revolución nacional.*

68. The back-and-forth between U.S. interventionism and isolationism is articulately argued in Louis Hartz, *The Liberal Tradition in America* (New York: Harcourt Brace, 1955). For Bolivia specifically, see Lehman, *Bolivia and the United States.*

Even though during the 1950s Bolivia had received quite a bit of U.S. assistance, Washington leaders did not control Bolivian policy. Bolivia, though a poor nation and increasingly dependent on U.S. economic assistance, in some instances manipulated the United States. Bolivian leaders quickly realized that for Washington, instability in the nation was anathema. A Bolivian government teetering on collapse, *norteamericano* leaders feared, could lead to a Cuban-style revolutionary nationalist takeover, and even communism. Indeed, because Bolivia had recently gone through a revolution, it was not surprising that U.S. leaders acutely feared political instability in the nation. Consequently, during times of political instability, Bolivian requests for assistance were granted by nervous Washington leaders wanting to avert another Cuba in the hemisphere.

A key goal of U.S. policy in Bolivia was stopping communism—which is not too surprising, since anticommunism was the overarching goal of the Alliance. To preserve a pro-U.S. government in La Paz, U.S. officials allocated assistance to the more conservative wing of the MNR, headed up by Paz Estenssoro.[69] This aid began to flow in 1952. Washington leaders thought assistance, targeted to support the Paz Estenssoro wing of the ruling party, would give the United States some leverage over the course of events in Bolivia.[70] Paz Estenssoro had broken the strength of the radical Bolivian labor movement (with miners at the movement's vanguard) in the late 1950s. In the 1960s, U.S. leaders firmly supported Paz Estenssoro's antilabor strategy.[71] Paz Estenssoro was the type of noncommunist, democratic, nationalist, pro-U.S. leader that the United States wanted to see throughout the Third World. (And Paz returned the favor—Paz had a photo of himself and Kennedy in the receiving room at his house in Tarija.) The new Kennedy administration, in order to woo the nations of the developing world into an escalating struggle with the communist bloc, wanted to make sure that democratic, pro-U.S. nations did not slip into the communist camp. Kennedy wanted to signal to the rest of the world

---

69. Lehman, *Bolivia and the United States*, 91–147.
70. Stephansky to the Secretary of State, July 16, 1962, "Bolivia and Democratic Processes," Folder "Bol-Gen, 8/62–12/62," Box 10, Country File: Bolivia, NSF, JFK Library.
71. Paz Estenssoro to JFK, October 5, 1961, Folder "Bol-Gen, 1/62–7/62," Box 10, Country File: Bolivia, NSF, JFK Library. Washington officials had been concerned about communist infiltration of labor movements in Latin America for decades. See Leslie Bethell, "From the Second World War to the Cold War: 1944–1954," in *Exporting Democracy: The United States and Latin America: Themes and Issues,* ed. Abraham F. Lowenthal (Baltimore: Johns Hopkins University Press, 1991), 61.

that the United States firmly supported noncommunist Third World nationalism, especially of the democratic type.[72]

Bolivia's Special Place in the Alliance

For U.S. officials, Bolivia was a special case—and a test case. Bolivia had successfully carried out a nationalist, democratic, social revolution. This was quite a feat for one of the world's poorest nations; because of the concentration of mining holdings in the hands of a few wealthy mining companies and the vast majority of lands in the hands of a tiny wealthy elite, its pre-1952 social and political system was one of the most unequal in the world. The revolution largely shattered this hierarchy. In addition, as discussed in previous chapters, the United States gave assistance to the MNR soon after it took power in 1952. U.S. leaders noted that "since the U.S. has been assisting the post-revolutionary government of Bolivia for nearly a decade, our own ability to assist a country to achieve development is also being tested by the Bolivian case. The seriousness of our commitment to assist countries which do make social and political reforms is under scrutiny."[73] If the United States could successfully implement its nation-building policy of fostering Western-style modernization in Bolivia, it could show the entire developing world the success of U.S. policy.

Bolivian officials understood their importance to U.S. officials. Because Bolivia had been receiving economic assistance from the U.S. government since 1942, they knew the arguments to make in order to get the *norteamericanos* to give them assistance.[74] More specifically, President Paz Estenssoro thoroughly comprehended Kennedy's desire to enlist Latin America in the worldwide anticommunist initiative. The Bolivian president, in a conversation with Benjamin Stephansky, U.S. ambassador to Bolivia in the early 1960s, stated, "Bolivia, more than most Latin American countries, can reach people by virtue of revolutionary changes which President Kennedy himself has recognized and alluded to in several communications."[75] The Bolivian head of state, in effect, told U.S. officials that Bolivia

---

72. Roland Egger, Special Representative to the President, to JFK, October 5, 1961, Folder "Bol-Gen-1961," Box 10, Country File: Bolivia, NSF, JFK Library.

73. "Experimental Policy Paper on Bolivia," July 19, 1962, Folder "Bol-Gen-Experimental Policy Paper 7/17/62," Box 10A, Country File: Bolivia, NSF, JFK Library.

74. James F. Siekmeier, "Responding to Nationalism: The Bolivian Movimiento Nacionalista Revolucionario and the United States, 1952–1956," *Journal of American and Canadian Studies*, no. 15 (Spring 1998).

75. U.S. Ambassador Benjamin Stephansky to SecSt, March 21, 1962, Folder "Bol-Gen, 1/61–7/62," Box 10, Country File: Bolivia, NSF, JFK Library.

had been well on the way to pursuing the goals of the Alliance with its 1952 revolution, nine years before the Alliance came into existence. Washington leaders concurred.

Therefore, Bolivia received special treatment from the United States during the Alliance years. Two examples will be discussed. First, starting in 1960, the United States worked with both the Inter-American Development Bank and the Federal Republic of Germany to implement the Triangular Plan in Bolivia (so called because it included the United States, Bolivians, and the FRG), which would funnel more investment money into the ailing mining industry. State Department official Thomas Mann noted in a memorandum to the Undersecretary of State Clarence D. Dillon that Soviet offers of assistance to Bolivia, specifically for a much-desired tin smelter, "had been most astutely timed to exploit the economic crisis in Bolivia."[76] Washington's assistance to Bolivia, then, was intended at least in part to counter a Soviet move.

The entities that loaned and granted funds to Bolivia as part of the Triangular Plan insisted that COMIBOL increase the power of its managers while laying off a large number of the rank-and-file.[77] The government-owned enterprise had become a "jobs program" for miners, who received higher wages and better benefits from COMIBOL than they would from its counterparts in the private sector. In addition, the plan called for using a part of COMIBOL's revenues to fund economic diversification projects, in particular in oil and agriculture, long a goal of the moderate wing of the MNR.[78]

Second, virtually upon taking office, President Kennedy sent not only a special representative, Roland Egger, to La Paz to ensure the success of U.S. policy, but also a "Special Mission." Both aimed to ensure that millions of dollars of U.S. assistance that flowed to Bolivia eventually produced "long-range development of the Bolivian economy."[79] In the mission's report, the officials stated that although "the political situation is worsening at an accelerating rate," it was "not hopeless." Given Bolivia's tumultuous era of the late 1950s, and U.S. officials' fear of the implications

---

76. Thomas Mann to Undersecretary of State Clarence D. Dillon, November 16, 1960, Folder Bolivia 1960 (ARA Files), Lots 62D418 and 64D15, Box 1, Subject Files of the Assistant Secretary, 1959–1962, Bureau of Inter-American Affairs, RG 59, NA.

77. Rotchin, *Clientelist State*, 77.

78. Melvin Burke, *The Corporación Minera de Bolivia (COMIBOL) and the Triangular Plan: A Case Study in Dependency* (Meadville, Pa.: Allegheny College, 1987).

79. Roland Egger, Special Representative to the President, to JFK, October 5, 1961, Folder "Bol-Gen-1961," Box 10, Country File: Bolivia, NSF, JFK Library.

of a breakup of the MNR, Washington leaders were understandably concerned about Bolivia devolving into chaos. As earlier discussed, U.S. foreign policymakers decided to build up the Bolivian military as insurance against a meltdown of the MNR. The mission concluded its report by calling for "the establishment of an integrated long-range plan for the economic development of Bolivia." It also concluded—as members of the Eisenhower administration had similarly concluded—that Bolivia was "our most potent demonstration in Latin America" of Washington's ability to promote pro-U.S. economic development that would serve the interests of the majority in a nation run by a democratic government.[80]

Bolivia Tries to Get What It Wants from the United States

During this period, Bolivia wanted two things from its relationship with the United States. First, because its economy was still largely dependent on exports of minerals, in particular tin, it desired that the United States refrain from any action that might lower the price of tin. That meant, foremost, that Bolivian officials most certainly did not want *norteamericano* leaders to sell tin from the U.S. government's strategic stockpiles.

Second, Bolivian leaders wanted economic and military aid. Economic aid would relieve Bolivian leaders of the need to raise capital to fund their government and the private sector economy and pay for the infrastructure development that the middle class wanted. It would also directly benefit working-class Bolivians and, hopefully, ensure a modicum of social peace in a nation traditionally rent with class-based conflict.[81] U.S. military aid would increase the status of military leaders and give the MNR's leaders the tools they needed to punish increasingly numerous and persistent demonstrators—often from the working class or poor sectors of society—who challenged the rule of the military. Bolivian military leaders, in short, claimed they needed weaponry for "internal assistance." Indeed, during the Kennedy administration, U.S. military assistance to Bolivia sharply increased, which included support not only for "civic action" programs but also for internal security purposes.[82]

80. Jack C. Corbett, Seymour J. Rubin, and Willard L. Thorp to President Kennedy, March 24, 1961, Decimal File 724.5MSP/3-2761, RG 59, DOS Central Files, NA.
81. Paz Estenssoro to JFK, October 5, 1961, Folder "Bol-Gen, 1/62–7/62," Box 10, Country File: Bolivia, NSF, JFK Library.
82. Memorandum of conversation regarding military assistance to the Bolivian Armed Forces, April 6, 1960, Decimal File 724.5-MSP/4-160, RG 59, DOS Central Files, NA. "U.S.

In the minds of Bolivia's leaders, economic aid was necessary because of Washington's decision to sell off increasing amounts of the U.S. government strategic mineral stockpile. Considering the importance U.S. officials attached to Bolivian stability, Washington's decision to sell down the stockpile, lowering tin prices and damaging the Bolivian economy, is interesting. Perhaps Washington leaders thought that they could get away with selling government-owned metals: they surmised a lower price might hurt Bolivia, but not to the extent that a weak Bolivian economy would foster a radically anti-U.S. movement. Second, U.S. foreign policymakers thought that it was important to somehow counteract large outflows of capital from the U.S. government for military and economic aid around the world.[83] One way for the government to partially offset this outflow would be to earn income from selling down stockpiles of strategic minerals. Finally, Washington officials, schooled in the principles of free-market economics, looked at the sale of stockpiled metals in ideological terms: these leaders saw free-market capitalism as superior to government-owned stockpiles.

Bolivian leaders were angry at the U.S. decision to sell the stockpiled tin, but they were not powerless. Arguably, as the *norteamericanos* sold more and more of the stockpiled tin, and in the process pushed down the price of tin and with it Bolivia's foreign exchange earnings, Washington ironically helped produce the very situation that it very much wanted to avoid: disintegration of pro-U.S. stability. Therefore, Bolivian leaders, could, and did, make the argument that their nation was on the verge of falling apart and they therefore needed more economic aid from the United States. Bolivia used its instability as a lever to get what it wanted from Washington.[84]

Getting the Gringos' Attention

For Bolivia's policy to be effective, top U.S. officials needed to care about the nation. They did. As the political situation in Bolivia became more and

---

military assistance from 1960 to 1963 jumped from $300,000 to $5 million." U.S. Agency for International Development, *U.S. Overseas Loans and Grants*, http://qesdb.usaid.gov/cgi-bin/broker.exe?_service = default&_program = gbkprogs.data_country_2.sas&unit = N&co code = 5BOL + &sscode = GBK419929 + &year = 1963.0 + &year = 1962.0 + &year = 1961.0 + &year = 1960.0 + &x = 43&y = 7 (accessed June 22, 2009).

83. Richard J. Barnet, *The Alliance: America, Europe, Japan—Makers of the Postwar World* (New York: Touchstone, 1983), 199–202; Rabe, *Most Dangerous Area*, 153–54.

84. Stephansky to Secretary of State, April 27, 1962, Folder "Bol-Gen, 1/62–7/62," Box

more tenuous, interestingly, this fragility gave the leaders of that nation much more access to top U.S. leaders than other Latin American nations and more control over U.S.-Bolivian relations. U.S. leaders' interest in Bolivia existed at the highest level. On March 3, 1961, Arthur Schlesinger Jr. wrote a memorandum to President Kennedy urging a "top-level" review of U.S. policy toward Bolivia. Schlesinger did a good job in getting the attention of the young president. He focused Kennedy's attention on Bolivia by warning that it "might well go the way of Cuba" if an increase in U.S. economic assistance was not immediately forthcoming. Fearing that a left-wing or unfriendly Bolivia "would be a base of subversion and revolution in Peru, Ecuador, Brazil, Chile, and Paraguay," Schlesinger closed by stating, "One can already imagine the speeches in Congress on the theme 'Who lost Bolivia?'"[85] When the Bolivian ministers of economy and rural affairs desired to see President Kennedy in 1962, the president's executive secretary, William H. Brubeck, pointedly informed White House officials that Kennedy had "a personal interest in Bolivian development," and noted "the still extremely precarious political situation" there.[86]

A concrete way to communicate to the United States that the Bolivian polity was on the verge of disintegration was for Bolivian military leaders to tell U.S. officials of a possible military *golpe,* or coup. Maintaining democratic governments in Latin America was very important to U.S. leaders. Noncommunist democratic nations in the developing world could be used by Western leaders to make the point that the U.S.-led "free" world bloc was superior to the communist bloc.

Bolivian leaders skillfully manipulated U.S. concern that a military coup would lead the South American nation down the road to military dictatorship. In August 1961, Bolivian colonel Juan Lechín Suárez (half-brother to Juan Lechín Oquendo, revolutionary leader and Bolivian vice president from 1961 to 1964) warned U.S. military leaders in Bolivia that the top Bolivian military brass intended to sweep the MNR government out of

---

10, Country File: Bolivia, NSF, JFK Library. In this memorandum, José Antonio Arze Murillo, the Bolivian minister of the interior, told the U.S. ambassador Ben Stephansky that he expected antigovernment riots to escalate through Labor Day (May 1). The Bolivian official noted that the protestors would have Czech light weapons. The U.S. ambassador feared that the Bolivian military units assigned to anti-riot duty were so poorly armed that they might even defect if street battles escalated! Consequently, he asked for extra aid money to purchase "riot guns, pistols, and ammunition" for these forces.

85. Memorandum, Schlesinger to JFK, "The Crisis in Bolivia," March 3, 1961, p. 2, *FRUS, 1961,* microfiche supplement to vols. 10, 11, and 12.

86. William H. Brubeck, Executive Secretary, to Kenneth O'Donnell, May 27, 1962, Folder "Bol-Gen, 1/62–7/62," Box 10, Country File: Bolivia, NSF, JFK Library.

power and bring in new leadership.[87] Not surprisingly, Washington officials feared a military coup could quickly lead to an ultranationalist, radical, or communist backlash. More broadly, and more ominously for Washington, a coup in La Paz would be hard evidence that all its support of the MNR stretching back to the early 1950s had been a failure, a failure U.S. policymakers very much wanted to avoid as the Alliance for Progress began to bog down by 1963–64. Because U.S. officials viewed Bolivia as a test case of their ability to help a democratic, noncommunist regime provide sufficiently for its people, the replacement of a democratic government with a military one would be a big psychological blow to Washington.

Bolivian officials, time and time again, tried to get the *norteamericano* leaders to allocate more economic assistance to their nation. They saw such aid as instrumental to jump-starting the Alliance (the benefits of which seemed to be accruing very slowly).[88] More important, Bolivian officials were successful. Whenever they notified U.S. officials of their growing economic and political problems, Washington sent more aid.

In addition to signaling Washington that it was in danger of collapse or military takeover, Paz Estenssoro's government made careful overtures to (or accepted overtures from) the Soviet bloc in order to compel the *norteamericanos* to increase the amount of aid. Castro's 1959 rise to power in Cuba, by exponentially increasing U.S. fears of Soviet expansion in the region, gave Bolivian leaders more of an opportunity to "play the Soviet card." In this regard, they were very skillful at making it seem as if Soviet leaders were coercing *them* into a relationship with the communist giant. Bolivian leaders knew full well that Washington would be very displeased if Bolivian officials openly requested assistance from the Soviet Union.

According to Bolivian leaders, Soviet officials talked to their Bolivian counterparts about bringing a (traveling) industrial and trade exhibit to their nation and establishing a permanent trade mission. Bolivian leaders passed this information on to Washington to focus *norteamericano* attention on Bolivia. Further, Bolivian officials told U.S. officials that the Soviet Union had claimed that the United States was overcommitted in Latin America. In other words, the Soviets told Bolivian leaders that the *norteamericanos* could never fulfill their promises. Finally, the coup de grace: according to Bolivian policymakers, the Soviets claimed they could make

87. Williams to Secretary of State, August 19, 1961, Folder "Bol-Gen-1961," Box 10, Country File: Bolivia, NSF, JFK Library.
88. William H. Brubeck, Executive Secretary, to Kenneth O'Donnell, May 27, 1962, Folder "Bol-Gen, 1/62–7/62," Box 10, Country File: Bolivia, NSF, JFK Library.

Bolivia the socialist "showpiece" of South America.[89] Bolivian efforts to adroitly "play the Soviet card" seemed to succeed. U.S. leaders, threatened by even hints of possible Soviet incursions into Latin America, responded by giving more economic assistance to the Andean nation.[90]

The main reason why the Bolivians ultimately put a stop to their "feelers" to the Eastern bloc was the prospect of significantly increased U.S. economic assistance under the Alliance for Progress. But two events provided the proximate causes. First, in 1961 Paz's government discovered documents linking the Partido Comunista de Bolivia (PCB) (Bolivian Communist Party) to Cuba and evidence that the two planned to overthrow the Paz government.[91] Second, the 1962 Cuban Missile Crisis largely ended Bolivian officials' attempts to play the "Soviet card." With Khrushchev's perceived capitulation—it was widely viewed that way at the time—the power of the Left in Latin America momentarily declined.[92] In addition, many Latin American leaders concluded that the missile crisis represented a slow exit on the part of the Soviets from Latin America. As a result these leaders concluded that playing the Soviet card would not be very effective. After the Cuban Missile Crisis came to an end, it was not credible to maintain that the Soviet Union would actually care enough about Latin America to seek another satellite (in addition to Cuba) there. The upshot was that Bolivia largely stopped courting the Soviets after 1962.[93]

89. Stephansky to Secretary of State, April 6, 1962, Folder "Bol-Gen, 8/62–12/62," Box 10, Country File: Bolivia, NSF, JFK Library.

90. Total U.S. assistance jumped from $15.3 million in 1960 to $39 million in 1962. U.S. Agency for International Development, *U.S. Overseas Loans and Grants,* http://qesdb .usaid.gov/cgi-bin/broker.exe (accessed May 17, 2008).

91. The documents were of doubtful authenticity, but they gave Paz an opportunity to crack down on the Left. Lehman, "U.S. Foreign Aid," 670.

92. Twenty-five years after the Cuban Missile Crisis, newly released evidence showed that Kennedy, while taking a firm public stance, was working behind the scenes to ensure war would not break out between the superpowers. A generation later, declassified documents and top U.S. officials revealed that Kennedy promised to dismantle Jupiter missiles at NATO bases in Turkey and Italy in exchange for Soviet withdrawal of its Cuban missiles. See Walter LaFeber, *The American Age: U.S. Foreign Policy at Home and Abroad,* 2nd ed. (New York: W. W. Norton, 1994), 2:601.

93. Stephansky to Secretary of State, December 18, 1962, Folder "Bol-Gen, 8/62–12/62," Box 10, Country File: Bolivia, NSF, JFK Library. However, U.S. fears of Soviet penetration in Bolivia did not evaporate with the end of the Cuban Missile Crisis. See Thomas L. Hughes, Department of State, Bureau of Intelligence and Research, January 9, 1963, "Soviet Bloc Economic Overtures to Bolivia," Folder "Bol-Gen 1/63–3/63," Box 10A, Country File: Bolivia, NSF, JFK Library.

A Tragic Denouement for the MNR, the 1964 *Golpe*, and Tighter U.S.-Bolivian Relations

The year 1962 represented an important turning point in U.S.-Bolivian relations in another sense. For a decade, the United States had tried to keep the MNR from falling apart—and to keep the cautious moderates of the party in the leadership positions. After 1962, Washington leaders, realizing that the left and the moderate wings of the MNR were on the verge of having a nasty divorce, gave up on the policy of maintaining MNR unity[94] and relied more and more on U.S. military assistance to increase the power of the Bolivian military. If the MNR collapsed, a pro-U.S. Bolivian military could stage a coup, keeping Bolivia noncommunist and friendly to the United States.

Another important turning point occurred in U.S.-Bolivian relations in 1963–64. U.S. leaders became less and less concerned with Bolivia's internal affairs by the mid-1960s. In the early, heady years of the Alliance for Progress, U.S. leaders criticized the MNR for its undemocratic rigging of elections.[95] As time went by, the Kennedy administration cared less and less about whether the Alliance promoted democracy or not. Firmly anticommunist "neighbors" were more important than weak, democratic neighbors that might "fall" to communism.

The traditional U.S. quest for pro-U.S. stability in Bolivia became much more difficult in 1963 and 1964. U.S. policy going back to the earliest years of the Bolivian revolution aimed to support the cautious moderate element of the MNR, headed up by Paz Estenssoro. But Paz's position was becoming weaker and weaker. As the left-wing segment of the MNR left the party in 1963, in part because Paz had used the military to break strikes, Paz's base began to erode significantly.[96] When the MNR engineered a constitutional change in 1961 to allow presidents to serve consecutive terms, many thought that this amendment to the constitution was

---

94. Memorandum from Ambassador Benjamin Stephansky to Assistant Secretary of State for Inter-American Affairs Edwin Martin, October 18, 1962, "Bolivia-1962, Splitting Paz from Lechín," Box 1, Lot 70 D443, RG 59, Records of the Department of State, NA.

95. Rusk to Amemb La Paz, July 16, 1962, Folder "Bol-Gen, 1/62–7/62," Box 10, Country File: Bolivia, NSF, JFK Library. Rusk was concerned that the MNR action would create anti-U.S. sentiment among the noncommunist opposition to the MNR in Bolivia. Also, support of a nondemocratic MNR would make the United States look hypocritical in criticizing authoritarianism in the hemisphere.

96. Salvador Angulo and Loreto Correa, "La política exterior norteamericano en América Latina: Los casos de Chile y Bolivia, 1960–1980," in *Visiones de fin de siglo: Bolivia y América*

specifically put in place to benefit Paz, and his support eroded even further.

Simultaneously, U.S. officials facilitated the erosion of the MNR's left-wing base. The move proved counterproductive to the U.S. goal of maintaining pro-U.S. stability in the nation. As Washington's fears of communism in Latin America grew, U.S. officials thought it more important to denude the Left of power than maintain support for the MNR. In a memorandum to McGeorge Bundy, Johnson's special assistant for national security affairs, Benjamin H. Read, executive secretary of the Department of State, noted that "United States pressure on the [Bolivian] Government to carry out reforms in the state-owned tin mines" was imperative, since "these reforms tended to undercut the power base" of the left wing of the MNR.[97]

U.S. support for the moderate segment of the MNR, dating back to 1952, easily transferred to General René Barrientos Ortuño when he ousted Paz in a coup on November 4, 1964. There is no evidence U.S. officials gave Barrientos a "green light" for the coup.[98] However, two important points need to be made. First, the Johnson administration quickly offered official diplomatic recognition to Barrientos. Both Kennedy and Johnson privileged pro-U.S. anticommunism in Bolivia over democracy. This was the case despite Kennedy's rhetoric in the early years of the Alliance promoting democracy in Latin America, and Johnson's statement upon Kennedy's death that the Alliance for Progress was to be continued in a Johnson presidency. As historian Matthew Gildner has concluded, "Washington's recognition of Bolivia's military government in the wake of the November 1964 coup illustrated that Lyndon B. Johnson shared the same problem as that of his predecessor, John F. Kennedy: he could not reconcile his obligation to political democratization under the Alliance for Progress with his commitment to regional security and anticommunism."[99]

Second, recently released U.S. government documents show that once Barrientos was in power the United States offered him significant

---

Latina en el siglo XX, ed. Dora Cajías, Magdalena Cajías, Carmen Johnson, and Iris Villegas (La Paz: IFEA / Coordinadora de Historia, Embajada de Espan~a en Bolivia, 2001), 417.

97. Benjamin H. Read to McGeorge Bundy, May 28, 1964, *FRUS, 1964–1968*, vol. 31, 337.

98. Lehman, *Bolivia and the United States*, 141, presents circumstantial evidence for a U.S. "green light" to coup plotters. However, Kirkland, in *Observing Our Hermanos de Armas*, categorically states that Washington did not encourage Barrientos.

99. Matthew Gildner, "Revolution, Recognition, and Reconciliation: Bolivia, the United States, and the Alliance for Progress, 1961–1964" (unpublished paper in possession of the author, n.d.), 3.

amounts of assistance. U.S. officials saw him as "the only apparent feasible alternative for the time being to chaos and the eventual domination of extremist groups."[100] Washington saw him as the heir, in a sense, to the cautious moderates of the now-deposed MNR. U.S. government support, in addition to economic and military assistance, included covert assistance to Barrientos to help him win the 1966 election and to forcibly, and violently, put down strike violence in Bolivia's mines.[101]

By the end of the 1960s, it was clear, Barrientos's repression of the miners notwithstanding, that the Bolivian revolution had made great strides. The land reform is an important example. By 1967, 7.2 percent of Bolivia's total land was redistributed to the landless, making it the most thorough land reform in South America to that time. According to Dwight B. Heath, 291,823 new land titles were distributed under the reform, and 191,459 families received titles.[102] More significantly, it broke the back of the quasi-feudal landholding structure that had held sway in Bolivia up to 1952. *Campesinos*, who had formerly been derisively referred to as "indios," were assuming the roles of citizens.[103] The structural changes of the revolution could not be reversed; and in some ways the Bolivian revolution lived on. Even as some observers noted the growth of a new elite, based on commercial success, in the countryside after the revolution, as Herbert S. Klein and Jonathan Kelly concluded, the nation "clearly experienced a profound and violent social revolution which abruptly and permanently changed the entire society."[104]

Barrientos's government continued the revolution in some ways. Even though he largely curtailed the land reform, his populist style endeared him to some segments of the *campesino* community and comported with previous Bolivian revolutionary leaders.[105] His popularity with the peasantry proved important, as his greatest challenge would be a rebellion in

---

100. "Memorandum Prepared for the 303 Committee," July 13, 1965, *FRUS, 1964–1968*, vol. 31, 359.

101. Editorial Note, *FRUS, 1964–1968*, vol. 31, 334–35; ibid., 349; "Memorandum Prepared for the 303 Committee," July 13, 1965, ibid., 359; Benjamin H. Read to McGeorge Bundy, June 19, 1965, ibid., 355–56.

102. See Dwight B. Heath, Charles J. Erasmus, and Hans C. Buechler, *Land Reform and Social Revolution in Bolivia* (New York: F. A. Praeger, 1969), 373–74.

103. Ibid., 376, 387.

104. Ibid., 386–87; Jonathan Kelley and Herbert S. Klein, *Revolution and the Rebirth of Inequality* (Berkeley and Los Angeles: University of California Press, 1981), 104.

105. For the curtailing of the land reform, see Healy, *Llamas, Weavings, and Organic Chocolate*, 13. For a good description of Barrientos's populist style and how it appealed to many in the *campo*, see Xavier Albó, "From MNRistas to Kataristas to Katari," in *Resistance, Rebellion, and Consciousness in the Andean Peasant World, 18th to 20th Centuries*, ed. Steve J. Stern (Madison: University of Wisconsin Press, 1987), 385–86.

the countryside. It was spearheaded by the Argentine revolutionary Ernesto "Che" Guevara. Although a foreign-backed insurgency was a new experience for a Bolivian leader, the battle against Guevara revealed that the dynamics of U.S.-Bolivian relations established since the 1952 revolution remained largely unchanged.

THE REBELLION IN THE COUNTRYSIDE

U.S.-Bolivian and U.S.–Latin American Relations in the Mid-1960s

Ernesto "Che" Guevara is one of the most divisive icons of our era, especially in Bolivia, where some see him as a liberator and others as an invader. He is idealized by the Left for his dedication to socialist revolution and condemned by the Right for the bloodiness of his revolutionary adventures.[1]

He is perhaps one of the most examined individuals in modern Latin American history. The literature on his life and activities is vast. Perspectives on his attempt to foment revolution in Bolivia tend to fall into two broad groups. One group focuses on how he saw his attempt to foment revolution in Bolivia as part of his broader goal of world socialist revolution.[2] Some who subscribe to this "school of thought" believe that his failure to connect with Bolivia's divided leftist movement doomed him from the beginning.[3] Others look more closely at the military's 1967 campaign to capture and execute him. Guevara's demise provides an interesting case study of the clash of the two major cold war blocs operating in the Western Hemisphere. On the one hand, Fidel Castro inspired and supported

---

1. A representative example of a critique from the right is Alvaro Vargas Llosa, "The Killing Machine: Che Guevara, from Communist Firebrand to Capitalist Brand," *New Republic*, July 11–18, 2005, 25–30.

2. Biographies of Guevara that discuss his vision for world socialist revolution include Jon Lee Anderson, *Che Guevara: A Revolutionary Life* (New York: Grove Press, 1997), and Jorge Castañada, *Compañero: The Life and Times of Che Guevara* (New York: Knopf, 1997).

3. Daniel James, "Introduction," in Che Guevara, *The Complete Bolivian Diaries of Che Guevara and Other Captured Documents* (New York: Cooper Square Press, 2000), 61–63.

attempts to spread revolution in the region. On the other, U.S. counterinsurgency policy—itself a reaction (at least to some extent) of Castro's revolution—aimed to thwart Castro's revolutionary hemispheric vision.[4]

This chapter examines Guevara's battle in Bolivia in a different context. It looks first at how the Bolivian leadership and citizenry responded to Guevara's incursion and how the Bolivian government—with U.S. assistance—successfully apprehended him and destroyed his nascent movement. Second, it looks at Washington's view of both the Bolivian scene and the threat Guevara represented. The Bolivian government's response to Guevara's challenge represented a great victory for the Bolivian military, government, and revolution. The irony is that not only did Guevara attempt to foment revolution in a nation with a popularly elected leader but he did so in a country still undergoing its own social revolution.

To understand the significance of Guevara's attempt to foment his style of socialist revolution in Bolivia, it is important to understand that both Bolivia and inter-American relations were in great flux in the mid-1960s. Going back a bit, in the early 1960s the United States had focused a great deal of attention on Latin America, a part of the world that during the cold war it had largely taken for granted. With President John F. Kennedy's Alliance for Progress, the young president proposed that the United States and Latin America work together to promote social, political, and economic reform—and implement the largest mutual assistance program ever conceived for the nonindustrialized world. At the same time, Kennedy aimed to immunize the hemisphere against communism, with U.S. military assistance a key part of that program.[5]

After Kennedy's assassination, President Lyndon Baines Johnson (LBJ) dropped the idealistic side of the Alliance for Progress while maintaining the hard-line anticommunist strain of Kennedy's efforts in the region. For example, in 1964, the United States gave both development assistance and covert assistance to Chile. The U.S. government, through the Central Intelligence Agency, gave $3.2 million in covert funding to support Eduardo Frei's campaign for president and to prevent socialist Salvador Allende

---

4. Henry Butterfield Ryan, *The Fall of Che Guevara: A Story of Soldiers, Spies, and Diplomats* (New York: Oxford University Press, 1998). Gary Prado Salmón, a military official who participated in the Bolivian military's defeat of Guevara, recounts his story in *The Defeat of Che Guevara: Military Response to Guerrilla Challenge in Bolivia*, trans. John Deredita (New York: Praeger, 1987). Felix I. Rodríguez, a Cuban military officer who worked for the CIA in Bolivia aiding the Bolivians in apprehending Che, recounts his story in Rodríguez and John Weisman, *Shadow Warrior* (New York: Simon and Schuster, 1989).

5. For Kennedy's policy toward the region, see Rabe, *Most Dangerous Area*.

Gossens (who headed up a left-wing coalition that included communists) from being elected.[6] Frei's reformist government proved useful to U.S. policymakers—indeed, U.S. support of his reformist, democratic government could score Washington some important points in the nonindustrialized world.

But by 1966, the year Che headed off to start a revolution in the Bolivian countryside, U.S. policy boiled down to one thing: anticommunism. Where Kennedy had at least done some hand-wringing over military *golpes de estado* in Latin America, Johnson easily accepted the 1964 coup in Brazil and the 1966 military takeover in Argentina—not to mention the 1964 coup in Bolivia.[7] A key figure in the policy shift away from some of the more idealistic aspects of the Alliance to a focus on private investment and anticommunism is Thomas Mann, Lyndon Johnson's top adviser on Latin America.[8] Basically, the Johnson administration wanted the countries of Latin America to increase economic growth through economic integration, lower tariffs, modernized education systems, increased agricultural efficiency, and increased private investment. In turn, the administration would offer a "carrot," in the words of Special Assistant to the President Walt W. Rostow, of "expanded economic assistance."[9] Stimulated economic growth would, according to U.S. officials, lay the groundwork for pro-U.S., anticommunist governments. Indeed, LBJ would go to great lengths to head off even a perceived increase in communist influence in Latin America, as he proved when he dispatched twenty-three thousand U.S. soldiers to the Dominican Republic in 1965. The controversial invasion—motivated largely by Washington's fear of "another Cuba" in the region—was the first U.S. landing of ground forces in a Latin American nation since the 1930s.[10]

    6. "Memorandum Prepared for the Special Group," April 1, 1964, *FRUS, 1964–1968*, vol. 31, 558; "Memorandum for the Record," May 12, 1964, ibid., 575; Editorial Note, ibid., 582.
    7. Tulchin, "Promise of Progress," 232–33.
    8. Walter LaFeber, "Thomas C. Mann and the Devolution of Latin American Policy: From the Good Neighbor to Military Intervention," in *Behind the Throne: Servants of Power to Imperial Presidents, 1898–1968*, ed. Thomas J. McCormick and Walter LaFeber (Madison: University of Wisconsin Press, 1993), 166–203.
    9. Walt W. Rostow to Lyndon B. Johnson, October 15, 1966, OAS Summit 5/66–12/66, Vol. 1, Box 15, International Meetings Files, National Security Files, Lyndon Baines Johnson Presidential Library, Austin, Tex. (hereafter LBJ Library).
    10. Standard accounts of the U.S. intervention in the Dominican Republic in 1964 include Piero Gleijeses, *The Dominican Crisis: The 1965 Constitutionalist Revolt and American Intervention* (Baltimore: Johns Hopkins University Press, 1978), and Abraham Lowenthal, *The Dominican Intervention*, 2nd ed. (Baltimore: Johns Hopkins University Press, 1995).

As it became clear that Washington had dispensed with the idealistic, reformist side of the Alliance, many Latin Americans lost faith in and interest in the program—as had many in the United States.[11] A cynic would say that from the point of view of cold war Washington, U.S.–Latin American relations had reverted back to the usual—U.S. officialdom had lost interest in the region and would not regain it before the next crisis in inter-American relations. One of the more famous journalists of the twentieth-century United States, James "Scotty" Reston, once said that people in the United States would do anything for Latin America, except read about it.[12] By the mid-1960s, the U.S. public had grown tired of the seemingly intractable problems in Latin America and the Latin Americans' criticisms of the inadequacy of the Alliance. After all, it was not surprising that U.S. observers would lose interest in a region that had benefited from billions of dollars of U.S. taxpayer largess while at the same time criticizing U.S. efforts.[13]

The changing nature of U.S. policy toward the region is important for understanding Guevara's attempt at instigating revolution in the Bolivian Oriente. One thread linked all of Guevara's attempts at fomenting revolution in Latin America and Africa: he found himself fighting U.S.-backed governments and rebellions. (Guevara only visited the United States once—for a few months in the 1950s as a traveler—and there is virtually no record of his experiences there.)[14] Guevara perceived the United States—in many respects accurately—as supporting reactionary regimes in the nonindustrialized world, regimes he considered nothing more than proxies of the United States.[15] Bolivia, in his mind, could be termed such a proxy, if only because it had received an extraordinary amount of U.S. assistance.[16]

This sets the stage for 1967. In many respects, 1967 marked a turning point in U.S.–Latin American relations. Conflicts at an inter-American summit in Punta del Este, Uruguay, caused a breakdown of multilateralism in the Western Hemisphere. Specifically, the Latin Americans did not

---

11. For a good overview of the Alliance, see Jeffrey F. Taffett, *Foreign Aid as Foreign Policy: The Alliance for Progress in Latin America* (New York: Routledge, 2007). In the mid- to late 1960s the Alliance was critized by many observers. Taffett's chapter 8 deals with such criticism: see especially 175–94.

12. Thomas Skidmore and Peter H. Smith, *Modern Latin America*, 5th ed. (New York: Oxford University Press, 2001), 1.

13. Edwardo Frei, "The Alliance That Lost Its Way," *Foreign Affairs* 45 (April 1967): 437–48.

14. Anderson, *Che Guevara*, 93–94.

15. Ryan, *Fall of Che Guevara*, 18.

16. Siekmeier, *Aid, Nationalism, and Inter-American Relations*.

want to participate with the United States in a free trade area—instead, they wanted to form an economic zone of their own that excluded the United States.[17] Because a series of right-wing coups soured Congress's mood on Latin America, assistance to the region was not forthcoming in large amounts. Consequently, the Johnson administration did not have a "sweetener" to induce the Latin Americans to join a U.S.-sponsored trading bloc. Moreover, the increasing attention placed on Vietnam—which, of course, had already become an obsession—meant that Latin America was rapidly falling to the bottom of the list of priorities of the United States.[18]

Guevara's Motives

Many investigators have attempted to discover why Guevara chose southeastern Bolivia as his "base for operations" for fomenting revolution in South America. It is important to note that Guevara's attempt to instigate an uprising in Bolivia that would spread across that nation and even the South American continent came after two important but ill-fated attempts in 1963 to incite revolution in South America—in Bolivia and in Argentina. Both were defeated by the militaries of their respective nations. It also followed Guevara's ill-fated attempt to start a revolution in Africa—a place that, because of its poverty and in some cases repressive governments, must have seemed like fertile ground. In addition, Guevara thought that the United States was poised to exert more control over that continent, and he wanted to thwart such an effort.[19]

Moreover, to understand Guevara's actions in Bolivia—he had been planning an insurgency there since 1964—one must understand his long-term vision for socialist revolution in the nonindustrialized world. Guevara, as is well known, thought and spoke in expansive terms. Put briefly, he aimed to destroy imperialism.[20] And Bolivia's role in this global project?

---

17. Robin L. Rosenberg, "OAS and Summit of the Americas: Coexistence or Integration of Forces for Multilateralism?" *Latin American Politics and Society* 43 (Spring 2001): 83.
18. Tulchin, "Promise of Progress," 239–41.
19. Gustavo Rodríguez Ostria, "Bolivia en el ciclo guerrillero, 1963–1970: Continuidades y diferencias," *La Prensa*, July 17, 2005, 1–2; Anderson, *Che Guevara*, 537–79; Ryan, *Fall of Che Guevara*, 26–29.
20. Paul J. Dosal states that Guevara aimed to set up a "covert network linking La Paz, Havana, Algiers, Brazzaville, Dar es Salaaam, Prague, Moscow, and Beijing" in order to destroy imperialism. Dosal, *Comandante Che: Guerrilla Soldier, Commander, and Strategist, 1956–1967* (University Park: Pennsylvania State University Press, 2003), 194–95; 252.

From Guevara's perspective, Bolivia could be the next Vietnam: Che aimed to force a U.S. intervention, thus further inciting the Latin American Left to join the guerrilla war. According to the diary of one of the Bolivians who joined Guevara's insurrection, Harry "Pombo" Villegas, Che said that Bolivia had to "sacrifice itself" to create the conditions for revolution in the surrounding countries—hardly an enticing scenario for Bolivia.[21]

A broader problem for Guevara's efforts in Bolivia was that he tried to impose the Cuban model on the Bolivian situation. In Cuba, in contrast to Communist ideology, the party was in many respects subservient to the army even after the revolution. The Bolivian communist party, however, refused to subject itself, as Guevara demanded, to his control.[22] Indeed, so confident was Guevara of Bolivia's potential for a revolution inspired by a small band of guerrilla leaders—the Cuban model—that he did not think it important to plan out essential elements of either strategy or tactics. A key example was his nearly complete lack of concern for developing a network of urban sympathizers, which had proved critically important in Cuba.[23]

Another reason why Guevara might have chosen Bolivia as a place to start his revolution was because, as a young man, he had visited Bolivia right after the 1952 revolution. In the words of Paul J. Dosal, Che was impressed with the "militancy of the miners" there, seeing the "revolutionary potential" of armed workers spearheading a revolutionary battle against an oligarchy.[24] However, Guevara chose not to work with Bolivia's miners in 1966–67. In a conversation with Bolivia's communist leader,

21. Pombo, quoted in James, "Introduction," in Guevara, *Complete Bolivian Diaries*, 16. Guevara's most compelling statement setting forth how he aimed to create multiple Vietnams is in his "Message to the Tricontinental," reprinted in *Guerrilla Warfare*, ed. Brian Loveman and Thomas M. Davies Jr. (Wilmington, Del.: Scholarly Resources, 1997), 165–66, 172, 175–76.

22. When Mario Monje asked that Che submit to his leadership in the campaign, Che replied, "Here I am adviser to no one." Guevara, quoted in Dosal, *Comandante Che*, 248. Dosal notes that Guevara refused to submit to local leadership because he blamed his failure to foment revolution in the Congo a year earlier on his deference to the Congolese guerrilla leadership (249). Dosal concludes that Guevara thought that if he simply presented the Bolivian communists with a fait accompli, they would rally to the rebellion. However, at no point did the Bolivian Communist Party rally to Guevara's cause (258).

23. Ryan, *Fall of Che Guevara*, 17. Guevara's lack of concern for strategy and tactics is particularly ironic given that he had written a thorough and thoughtful manual for guerrilla warfare that had achieved wide readership by the time he began his Bolivia rebellion. First published as *La guerra de guerrillas* in 1960, it was published in English the following year as *Guerrilla Warfare* (New York: Monthly Review Press, 1961). Dosal discusses Guevara's lack of interest in an urban support network in *Comandante Che*, 258–59.

24. Dosal, *Comandante Che*, 32–33.

Mario Monje Molina, at the end of 1966, Guevara identified a number of reasons why Bolivia was a good place to start his continent-wide rebellion. He noted the economic distress of the people, in part caused by exploitation of foreign-owned businesses, as a key reason why Bolivia would provide fertile ground for revolution. Moreover, the weakness of Bolivia's government, he maintained, was an important factor.[25] In addition, there were other factors Guevara did not mention in his conversation with Monje. The Bolivian army was one of the weakest in the region.[26] Even though the Andean nation was headed by a democratic leader, when Guevara began his initial planning for his *foco* (insurgency) in Bolivia, representative rule was faltering; and in November 1964 the Bolivian military ousted President Víctor Paz Estenssoro. Thus, Bolivia was led by a military government—one of the few in Latin America at that time.[27] Guevara probably assumed that the Bolivian citizenry would be more likely to rally to his cause in a nation headed up by a military leader (Cuba's hated dictator, Rubén Fulgencio Batista, whom Guevara worked to overthrow, had been such a military leader) than if they lived in a democracy. With regard to the United States, Guevara also thought that since the United States had few economic or strategic interests in Bolivia, it would not respond quickly to a guerrilla incursion, giving the *foco* time to establish itself.[28]

Guevara's Many Problems

Guevara's assessment of Bolivia proved inaccurate. Indeed, that nation was perhaps the worst possible choice for Guevara's war. First, Bolivia's 1952 revolution had not stopped with the 1964 coup by General René Barrientos Ortuño; indeed, in many respects it continued up through the late 1960s. An interesting personal connection with regard to revolutionary

---

25. Douglas Henderson to the Department of State, February 10, 1968, Subject Numeric File POL 12–6 BOL, RG 59, DOS Central Files, NA.

26. Ryan, in *Fall of Che Guevara*, 40–41, succinctly summarizes the Bolivian military's weaknesses. Bolivia's military had never won a war and had been soundly defeated by the revolutionaries in 1952.

27. In March 1964, the U.S. government so feared a collapse of the Paz regime that it undertook a high-level study of how it might respond if Paz Estenssoro were assassinated or otherwise incapacitated before the August 1964 elections. Latin American Policy Committee, "Bolivia—Pre-Election Contingency Plan," March 20, 1964, Cables, Vol. 1, 12/63–7/64, Box 7, Bolivia, County Files, National Security Files, LBJ Library.

28. Dosal, *Comandante Che*, 253.

continuity can be seen in Barrientos himself, who became president in 1964. He had been a Bolivian revolutionary going back to 1946—he even piloted the plane that brought President Víctor Paz Estenssoro out of exile from Buenos Aires in 1952 to lead the poor Andean nation through its first momentous years of revolution.[29] Barrientos's November 1964 coup proved remarkably easy, and he enjoyed quite a bit of support throughout the country. Factors that explain Barrientos's popularity include Paz's failure to cultivate peasant support, the exit of Juan Lechín Oquendo's left-wing segment of the party, Paz's underestimation of the political ambitions of some of the officers' corps, and most particularly Barrientos's own charisma and ambition.[30]

Even as opposition to Barrientos rose, it remained fragmented during his time in office. The opposition included the ousted MNR; the Falange Socialista Boliviana (FSB), a fascist group; and the leftist Partido Revolucionario de la Izquierda Nacional (PRIN).[31] A divided opposition helped him get elected in 1966 with a large percentage of the vote. But Barrientos's charisma and knowledge of Quechua, the most widely spoken Indian language in Bolivia, probably proved as important, especially among the working class and *campesinos* (poor famers). He attempted to fold the *campesinos* into his governing coalition with his *pacto militar-campesino*. This informal agreement was actually a continuation of an alliance that the MNR leadership had forged between the moderate elements of the MNR, the military, and the *campesinos*. Although its roots ran back to the late 1950s, the *pacto militar-campesino* came into its own in the early 1960s.[32] By moving away from Paz Estenssorro's technique of playing regional *campesino* leaders off against one another and instead negotiating

29. James, "Introduction," in Guevara, *Complete Bolivian Diaries*, 19.

30. Rotchin, *Clientelist State*, 84. Moreover, because Bolivia's constitution was only amended in 1961 to allow presidents to run for consecutive terms in office, some Bolivians feared *continuismo*—that Paz would entrench himself in power. Consequently, his support further eroded. Lehman, *Bolivia and the United States*, 138.

31. Memorandum from Thomas L. Hughes to Secretary of State, July 24, 1968, Subject Numeric File POL 12 BOL, RG 59, DOS Central Files, NA. A U.S. government intelligence threat assessment noted that because Barrientos thought that a public announcement of the existence of guerrillas in southeastern Bolivia would invite criticism from the MNR, he was slow to rally support for a fight against the guerrillas, which gave them an opportunity to establish and thus strengthen themselves. "Cuban-Inspired Guerrilla Activity in Bolivia," June 14, 1967, Guerrilla Problems, Box 23, Intelligence Files, National Security Files, LBJ Library.

32. Rotchin, *Clientelist State*, 83; Whitehead, "Bolivian National Revolution," 33. See also Timothy P. Wickham-Crowley, *Guerrillas and Revolution in Latin America: A Comparative Study of Insurgents and Regimes Since 1956* (Princeton: Princeton University Press, 1992), 151.

truces, he reached out directly to the peasants, as an old-fashioned patron would seek clients among those in society with little power.[33]

In recent years, the diaries and interviews of members of Guevara's band have been reissued, helping to generate more interest in Guevara's activities in Bolivia.[34] Although some do discuss the revolutionary changes implemented by Bolivia's governments since 1952, including land reform, Guevara's revolutionaries did not see the Bolivian revolution as having had much effect on the Bolivian countryside. Even though the land reform was not thoroughly implemented in the Oriente,[35] it is clear that the reform, by giving landless Bolivian Indians access to land, had given them a solid stake in a key part of Bolivia's national patrimony for the first time. Consequently, the indigenous people had little to gain from a Che-style uprising.[36] Moreover, peasants in the Oriente did not lack for access to land. Observers noted, in fact, that it was an area of abundant land. Large landowners could not even cultivate the entirety of their own holdings. Even the poorer *campesinos* in the Oriente enjoyed greater access to land than the rural residents of the western cordillera. One critic of Guevara's efforts to foment revolution in the eastern lowlands caustically concluded, "What was Che going to offer these peasants, still more land they could not use?"[37]

Moreover, some *campesinos* actively resisted Guevara's incursion and called for their fellow agriculturalists to back the Bolivian government against what they saw as a foreign invasion. After all, many Bolivians saw the Barrientos government as legitimate because it had been recently popularly elected.[38] And Barrientos, by continuing the land reform, maintained a key element of the 1952 revolution.[39]

33. Dunkerley, *Rebellion in the Veins*, 116, 133. Also see Albó, "From MNRistas to Kataristas to Katari," 386.
34. For example, Rodolfo Saldana, *Fertile Ground—Che Guevara and Bolivia: A Firsthand Account by Rodolfo Saldaña* (New York: Pathfinder, 2001); Harry Villegas (Pombo) Tamayo, *Pombo: A Man of Che's Guerrilla: With Che Guevara in Bolivia, 1966–1968* (New York: Pathfinder, 1997).
35. Ernest Feder concluded that in the Oriente there was a "counterreform" after the 1952 land reform. Feder stated, "A conjuncture of politics and traditions successfully resisted implementation of the land reform in the Oriente." Quoted in Kevin Healy, *Caciques y patrones, una experiencia de desarrollo rural en el sur de Bolivia* (Cochabamba: Ediciones El Buitre, 1983), 40 (my translation). As a result, unlike in Bolivia's western mountain ranges, the traditional rural elite in the Oriente maintained its power after the land reform.
36. James, "Introduction," in Guevara, *Complete Bolivian Diaries*, 59.
37. Luis Mercier Vega, quoted in Wickham-Crowley, *Guerrillas and Revolution in Latin America*, 117.
38. James, "Introduction," in Guevara, *Complete Bolivian Diaries*, 60–61.
39. Klein, *Concise History*, 223–24.

Guevara faced a second major set of problems as he squared off against the Bolivian military. Although observers noted that the Bolivian military was ill-trained and ill-equipped, it proved an effective fighting force.[40] It had benefited since the late 1950s from materiel and training by the U.S. military under the Military Assistance Plan (MAP). One facet of the Bolivian army that both made it more effective and improved its image with the Bolivian people was "civic action." Since 1961, the Bolivian army had used some of its U.S. support to implement "civic action" projects—irrigation, road, and other infrastructure development. A significant chunk of the army's time (about one-fifth) was devoted to such projects. This activity helped the army bulwark its revolutionary credentials—indeed, it was a creature of the MNR. Such credentials presumably gave it increased support among the Bolivian populace, who to a great extent supported the 1950s revolutionary vision of the MNR. Indeed, one observer even termed the Bolivian army "a people's army."[41]

This idea of a "people's army" has deeper roots than civic action. After Bolivia's disastrous loss in the 1932–35 Chaco War, a group of influential reformist military leaders formed an organization, Razón de Patria (RADEPA), dedicated to fostering a more egalitarian Bolivian society with a more democratic government. In part because of RADEPA's influence, the post–Chaco War military began to concern itself with how to teach poor rural *mestizos* and Indians the rights and responsibilities of Bolivian citizenship—in the language they used, how to create "the new Bolivian man."[42]

As a consequence, the Bolivian peasantry viewed the Bolivian military as a patriotic institution and would not flock to Che's movement. Indeed, the *campesinos* feared both the Bolivian military and Che's band, but feared the Bolivian military a bit less since it contained no foreigners.[43] And without active *campesino* participation, which of course had proved crucial in

40. Ryan, *Fall of Che Guevara*, 40–41.

41. James, "Introduction," in Guevara, *Complete Bolivian Diaries*, 22–23. When the Bolivian government publicly announced that the guerrilla band included Cubans, it offered Barrientos an opportunity to, in the words of Gary Prado Salmón, "exploit the nationalist sentiment of the people." Indeed, left-wing political parties shied away from openly supporting Guevara's insurrection. Prado Salmón, *Defeat of Che Guevara*, 134. See also Wickham-Crowley, *Guerrillas and Revolution in Latin America*, 65.

42. Juan Ramón Quintana T., "El servicio militar obligatorio en América Latina y Bolivia: Una aproximación al estado de la cuestión a fin de siglo," in *Visiones de fin de siglo: Bolivia y América Latina en el siglo XX*, ed. Dora Cajías, Madalena Cajías, Carmen Johnson, and Iris Villegas (La Paz: IFEA / Coordinadora de Historia, Embajada de España en Bolivia, 2001), 276.

43. Ryan, *Fall of Che Guevara*, 42–43.

the revolution in Cuba, Che's efforts in the Bolivian lowlands were doomed.

The U.S. View, Barrientos, and Guevara

Soon after the Bolivian government became aware of Che's activities in southeastern Bolivia, it requested U.S. communications support and materiel. U.S. ambassador Douglas Henderson at first demurred.[44] In discussing in May 1967 the possible beneficial and detrimental aspects of training an elite Bolivian military unit to aid the Bolivian armed forces apprehend Guevara, Washington leaders expressed some trepidation that U.S. military assistance in counterinsurgency efforts could represent a potential quagmire.[45] U.S. leaders' fears of a potential quagmire in Bolivia proved ironic because Washington was deepening its commitment in Vietnam exactly at that time. U.S. officials also fretted over the possibility that a U.S.-trained group of Bolivian elite military leaders would only accentuate jealousies within the Bolivian military, making them increasingly ineffective.[46]

Eventually, the U.S. government provided communications equipment, rations, and ammunition; expedited the delivery of four helicopters that Bolivia had already purchased; and trained the Bolivian Second Ranger Battalion.[47] Of the assistance provided by the United States, the two elements that proved the most important when it came to fighting Guevara's insurgency were the training of the elite Ranger units and the U.S. Central Intelligence Agency's (CIA) intelligence support.[48]

The back story to this assistance is important because it illustrates important trends in Bolivia's relationship with the United States. The U.S. military had begun preliminary counterinsurgency training of the Bolivian military leadership in 1962. Bolivia had been on a list maintained by the

---

44. Editorial Note, *FRUS, 1964–1968*, vol. 31, 369–71.
45. Ryan, *Fall of Che Guevara*, outlines U.S. government officials' fears of U.S. soldiers being captured or becoming causalities in the effort to apprehend Guevara. The fear of "another Vietnam" was particularly strong. See pp. 49–57.
46. Telegram from the U.S. Embassy in La Paz to the Department of State, May 24, 1967, Subject Numeric File POL 23 BOL, RG 59, DOS Central Files, NA.
47. Editorial Note, *FRUS, 1964–1968*, vol. 31, 376. According to the assistant secretary for congressional relations, William B. Macomber Jr., over half of Bolivia's army had received some U.S. military training. Macomber to Howard Baker, October 5, 1967, Subject Numeric File POL 23 BOL, RG 59, DOS Central Files, NA.
48. Prado Salmón, *Defeat of Che Guevara*, 218.

Department of Defense's "Special Group for Counterinsurgency" of countries in particular danger of communist infiltration since 1964.[49]

Consequently, by 1966, Washington was primed to provide effective training and some useful materiel for the Bolivian military when the Guevara threat materialized.[50] In addition, Barrientos exaggerated the extent and power of Guevara's forces in Bolivia to prod U.S. officials to increase military assistance. Knowing of U.S. concern with insurgency in Latin America since the early 1960s, Barrientos portrayed the Bolivian military's efforts to defeat Che as part of a broader hemispheric effort. Thus, it was not surprising that Washington officials quickly focused on Bolivia as soon as the existence of Guevara's insurgency was confirmed.[51]

The timing of U.S. military assistance was especially significant for Barrientos's political career, in that he had been curtailing the military's budget from the beginning of his time in office. Such curtailments were risky. As any observer of Latin American politics knows, a disgruntled military can at best erode, and at worst threaten, the leader's power.[52] U.S. military assistance, in short, could help forestall a coup. And finally, U.S. efforts to set up an intelligence-gathering network proved instrumental for the Bolivian military in apprehending Guevara. In 1967, Secretary of State Dean Rusk impressed Bolivian vice president Luis Adolfo Siles Salinas (half-brother of Hernán Siles Zuazo) with the importance of such a network. Rusk averred that U.S. intelligence support in Vietnam, Laos, and Greece

---

49. Telegram of the U.S. Embassy in La Paz to the Department of State, June 30 1962, Decimal File 724.5/6-312, RG 59, DOS Central Files, NA; Dosal, *Comandante Che*, 278.

50. Wickham-Crowley, *Guerrillas and Revolution in Latin America*, 69–84. The Special Group for Counterinsurgency was created by the Kennedy administration in 1962 in the wake of the defeat of the U.S.-sponsored forces made up of Cuban nationals at the Bay of Pigs in 1961. Ryan, *Fall of Che Guevara*, 23–24, 59. Prado Salmón, a Bolivian military leader who helped organize the hunt for Guevara's brigade, in his *Defeat of Che Guevara*, 23, 25, maintains that despite U.S. counterinsurgency training, up through 1966 the Bolivian military did not take the threat of subversion in Bolivian seriously.

51. Even as there were larger insurgencies in Colombia, Venezuela, and Guatemala, in June 1967, Walt W. Rostow, President Johnson's National Security Adviser, moved Bolivia to the "top of the list" of dangerous Latin American insurgencies. Certainly the supposed presence of Guevara, which CIA sources confirmed in May, influenced the Johnson administration's decision in this regard. See Dosal, *Comandante Che*, 286, and Editorial Note, *FRUS*, 1964–1968, vol. 31, 371.

52. Barrientos's masterful political skills helped him maintain a degree of control over the military. He skillfully managed to neutralize one opponent of his in the military, General Alfredo Ovando Candia, by allowing him to take credit for a number of civic action projects. Telegram from Henderson to Department of State, March 31, 1967, Subject Numeric File POL 23-9 BOL, RG 59, DOS Central Files, NA.

had greatly helped efforts to track down and capture insurgents in those nations.[53]

Although the increased effectiveness of the Bolivian military and Barrientos's popularity figure prominently in Guevara's failure, the refusal of the peasantry to support him was the main reason his movement was easily crushed by the Bolivian armed forces. The U.S. Embassy in La Paz proved remarkably prescient in a May 1967 cable to the State Department. After affirming that U.S. military training of Bolivian elite units could be an important counterinsurgency strategy, Ambassador Douglas Henderson concluded that "unless guerrilla force disintegrates due to rugged and unhealthy terrain and lack of support (which is a possibility), we see no short term (within the next four months) solution with a reasonable chance of success."[54] Interestingly, Henderson's "possibility" came true—he even got the timing right. Indeed, a bit more than four months later, in early October, Guevara was captured and executed by Bolivian officials.

Militarily and politically, Guevara's movement was a sword that cut two ways for Barrientos. On the one hand, it exposed the risk he had taken in scaling back military budgets in an austerity effort.[55] The rebel movement could expose a weaker military to embarrassing defeat. On the other hand, Guevara's threat unified the Bolivian military and government in a common cause.

Another element of Guevara's incursion in Bolivia needs to be investigated—the issue of Cuban support. Cuba was, in the mid-1960s, caught between the main Communist antagonists of that era, the Soviet Union and the People's Republic of China. Although Cuba supported guerrilla movements in the nonindustrialized world, it depended on Soviet economic and military assistance. Cuban leader Fidel Castro "squared the circle" by agreeing to the "peaceful coexistence" doctrine of the Soviet Union in January 1964, while continuing to aid revolutionary movements in the nonindustrialized world.[56]

The Bolivian Communist Party, realizing the nationalistic and xenophobic nature of many Bolivians, feared that a Cuban-inspired attempt at revolution in Bolivia, especially in the countryside, would be doomed. In fact,

---

53. Ryan, *Fall of Che Guevara*, 95.
54. Telegram from the U.S. Embassy in La Paz to the Department of State, May 24, 1967, Subject Numeric File POL 23 BOL, RG 59, DOS Central Files, NA.
55. Telegram from Henderson to Department of State, March 31, 1967, Subject Numeric File POL 23-9 BOL, RG 59, DOS Central Files, NA.
56. Dosal, *Comandante Che*, 198–99, 210, 214. Dosal states, "Castro vacillated between Soviet orthodoxy and Guevarism" (213).

Bolivian communist leader Mario Monje Molina, asserted that Guevara's efforts had no hope of succeeding. Guevara's attempts at fomenting rebellion would be perceived as a foreign threat; and, therefore, his movement would not receive sympathy from the Bolivian peasantry. He correctly predicted Guevara's defeat.[57]

Given how precarious a Cuban-inspired attempt at revolution in South America would be, one might ask—was Guevara acting on his own? Although some observers have attempted to make the case that Guevara and Castro had a falling out as early as 1964, the evidence for this position is weak.[58] Guevara resigned from his positions in the Cuban government in November 1964 not because of conflict with Castro, but because he wanted to lead revolutionary cadres in the nonindustrialized world.[59] Castro saw Guevara's Bolivian incursion as necessary. Indeed, after the failure to foment revolution in Africa, the Cuban leader now thought that Latin America had to take center stage in Cuba's efforts to stimulate revolution in other countries.[60] Castro's support of Guevara's Bolivian rebellion further strained Cuba's relations with the Soviet Union. In an effort to improve relations with the United States, the Soviets had been attempting to rein in Cuba's attempts at spreading revolution in the nonindustrialized world.[61] Consequently, the Soviets were unhappy that Castro had not informed them beforehand of Che's plans.[62] The Soviet Union's displeasure with Cuba's efforts to stimulate revolution abroad, in particular Che's efforts in Bolivia, grew so great that Moscow curtailed its assistance to Cuba and stalled on signing a Cuban-Soviet trade agreement.[63]

---

57. Ibid., 264.
58. Ryan, *Fall of Che Guevara*, 33–36. Dosal asserts that "Che Guevara did not leave Cuba [in 1965, to assist guerrilla movements in Africa] because of a violent disagreement with Fidel or Raúl [Castro]" (*Comandante Che*, 203).
59. Dosal, *Comandante Che*, 202–3; 209–10.
60. Piero Gleijeses, *Conflicting Missions: Havana, Washington, and Africa, 1959–1976* (Chapel Hill: University of North Carolina Press, 2002), 216–17.
61. James G. Blight and Philip Brenner, *Sad and Luminous Days: Cuba's Struggle with the Superpowers After the Missile Crisis* (Lanham, Md.: Rowman and Littlefield, 2002), 121–22, 133.
62. Ryan, in his *Fall of Che Guevara*, 61–63, notes that top adviser to Lyndon Johnson, Walter Rostow, informed the president that the Soviets were very unhappy with the Cubans for not consulting with them before Guevara's incursion into Bolivia.
63. Blight and Brenner, *Sad and Luminous Days*, 133; Daniela Spenser, "The Caribbean Crisis: Catalyst for Soviet Projection into Latin America," in *In from the Cold: Latin America's New Encounter with the Cold War*, ed. Gilbert M. Joseph and Daniela Spenser (Durham: Duke Unversity Press, 2008), 103. Probably in response to the Soviet Union's displeasure with Cuba's support for revolutionary movements in Latin America, in particular Che's in Bolivia, Castro softened his anti-Soviet position after Che's death. Specifically, Castro kept secret an important January 1968 speech to the Central Committee of the Communist Party of Cuba

The issue of Cuban support has another side to it—how the Bolivian leadership portrayed Che's insurgency to its people. Barrientos, after Che's capture and execution, not surprisingly emphasized how his defeat redounded to the glory of the Bolivian military and nation. Barrientos attacked Guevara as a renegade who "invaded the nation's territory with mercenaries and traitors who sowed mourning and blood in *campesino* villages.... This invasion was met by our Armed Forces, whose triumph can be blemished by nothing and by no one but those who act out of spite, mediocrity and cowardice."[64]

It is important to note that U.S. and Bolivian officials often did not see eye to eye with regard to tactics in the counterinsurgency effort. Concerned about the poor level of counterinsurgency training of Bolivian troops, U.S. leaders stressed the importance of training, whereas Bolivian leaders wanted more modern and powerful weaponry. Even as Bolivians indicated they agreed with U.S. leaders, they continued to request higher-technology arms.[65]

However, the two nations did agree that the Bolivian military should fight the battle against Che alone. U.S. troops did not enter the fray. In addition, the regular Bolivian military had already had Guevara on the run before the U.S.-trained Ranger units engaged the guerrillas. It was they, not the Rangers, who had found the guerilla bases early on and prevented the movement from establishing a foothold, and it was they who scored the important victories on the battlefield.[66]

Turning to the diplomacy surrounding the counterinsurgency effort, the Bolivian Foreign Ministry ensured that the Bolivian military's victories in the battles against the guerrillas were well advertised. Indeed, the Bolivian Foreign Ministry stated that its primary goal during mid-1967 was to "manage international opinion" so that the world knew that the Bolivian military was effectively countering Guevara's rebellion.[67] The Bolivian government's emphasis on the public-relations aspect of the conflict in southeastern Bolivia helps to explain the Bolivian military's decision to execute

---

that criticized the Soviets, probably to avoid an open break with the Soviet Union. Blight and Brenner, *Sad and Luminous Days*, 133–37.

64. Barrientos, quoted in Prado Salmón, *Defeat of Che Guevara*, 212.
65. Dosal, *Comandante Che*, 277, 281–82.
66. Memorandum from Walt W. Rostow, Special Assistant to the President, to President Johnson, June 23, 1967, *FRUS, 1964–1968*, vol. 31, 373; ibid., 377; Dosal, *Comandante Che*, 301; Richard Harris, *Death of a Revolutionary* (New York: W. W. Norton, 2000).
67. Letter from Alberto Crespo Gutiérrez of the Foreign Ministry, July 27, 1967, *Reservados–1967*, ARE.

Guevara. U.S. Central Intelligence Agency "contract personnel," who worked with the Bolivians to improve their intelligence-gathering capabilities, urged that Guevara be taken prisoner, not executed on the spot.[68] Yet the famous revolutionary was executed soon after he was captured. One of the top Bolivian officials who participated in the effort to defeat Guevara, Gary Prado Salmón, explained that the Bolivian military decided to execute Guevara because it was important for them to show that Che had been defeated in battle. Moreover, Prado Salmón stated, Bolivian military leaders felt that if Che were held captive, his supporters would attempt to free him. The worst-case scenario from Bolivia's perspective would be that the victory of the Bolivians over the insurgency would be forgotten if Che managed to escape.[69]

The Bolivian Military, the Demise of Guevara, and Increasing Anti-Americanism

The significance of the fall of Guevara can be seen by examining the inter-American context. Guevara's uprising in Bolivia represented a turning point in U.S. relations with Latin America. No longer would Cuba directly sponsor any major attempts to spread revolution in the hemisphere. Nevertheless, Latin America leftists still perceived Castro's Cuba as an attractive alternative model for development and the United States as a force for reaction.[70] In Bolivia, starting in 1969, the Left became more predominant in Bolivian politics, and a segment of Bolivia's anti-U.S. Left continued to draw its inspiration from Castro's revolution.

The significance of Guevara's defeat can be put in broader perspective in a different way—by examining broad trends in Latin American political culture. Scholars have spent a great deal of time pondering why, given the inequities in Latin America, there has been a dearth of social revolutions that have radically altered the relationship between the players in the social, political, and economic milieus. Bolivia has one of the most unequal distributions of income in Latin America, if not in the entire world. Consequently, the failure of Guevara's revolution in Bolivia for socialism—and, it is important to note, socialism was his ultimate goal—begs the question

68. Editorial Note, *FRUS, 1964–1968*, vol. 31, 381.
69. Prado Salmón, *Defeat of Che Guevara*, 182.
70. Tulchin, "Promise of Progress," 242.

of why he failed. Although many reasons for his failure have been mentioned, there are some broader answers to this important question. Some scholars have posited that the corporatist bent of Latin American society and government, in which groups in society cede authority to the state or ruling party in exchange for a modicum of legitimacy, security, or other benefits, explains why there have been relatively few violent, social revolutions in the region.[71] Certainly, the corporatist explanation has some explanatory usefulness in Bolivia.

The most important conclusion to draw from Guevara's defeat, however, is that it was the Bolivian military and government's victory. In the end, despite missteps at the beginning of the insurgency, it has proved to be the most significant military victory in the nation's recent history.[72] As Prado Salmón concluded, it represented the most important Bolivian military campaign since the 1930s Chaco War and proved an important victory for a military much derided for its poor record on the battlefield.[73] In addition, the defeat of Guevara meant a victory for the ongoing Bolivian revolution. Despite Barrientos's coup in 1964, the Bolivian revolution lived on—in particular in the *campo*. Indeed, the victory over Guevara's insurgency was a *Bolivian* victory—and the decision by the Bolivian military to execute Guevara, against the advice of U.S. officials—was a demonstration of the independence of *Bolivian* decision making.

In the end, the Bolivian military's defeat of Guevara strengthened not only the Bolivian government but the Bolivian revolution. Glen Rotchin has argued that the military's civic action programs, which had been in full swing well before Guevara entered Bolivia, "contributed to the military's self-perception as the only viable and indeed, legitimate heir to the

---

71. Howard J. Wiarda has referred to corporatism as an "apparently dominant political culture" in Latin America. He defines "corporatism" as "a system of authority and interest representation, derived chiefly (though not exclusively) from Catholic social thought, stressing functional representation, the integration of labor and capital into a vast web of hierarchically ordered, 'harmonious,' monopolistic, and functionally determined unions (or corporations), and guided and directed by the state." He adds that corporatism's "cultural-historic tradition stretching back to the origins of the Iberic-Latin systems and embodying a dominant form of sociopolitical organization . . . is similarly hierarchical, elitist, authoritarian, bureaucratic, Catholic, [and] patrimonialist." Howard J. Wiarda, "Corporatism and Development in the Iberic-Latin World: Persistent Strains and New Variations," in *The New Corporatism: Social-Political Structures in the Iberian World*, ed. Frederick B. Pike and Thomas Stritch (Notre Dame: University of Notre Dame Press, 1974), 33, 6.

72. A U.S. government intelligence report noted that a lack of counterinsurgency training hampered the early efforts of the Bolivian military to apprehend the guerrillas. "Cuban-Inspired Guerrilla Activity in Bolivia," June 14, 1967, Guerrilla Problems, Box 23, Intelligence Files, National Security Files, LBJ Library.

73. Prado Salmón, *Defeat of Che Guevara*, 240.

MNR."[74] That is to say, the military was in some ways the heir to the revolution, and its victory over the insurgents in the Oriente stimulated Bolivian nationalism.

In the wake of the demise of Guevara's insurgency, one might be tempted to conclude that U.S.-Bolivian relations would improve. After all, the two nations had effectively worked together to quell a threat to both. Moreover, U.S. officials perceptively realized that if they sent U.S. troops to Bolivia, it would arouse Bolivian nationalism sentiment and perhaps even threaten the survival of the Barrientos government.[75] However, a resurgence of Bolivian nationalism after Guevara's defeat caused a deterioration in Bolivia's relationship with the United States. To exacerbate the anti-U.S. sentiment, Minister of the Interior Antonio Arguedas sent a copy of Che Guevara's Bolivia diary to Castro in Cuba while shockingly claiming that a number of Bolivian officials and U.S. officials stationed in Bolivia were CIA agents. Although his allegations were unproven, they raised the specter of undue U.S. control over Bolivian affairs.[76]

Despite significant U.S. economic and military assistance to Bolivia in the 1960s, a number of factors caused a deterioration in U.S.-Bolivian relations after the fateful month of October 1967. In that month Henderson perceptively noted that even as the glow of the Bolivian military's victory over the guerrillas was still radiant, "a resurgence of nationalist sentiment" in Bolivia not only threatened the stability of Barrientos's government, but could stimulate anti-U.S. feeling as well.[77]

The assistance nexus was key in this regard. The Bolivians' desire for U.S. aid—or dependence on U.S. assistance—drove the relationship between the two nations. Indeed, the U.S. Embassy in August 1968 concluded that the "central element in our relations with Barrientos over [the] medium term is material assistance and our inability to meet his expectations for additional new amounts."[78] The Bolivian military's unhappiness mounted as soon as it discovered it would not be rewarded with increased

---

74. Rotchin, *Clientelist State*, 91.

75. Henderson noted in a telegram to the Department of State that "it is a fact of life in this super-nationalistic country that any invitation to foreign government [sic] to put troops on Bolivian soil is political dynamite which could readily blow [the] leader responsible for it off the scene." Telegram 507 from La Paz to the Department of State, September 30, 1967, Subject Numeric File POL 23-9 BOL, RG 59, DOS Central Files, NA.

76. Lehman, *Bolivia and the United States*, 157.

77. Henderson to the Department of State, Airgram A-138, October 28, 1967, Subject Numeric File POL 23-9 BOL, RG 59, DOS Central Files, NA.

78. U.S. Embassy in La Paz to Department of State, August 22, 1968, Subject Numeric File POL 1 BOL-US, RG 59, DOS Central Files, NA.

military assistance after Guevara's capture. In fact, U.S. assistance fell. The decline in U.S. assistance (termed "drastic" by Ambassador Henderson) proved especially painful as Bolivia had been favored by U.S. aid officials up to 1968. In addition, problems in consummating a few high-profile assistance projects plagued U.S.-Bolivian relations. To make matters worse, Bolivians also blamed the United States for the falling price of tin.[79] By mid-1968, U.S. officials in La Paz reported that "anti-American elements are being revitalized in Bolivia at a truly surprising rate."[80] The seeds of a nascent anti-Americanism had been planted. The discontent evident in 1968 was but a pale harbinger of what would come as President Richard M. Nixon entered the White House the following year, and a series of Bolivian military leaders would steer the nation on a leftward course that stoked already existing anti-U.S. feeling.

A New U.S. Administration and U.S.-Bolivian Relations

There are two misconceptions about Bolivia and U.S.–South American relations in the late 1960s and early 1970s. The first is that the only significant guerrilla movement in Bolivian history was Che Guevara's ill-fated escapade in the Santa Cruz province in 1966–67. The second is that the Nixon administration (with the exception of U.S.-Chilean relations during the thoroughly investigated period of socialist Salvador Allende Gossens's presidency in Chile) did not care about South America. Instead, there were significant guerrilla movements in Bolivia both before and after Guevara's revolt, and the guerrilla activity after Che's debacle had a significant impact on Bolivian politics. And the Nixon administration, although very busy with overhauling U.S. policy in Vietnam, the Soviet Union, and the People's Republic of China, did devote considerable time and concern to South American affairs.

A bit of context with regard to the history of U.S. foreign policy is important to understand how it changed during the Nixon administration. As has been aptly demonstrated by other scholars, Nixon's policy of détente very much changed the nature of the containment policy that had been the bedrock of U.S. foreign policy since World War II. With regard to the "great powers," the Nixon administration put much more emphasis

79. Ibid.
80. U.S. Embassy in La Paz to the Department of State, June 6, 1968, Subject Numeric File POL BOL, RG 59, DOS Central Files, NA.

on negotiation than had previous administrations. However, with regard to U.S. policy toward Latin America, continuity proved more important than change. In particular, the Nixon administration's policy toward leftwing regimes in Latin America was the same as its predecessors'. The administration feared that left-wing movements in the region would spur the growth of communism in Latin America, thus empowering the world communist movement. Consequently, it undercut leftist regimes and shored up right-wing regimes with economic and military assistance. U.S.-Bolivian relations fit squarely within this context.

To understand the fascinating and fluid political situation in Bolivia in the late 1960s and early 1970s, one must look at the South American context. It can best be understood by investigating the intersection of two important trends. First, there was a lurch to the left politically in South America in the late 1960s and early 1970s, most particularly in the Andes. Second—which is connected—there is the interesting and important history of guerrilla activity in Bolivia in the 1960s. U.S.-Bolivian relations hit their nadir at this critical juncture in history as tensions increased between the United States and the countries of South America.

The leftward shift in politics in Latin America can be seen in Bolivia's neighbors. In Argentina, strike activism in the late 1960s began to move the country to the left after the 1966 military coup overthrew the democratically elected government in Buenos Aires. The Argentine labor movement, inspired by the extreme repression of a general strike in Cordoba in 1969, named *el cordobazo*, greatly expanded its power by the early 1970s.[81] Activists from the popular sectors effectively resisted the repression of the military dictatorships of Generals Alejandro Agustín Lanusse and Roberto Levingston, paving the way for the return of Juan Perón to the country in late 1972 and his return to power the following year.[82] In Bolivia, a series of left-wing military dictatorships from 1969 to 1971 culminated in the creation of a Popular Assembly to push for fairer treatment of the impoverished Indian majority and the popular sectors.[83] In Peru, the 1968 coup by Juan Velasco nationalized the petroleum industry and promoted the most thorough land reforms in the nation's history.[84] And of course, in Chile, socialist Salvador Allende's election in 1970

81. Daniel Castro, ed., *Revolutions and Revolutionaries: Guerrilla Movements in Latin America* (Wilmington, Del.: Scholarly Resources, 1999), xxxvi.
82. Dunkerley, *Rebellion in the Veins*, 159.
83. Klein, *Bolivia*, 250–53.
84. Dirk Kruijt, *Revolution by Decree: Peru, 1968–1975* (Amsterdam: Thela, 1994).

(heading up a coalition of socialists and communists) brought about populist policies—including land reform—to improve the economic well-being of Chile's dispossessed.[85]

The leftward move in politics in the region provided "ideological cover" for an already existing guerrilla movement in the Andean region. The 1960s saw increased guerrilla activity in the Andes that, in some areas, reverberates to the present day. Most of the movements were inspired by Castro's victory in Cuba. In Colombia, the Ejército de Liberación Nacional was formed in 1964 and the Fuerzas Armadas Revolucionarias de Colombia, or FARC, was organized in 1966.[86] Around the same time the Ejército Popular de Liberación was formed.[87] In Peru in 1965, another group calling itself the Ejército de Liberación Nacional sprung up, as did the Movimiento de Izquierda Revolucionaria.[88] Although inspired by Castro's revolution in Cuba, they were almost entirely products of local conditions in their respective regions.

However, the focus here is on Bolivia, in particular on its less well-known guerrilla movements—that is to say, the ones before and after Che Guevara's uprising. The history of guerrilla activity in Bolivia in the 1960s can only be understood if one examines the relative powerlessness of the MNR after 1964. When it came to power in 1952, the MNR had a near consensus of support. But it was racked by political crisis in the early 1960s, and in November 1964 the military staged a coup that tossed the weak MNR out of power relatively easily. In fact, the MNR had lost its legitimacy as a revolutionary movement well before 1964. In the early 1960s, weakened with factionalism, it had to confront the rising power of the popular sectors now more willing than ever to work outside the MNR framework.[89] More important, it had lost its ability to inspire the average Bolivian. With the decline of the MNR, political space was created for guerrilla movements.[90]

85. Simon Collier and William R. Sater, *History of Chile, 1880–2002*, 2nd ed. (Cambridge: Cambridge University Press, 2004), 330–58; Brian Loveman, *Chile: A History of Hispanic Capitalism*, 3rd ed. (New York: Oxford University Press, 2001), 248–58.
86. Thomas C. Wright, *Latin America in the Era of the Cuban Revolution*, rev. ed. (New York: Praeger, 2001), 78–79.
87. Timothy P. Wickham-Crowley, "Terror and Guerrilla Warfare in Latin America, 1956–1970," *Comparative Studies in Society and History* 32 (April 1990): 202. This article is a very useful survey of Latin American guerrilla warfare in the 1960s.
88. Castro, *Revolution and Revolutionaries*, 105–34.
89. Fernando Calderón Gutiérrez, "Actores sociales: un siglo de luchas sociales," in *Bolivia en el siglo XX*, ed. Fernando Campero Prudencia (La Paz: Harvard Club of Bolivia, 1999), 435.
90. Dunkerley, *Rebellion in the Veins*, 161.

The most notable example, of course, was Guevara's incursion into Bolivia in 1966–67. What few scholars have examined, however, is that Guevara's attempt at fomenting rebellion inspired Bolivians to imitate his efforts. The 1969–70 era was typified by a more independent, home-grown Bolivian *guerrillismo*.[91] In 1969–70, in this last rendition of Bolivian guerrilla activity, Cuban participation was prohibited by the Soviet Union's attempt to curtail Castro's adventurism in Latin America.[92] Even though this last spasm of revolutionary violence was, like previous revolutionary episodes, put down by the Bolivian military, nonetheless, because of its timing, the guerrilla movement had an important impact on Bolivian history and U.S.-Bolivian relations.

In order to understand U.S.-Bolivian relations in the late 1960s and early 1970s, one must understand Nixon's overall foreign policy toward Latin America. In a memorable 1969 episode, before Allende came to power, National Security Adviser Henry A. Kissinger informed a startled and insulted Chilean foreign minister Gabriel Valdés Subercaseaux that the march of history had moved from Europe westward, to North America, and then to Asia, and that nothing of importance happened in the Southern hemisphere.[93] Most historians investigating this period conclude that Kissinger's disregard of Latin America as evidenced in his conversation with Valdés reflected the administration's general view.

However, Kissinger's arrogant dismissal of all things Latin American belies the Nixon administration's keen interest in the region—in Chile and in the rest of Latin America. Indeed, given the rising intensity in the pace of left-wing movements in South America in the 1960s and early 1970s and with the growth of guerrilla movements in the Andes, it is not surprising that the Nixon White House was very concerned with U.S.-Latin American relations and aimed to improve them.

With the exhaustion of the Alliance for Progress by the late 1960s, the high hopes it raised increased the already considerable gap between expectations and reality. Consequently, many in Latin America began to criticize the United States. As relations worsened, the Nixon administration aimed

91. Rodríguez O., "Bolivia en el ciclo guerrillero," 3–4.
92. Gustavo Rodríguez Ostria, "Teoponte: La otra guerrilla guevarista en Bolivia," *La Prensa*, July 17, 2005, 3.
93. Kissinger, in a private meeting with Valdés, told him that history moved from East to West, in the Northern Hemisphere, and that "nothing important comes from the South [Southern Hemisphere]." Kissinger, quoted in Seymour M. Hersh, *The Price of Power: Kissinger in the Nixon White House* (New York: Summit, 1983), 263.

to improve ties with Latin America, while maintaining a healthy flow of both economic and military assistance to the friendly governments in the region.

The administration tried to make U.S. assistance programs more effective by removing the requirement that Latin American aid recipients spend their assistance on U.S. products.[94] Arguably, this did little to improve the well-being of the nonelite majority in the region, but the point is Nixon was trying to do something to improve U.S. relations with Latin America. Nixon did a number of other things that signaled his interest in improving U.S. relations with the nations to the south. For example, he initiated a government-wide study of Latin American programs with National Security Study Memorandum 108 in December 1970.[95] He even initiated a study of the increasingly powerful Liberation Theology movement in the Catholic Church.[96]

Yet Nixon's concern and actions did not produce more harmonious relations with the Andean nations. In fact, these relations entered their tensest phase since the 1920s. With Velasco's takeover in Peru in October 1968 and prompt expropriation of the petroleum industry, Washington, in protest, reduced U.S. economic assistance.[97] With Allende's election in Chile in September 1970, Washington curtailed assistance programs for that country. Moreover, the United States implemented a covert action program to undermine the Allende regime. As the United States feared it faced rising anti-U.S. sentiment in the hemisphere, it not surprisingly began to increase military assistance to friendly regimes in the region, as Washington saw military assistance as the most reliable bulwark of such regimes.[98] Nixon's administration, fearing increased anti-Americanism in the region, tightened relations with Latin America's most powerful nation, Brazil, which was also very pro-U.S. under the leadership of General Emilio Garrastazu Medici.

94. National Security Decision Memorandum 30, November 5, 1969, Box H-211, NSC Institutional Files (H-Files), Nixon Presidential Materials, NA.
95. National Security Study Memorandum 108, December 10, 1970, Box H-178, NSC Institutional Files (H-Files), Nixon Presidential Materials, NA.
96. National Security Study Memorandum 68, July 12, 1969, Box H-159, NSC Institutional Files (H-Files), Nixon Presidential Materials, NA.
97. Blasier, *Hovering Giant*, 260–62.
98. Angulo and Correa, "La política exterior norteamericana en América Latina," 413. Military assistance to Latin American nearly tripled during the Nixon administration, rising from 45.7 million in 1969 to $134 million in 1974. U.S. Agency for International Development, *U.S. Overseas Loans and Grants*, http://qesdb.usaid.gov/cgi-bin/broker.exe (accessed July 4, 2008).

U.S.-Bolivian Relations: A Turning Point

In Bolivia, the deterioration in U.S.-Bolivian relations was as dramatic as that of U.S.-Chilean relations under Allende.[99] General René Barrientos, who served as president from 1964 to 1969, collaborated closely with the United States, allowing U.S. assistance to be used for internal security—for example, it was used to put down strikes, which angered leftists.[100]

After Barrientos's death in office, the State Department noted that because he had dominated Bolivian politics since his coming to power in 1964, a political vacuum would lead to political uncertainty and instability in the nation.[101] Indeed, from 1969 to 1971, Bolivia was ruled by a string of weak leaders. They came out of a long Andean tradition of left-wing military leaders. (There were some left-wing military leaders in Bolivia in the years following the Chaco War.) Their radical policies tended to accentuate a split in the Bolivian military between the nationalists (who advocated leftist reform) and the traditionalists (who supported Bolivia's landed and other elites).[102]

The radical military leaders from 1969 to 1971 fostered, or openly incited, "radical," anti-*norteamericano* sentiment. Two concrete examples include Bolivia's expropriation of Gulf Oil in 1969 and the expulsion of the Peace Corps in 1971. Both events strained Bolivia's relations with the United States. The run-up to the nationalization of Gulf Oil went back to the late 1950s. In 1958, the petroleum workers union demanded a new petroleum code less favorable to foreign investment. The Bolivian government complied by 1962, extending the state petroleum reserve to all areas of the nation not already allocated to private companies. This move built up the power of the Yacimientos Petrolíferos Fiscales Bolivianos (YPFB), the state-run oil company, while inhibiting joint ventures between it and foreign oil companies. In 1967, Bolivian leaders called for increasing Gulf Oil's payments to the Bolivian government, and some called for expropriation of the company's assets.[103] The Bolivian government put pressure on

---

99. Lehman, *Bolivia and the United States*, 162.
100. Editorial Note, *FRUS, 1964–1968*, vol. 31, Document 155, discusses U.S. assistance to the Bolivian military in repressing labor agitation. For an example of how Barrientos's labor repression angered the Left, see Domitila Barrios de Chungara, *Let Me Speak! Testimony of Domitila, a Woman of the Bolivian Mines* (New York: Monthly Review Press, 1978), 93–95.
101. Telegram 2821 from the Embassy in La Paz to the Department of State, May 7, 1969, Subject Numeric File POL BOL, RG 59, DOS Central Files, NA.
102. Angulo and Correa, "La política exterior norteamericana en América Latina," 419.
103. Airgram A-148 from the Embassy in La Paz to the Secretary of State, November 10, 1967, Subject Numeric File POL 2–1 BOL, RG 59, DOS Central Files, NA.

Gulf Oil to increase payments to the state, and the company complied in 1968.¹⁰⁴

Gulf Oil was expropriated for two reasons. First, there was deep resentment in Bolivia toward Gulf Oil, the largest foreign company operating in the nation. It was perceived as a usurper of the rights and property of YPFB. The Bolivian Oil Company, an offshoot of the YPFB, garnered only about 11 percent of the production of YPFB's fields. Because Gulf Oil had negotiated a better deal, around 50 percent of the production from the YPFB's fields flowed into Gulf Oil's coffers. Therefore, Gulf Oil was perceived as a rich and wealth foreign company muscling aside the struggling Bolivian company.¹⁰⁵ Second, Alfredo Ovando's decision to nationalize the company largely reflected his weak political position. After he resigned as head of the military after his September 1969 coup, he could not count on military support.¹⁰⁶ Returning to the revolutionary tradition of 1952 (the Gulf Oil expropriation was the first since the expropriation of the three largest mining companies in the heady days just after the revolution), Ovando thought, would be a winning political proposition.¹⁰⁷

Although the nationalization had largely domestic roots, it had a significant impact on Bolivia's relationship with the United States. Washington officials saw it as inhibiting future U.S. and other foreign investment in Bolivia. Gulf Oil's spokesman condemned the expropriation as "illegal."¹⁰⁸ His statement provoked a response from Ambassador Julio Sanjines Goitia, who responded that Bolivia had the right to nationalize (with compensation) foreign-owned businesses if it thought it was in the national interest.¹⁰⁹ Even as Gulf Oil and the Bolivians slowly worked their way toward a settlement, not surprisingly, Washington cut assistance to the Andean nation to a bare-bones level.¹¹⁰

104. Ingram, *Expropriation of U.S. Property*, 161.
105. Ibid., 170.
106. George C. Denny Jr. to Secretary of State, "Domestic Politics Forced Nationalization," October 30, 1969, Subject Numeric File PET 15–2 BOL, RG 59, DOS Central Files, NA.
107. Angulo and Correa, "La política exterior norteamericana en América Latina," 419.
108. Telegram from the Department of State to the Embassy in La Paz, October 30, 1969. Subject Numeric File PET 6 BOL, RG 59, DOS Central Files, NA.
109. Sanjinés's statement was transmitted from the Department of State to the Embassy in La Paz in telegram 184304, October 31, 1969, Subject Numeric File PET 6 BOL, RG 59, DOS Central Files, NA.
110. Telegram from the Embassy in La Paz to the Department of State, October 30, 1969, Subject Numeric File AID (US) BOL, RG 59, DOS Central Files, NA; telegram from the Department of State to the Embassy in La Paz, November 8, 1969, Subject Numeric File AID (US) BOL, RG 59, DOS Central Files, NA.

However, both Bolivian and U.S. officials desired a rapprochement. Washington officials worked quietly behind the scenes to get Gulf Oil and the Bolivians to come to an agreement on compensation, which they did.[111] In September 1970, the Bolivian government announced it would indemnify Gulf Oil in the amount of $78,622,171.44, payable over twenty years, with no interest.[112]

A year later, U.S.-Bolivian relations deteriorated further. Juan José (J. J.) Torres came to power in early October 1970 and ruled until late August 1971.[113] There was rarely a dull day in the tumultuous eleven months he was in office. In fact, in the first month after Torres took power, protestors celebrated his new government by attacking the U.S. Marine barracks in La Paz, as well as U.S. Information Service offices and offices of the Centro Boliviano Americano (the binational centers) in a number of Bolivian cities, causing several thousand dollars of damage.[114] These centers had been set up by the U.S. government to facilitate understanding between the two nations. More substantially, the Nixon administration feared that the Torres government would extend and deepen the anti-*norteamericano* sentiment and economic radicalism of the Ovando regime. The Nixon administration signaled its displeasure of the Torres regime by freezing all aid projects (aside from PL 480 disbursements) and abstaining on a vote on a World Bank loan for economic development in mid-1971.[115]

Although both Torres and Barrientos shared a similar background, having grown up in poor families from Cochabamba, the two leaders were polar opposites in Bolivia's relations with the United States.[116] Barrientos

---

111. Telegram 8579 from the Embassy in La Paz to the Secretary of State, December 27, 1969, Subject Numeric File POL BOL-US, RG 59, DOS Central Files, NA.

112. Ingram, *Expropriation of U.S. Property*, 181.

113. For one Torres official's view of the Torres regime, and the coup by Banzer, see Jorge Gallardo Lozada, *De Torres a Banzer: Diez meses de emergencia en Bolivia* (Buenos Aires: Ediciones Periferia, 1972). Lozada served as minister of the interior in Torres's government.

114. Minister of Foreign Relations David La Fuente to Minister of the Interior Jorge Gallardo [Lozada], October 30, 1970, *Documentos Reservados—1970*, ARE. The U.S. Embassy estimated that $47,000 worth of damage was done to U.S. property alone. Telegram from the U.S. Embassy in La Paz to the Department of State, October 20, 1970, Subject Numeric File POL BOL-US, RG 59, DOS Central Files, NA.

115. Memorandum from the U.S. Department of State to the U.S. Embassy in La Paz, January 16, 1971, Subject Numeric File POL BOL-US, RG 59, DOS Central Files, NA; Fernando Berckemeyer, ambassador from Peru to the United States, to the Peruvian Foreign Ministry, June 25, 1971, República de Peru, Ministero de Relaciones Exteriores, Archivo Central Raul Porras Barrenechea, Correspondencia desde la Embajada de Perú en Washington DC al Ministerio de Relaciones Exteriores en Lima, 5–3-A, 410, Lima, Peru; Berckemeyer to Foreign Ministry, June 29, 1971, ibid., 5–3-A, 426, Lima.

116. Dunkerley, *Rebellion in the Veins*, 115, and Lehman, *Bolivia and the United States*, 161, discuss Barrientos's and Torres's humble *cochabambino* origins.

worked hard to solidify relations with the United States, whereas Torres, for his part, did whatever he could to ruffle the North American eagle's feathers.

Another Insurgency Complicates U.S.-Bolivian Relations

Into this heady mixture of rapidly growing leftist sentiment and tense relations with the United States stepped a Bolivian guerrilla group, the Bolivian Ejército de Liberación Nacional (ELN). The ELN's poorly planned attacks in Teoponte, in the sparsely populated northern part of La Paz province, were in keeping with the experiences in 1963 and 1967. Its main goal was Cuban-style socialist revolution. However, its short-term objective was to force the Bolivian political system and military to the left.[117] Its mission squared with those of previous guerrilla groups. Despite the disastrous experiences of previous guerrilla uprisings, the ELN strictly adhered to the *foco* theory of revolution, which posited that an uprising that could defeat local authorities would attract local *campesinos* and quickly spread.[118] In addition, the ELN resembled earlier guerrilla movements in that a principle source of its support was from student revolutionaries.[119]

The ELN's impact on Bolivian national politics has not been thoroughly investigated.[120] Because the ELN's uprising in 1969–70 occurred in one of the most highly charged political periods in Bolivia's recent history, and at (arguably) the lowest point in U.S.-Bolivian relations, the hapless ELN actually helped pave the way for the most radical government in Bolivia's recent history.

Indeed, the Bolivian military, not surprisingly on "high alert" because of the guerrilla movements in the countryside, had made short work of the ELN by November 1970. However, with the collapse of the Alfredo

---

117. Néstor Paz, *My Life for My Friends: The Guerrilla Journal of Néstor Paz, Christian*, ed. and trans. Ed Garcia and John Eagleson (Maryknoll, N.Y.: Orbis, 1975), 10.

118. Although definitions vary, the *foco* was a guerrilla technique, successfully pioneered by the Cuban rebels in the 1950s, which relied on the use of force to impress upon the peasantry the power of the guerrilla movement while simultaneously drawing the military into battle. In addition, during a *foco*, the *foquistas* aimed to identify and train potential leaders through military struggle while educating the populace on the importance of guerrilla victory.

119. Rodríguez, "Bolivia en el ciclo guerrillero," 3.

120. However, Gustavo Rodríguez Ostria has published a new book on the subject. *Sin tiempo para las palabras: Teoponte, la otra guerrilla guevarista en Bolivia* (La Paz: Grupo Editorial Kipus, 2006).

Ovando government in October, there was enough disorder in the countryside that General (soon to be president) Torres managed to allow the remnants of the ELN to escape.[121] This helped to build his support among Bolivia's Left. More broadly, the ELN's revolutionary outburst helped to provoke a right-wing reaction to the increasingly squeezed Ovando regime—squeezed between the growing power of the Left and the fearful Right. Taking advantage of Ovando's waning support, a junta of right-wing generals swept the hapless Ovando out of power on October 6, 1970. But the political cauldron continued to boil at an intense rate—as it can only do in the traditionally unstable Bolivia. The right-wing power-grab only provoked a left-wing response the next day, led by none other than Torres.[122] Thus, the ELN's rebellion, because it occurred during a very fluid period of Bolivian history, reverberated much more forcefully through Bolivian society than would otherwise have been the case.

After its defeat, the ELN decamped to the cities, engaging in little revolutionary activity. Its move to urban areas, however, did reflect a growing trend in urban guerrilla movements in South America in the early 1970s.[123] More significantly, the ELN represented the end of an era: the *foco*-style rebellions led by *mestizos* or whites from the middle class would be replaced by ethnically based movements headed up by Indian leadership.[124] The ELN never achieved its basic objective of anti-imperialist revolution, of course, but it did achieve its short-term goal of having a deep impact on the Bolivian political scene.

From Washington's point of view, the Bolivian army's quick repression of the ELN was a relief. Not surprisingly, U.S. officials responded as they had to Guevara's uprising three years earlier: they accelerated the deliveries of Military Assistance Program equipment already in the pipeline.[125] After all, U.S. policymakers feared mushrooming South American radicalism in Allende's Chile and Velasco's Peru—as well as Torres's Bolivia.[126] However, it is clear that the 1960s guerrilla movements in Bolivia never

---

121. Dunkerley, *Rebellion in the Veins*, 174.
122. Ibid., 176–77.
123. Wright, *Latin America in the Era of the Cuban Revolution*, 93–109, provides a useful overview of Latin American urban revolutionaries at this time.
124. Xavier Albó investigates this transition in "Etnias y pueblos originarios: Diversidad étnica, cultural y lingüística," in *Bolivia en el siglo XX*, ed. Fernando Campero Prudencia (La Paz: Harvard Club of Bolivia, 1999), 471–72.
125. Memorandum from the Executive Secretary Theodore L. Eliot Jr. of the Department of State to National Security Adviser Kissinger, June 7, 1971, Subject Numeric File POL 1 BOL-US, RG 59, DOS Central Files, NA.
126. Lehman, *Bolivia and the United States*, 162.

really stood a chance of spreading revolution very far. A symbiotic relationship between the guerrillas and the various radical movements percolating in Bolivian society at the time could have strengthened both causes. But the guerrillas, like Che in the Oriente, did a poor job of building networks with supporters in either the *campo* or the cities, and as a consequence they were too cut off from Bolivian society to create such a self-reinforcing relationship.[127]

The late 1960s and early 1970s proved to be an important turning point in recent Bolivian history and U.S.-Bolivian relations. Anti-Americanism rose to such a fever pitch by 1971 that the U.S. ambassador, Ernest Siracusa, wrote the Department of State that left-wingers had considerable power in the nation and that "a rapidly deteriorating situation" led him to conclude that "the extremists . . . have no other objective than the complete elimination or US influence and even presence in Bolivia."[128] However, Hugo Banzer Suárez, who deposed Torres in August 1971, proved to be as friendly as Ovando and Torres had been hostile. Banzer wanted to promote internal security in Bolivia itself. He feared a revival of the guerrilla activity of the 1960s and therefore rigorously and brutally put down anything that looked like it might become a guerrilla movement. Although many on the Left were appalled, many middle-class Bolivians looked on with approval. Moreover, Banzer, as a firmly anticommunist leader who maintained effective if sometimes brutal control over Bolivia, would receive a great deal of economic and military support from the United States. In later years, Bolivia would look back nostalgically on his government as a stable period of economic development and relative political calm after the instability and uncertainty of the late 1960s and early 1970s. (Banzer skillfully used this nostalgic haze for his own political ends, declaring himself a democrat after Bolivia became a democracy, and winning the presidency in 1997.) As a consequence, the tragic embrace of right-wing dictatorship by U.S. policymakers was tightened.

From 1950 to 1970, the United States gave Bolivia around $525 million in economic assistance.[129] However, it seems that one cannot buy love, for by the early 1970s the relations between the two countries had reached

---

127. Rodríguez, "Teoponte," 6. However, when eight of the guerrillas were killed by the military in August 1970, the families of the guerrillas, supported by the leadership of Bolivia's national labor federation, the Central Obrero Boliviano (COB), organized a hunger strike. Paz, *My Life for My Friends*, 83.
128. Ernest Siracusa to the Department of State, June 3, 1971, Subject Numeric File POL BOL-US, RG 59, DOS Central Files, NA.
129. Ingram, *Expropriation of U.S. Property*, 210.

their lowest point in decades. The Nixon administration even allocated covert assistance to a group of anti-Torres Bolivians in mid-1971, hoping to cement support with this group if the Torres government were to fall. It is unclear if any of the assistance was actually transferred to the anti-Torres group.[130] Although evidence of the Nixon administration's allocation of covert assistance to foment a coup did not surface until 2009, rumors of U.S. attempts to secretly undermine Torres helped to increase anti-American sentiment in Bolivia.

---

130. Memorandum from Arnold Nachmanoff of the NSC Staff to the President's Assistant for National Security Affairs (Kissinger), August 19, 1971, *FRUS, 1969–1976*, vol. E-10, *Documents on American Republics, 1969–1972*, Document 107, http://history.state.gov/historicaldocuments/frus1969-76ve10/d107 (accessed July 14, 2010).

BOLIVIA'S LINE IN THE SAND

The Peace Corps and U.S. Foreign Policy

In April 1971, leftist students briefly occupied the Centro Boliviano Americano in Cochabamba. The students claimed that the Centro was teaching an "alien ideology" to the Bolivian people. In other words, the left-wing students feared the dissemination of U.S. culture at the expense of the Bolivian way of life.[1]

Less than two months later, J. J. Torres's government abruptly terminated its contract with the U.S. Peace Corps and expelled the Peace Corps volunteers working in the country. One explanation for Bolivia's abrupt dismissal of the volunteers is that the Torres government was responding to the fear on the part of many Bolivians that the Peace Corps was, like the Centro Boliviano Americano, spreading an alien ideology. Torres concluded that the only way to calm this fear was to get the Peace Corps volunteers out of Bolivia as quickly as possible.

In her recent book on the history of the U.S. Peace Corps, Elizabeth Cobbs Hoffman argues that in most cases the Peace Corps significantly helped the United States improve relations with the developing world.[2] In Bolivia, however, the opposite occurred. The Peace Corps was both a cause and a symptom of deteriorating U.S.-Bolivian relations in the early 1970s. In fact, the Peace Corps came to symbolize the degeneration of relations

---

1. Telegram from the U.S. Embassy in Bolivia to the Department of State, May 1, 1971, Subject Numeric File CUL 11 BOL, RG 59, DOS Central Files, NA.
2. Elizabeth A. Cobbs, "Decolonization, the Cold War, and the Foreign Policy of the Peace Corps," *Diplomatic History* 20 (1996): 80; Elizabeth Cobbs Hoffman, *All You Need Is Love: The Peace Corps and the Spirit of the 1960s* (Cambridge: Harvard University Press, 1998), 1–38, 251–59.

between the two nations, despite the good intentions of many Peace Corps volunteers—and even though the Peace Corps's development projects helped poor, rural Bolivians. As discussed in the previous chapter, during the late 1960s and early 1970s, U.S.-Bolivian relations were as poor as they had ever been. Bolivian government officials, under pressure from the Left, concluded that they had to do something to show that the United States was not controlling Bolivian economic and social development, and expelling the Peace Corps seemed to be the most effective way to do that.[3]

When the Kennedy administration established the Peace Corps in 1961, Bolivia seemed like the perfect laboratory for the intelligent, young, energetic Peace Corps workers. Over a hundred volunteers were sent there in the first two years of the program.[4] This contingent was one of the largest in Latin America and thus provided a way for the United States to show its support for a noncommunist, pro-*norteamericano*, democratic country (which Bolivia was in the early 1960s) that many perceived as having a progressive leadership. Sending so many volunteers would thus send a signal to Latin America that the United States did not just support repressive dictators but had a deep interest in the success of progressive democracies trying to implement deep social change. And indeed, for a decade both nations saw the benefits of a Peace Corps presence in the Andean nation.[5]

Although the Peace Corps is now an accepted part of U.S. diplomacy, in the 1960s it was an experimental institution. For the first time, U.S. citizens, nonexperts in foreign relations, were thrust onto the stage of U.S. diplomacy.[6] The Peace Corps intended to tap the energy of well-educated

---

3. Since its inception, the Peace Corps has served in 132 countries. Sixteen have asked the Corps to leave. Those countries were Bolivia, Burkina Faso, Ceylon (Sri Lanka), Gabon, Guinea, Indonesia, Iran, Libya, Malawi, Malaysia, Mauritania, Peru, Somalia, South Korea, Tanzania, and Turkey. Seven of them, including Bolivia, eventually asked the Peace Corps to return. See Hoffman, *All You Need Is Love*, 119, 280.

4. Oficina del Cuerpo de Paz, *Dos años del Cuerpo de Paz en Bolivia*, 10 July 1964 (La Paz: Cuerpo de Paz, 1964). Bolivia had a population of only about three million at this time. The number of volunteers jumped to 350 by the middle of the 1960s. Matilde Arze, a Bolivian official who worked in the Peace Corps office in Bolivia, interview, May 15, 1997, La Paz. See also Kevin Lowther and C. Payne Lucas, *Keeping Kennedy's Promise: The Peace Corps and the Unmet Hope of the New Frontier* (Boulder, Colo.: Westview Press, 1978), 42.

5. On the point of the Peace Corps as a means of fighting communism or Soviet expansion in the developing world, see Cobbs, "Decolonization," 90–94. Derek Singer, Latin American director of the Peace Corps for part of 1961, and Bolivia country director for the Peace Corps in 1962–64, noted that Washington leaders wanted other Latin American nations to perceive that the United States was supporting a democratic government, one generally seen as progressive. Derek Singer, interview, July 2, 1997, Arlington, Va.

6. Singer stated that, from the beginning, John F. Kennedy and his advisers wanted to keep the Peace Corps institutionally separate from the traditional agencies that ran U.S. diplomacy—most notably the State Department and the Foreign Service. The idea was to

young people to promote economic development in poorer areas of the world. For nearly all Peace Corps volunteers, often idealistic youths in their twenties, it was the first time they had lived abroad—and their first exposure to cultures that contrasted sharply with the U.S. way of life. At the same time, for residents of the small, isolated villages in nonindustrialized nations in Asia, Africa, and Latin America, the Peace Corps volunteers were often the first Americans they had ever met.

The U.S. Congress set forth the goals of the Peace Corps in 1961. Above all, the Peace Corps was to help the people of interested, nonindustrialized countries meet their nations' needs for trained manpower. The lawmakers also stipulated that the Peace Corps was to promote a better understanding of Americans wherever they served. Finally, Congress hoped the members of the Peace Corps would, after their tours of duty, educate the U.S. citizenry on Third World affairs.[7] President Carlos Lleras Restrepo of Colombia touted the Peace Corps in high-flying rhetoric: The organization would "awaken the civic spirit . . . orient the community in the realization of its own effort . . . overcome the problems of ignorance, sickness and backwardness . . . introduce new aspirations and new ideals to the popular masses, all with the desire to start forming a more equal society, more identified with the same purposes of excelling."[8]

In the end, the U.S. State Department, and more generally the executive branch, proved to be much more hard-headed when it came to the motivations behind setting up the Peace Corps. From their perspective, the Peace Corps was to solidify relations between the United States and its traditionally close allies in the developing world—such as the Philippines, the first nation that received Peace Corps volunteers. In addition, the development work of the Peace Corps would be an important tool in the worldwide fight against communism, promoting "Western economic influence," especially in rural areas.[9] In Latin America, and particularly in Bolivia, the Peace

---

keep the Peace Corps as apolitical as possible. Derek Singer, interview, July 2, 1997, Arlington, Va.

7. Gerard T. Rice, *Twenty Years of the Peace Corps* (Washington, D.C.: Peace Corps, U.S. Government Printing Office, 1981), 3.

8. Carlos Lleras Restrepo, quoted in *U.S. Peace Corps, Peace Corps Seventh Annual Report, June 30, 1968* (Washington, D.C.: Peace Corps, U.S. Government Printing Office, 1968), 53.

9. Telegram from the Embassy in the Philippines to the Department of State, May 18, 1961, *FRUS, 1961*, vol. 23, *Southeast Asia*, 23; telegram from the Department of State to the Embassy in the Philippines, August 5, 1961, ibid., 779n; for the quotation, see "Memorandum from the Under Secretary of State (Ball) to President Kennedy," Washington, October 10, 1962, *FRUS, 1962*, vol. 23, *Southeast Asia*, 635. For an analysis of U.S. intervention in the Philippines, and U.S. attempts to prevent the spread of communism and cement close

Corps focused on health, agriculture, and community development in the countryside, and on education in both rural and urban areas.[10]

The Peace Corps harmonized nicely with U.S. goals in Latin America. In 1961, despite the failures of earlier U.S. economic assistance programs in Latin America, the *norteamericanos* had established the Alliance for Progress.[11] Although later many would doubt the efficacy of aid, in 1961 the United States government and its citizenry thought that economic aid could help the nonindustrialized world develop along Western, capitalistic lines, stem the spread of communism in the developing world, and foster good relations between the United States and the emerging nations.

The U.S. public thought the same about the Peace Corps. Yet the Peace Corps represented something else for many in the United States, particularly those who did not work in the U.S. government. Domestically, the Peace Corps fulfilled a need among many *norteamericano* citizens of the early 1960s to feel that at least one part of their foreign policy was helpful to the world. The cold war had forced many Americans to come to terms with aspects of the dark underside of U.S. diplomacy, most notably the threat to use nuclear weapons and the increasing reliance on covert and military operations (in Latin America the two most prominent examples were Guatemala in 1952–54 and the Dominican Republic in 1965). Many in the United States wanted to feel good about their nation's relations with other countries, and the Peace Corps provided them such an opportunity. To many, the Peace Corps implemented the nation's best ideals and sent abroad some of its smartest people—a great example of the world's wealthiest nation serving the world.[12]

U.S.-Philippine relations, see D. Michael Shafer, *Deadly Paradigms: The Failure of U.S. Counterinsurgency Policy* (Princeton: Princeton University Press, 1988), 205–39.

10. Warren W. Wiggins, Associate Director, Office of Program Development and Operations, to the Director [of the Peace Corps], March 29, 1965, folder AID (US) 14 Peace Corps 1/1/64, Box 536, Central Foreign Policy Files, 1964–1966, Economic, General Records of the Department of State, RG 59, NA.

11. Two studies that discuss the failure of U.S. economic aid to Latin America in the 1950s are James F. Siekmeier, "Fighting Economic Nationalism: United States Economic Aid and Development Policy Toward Latin America, 1952–1961" (Ph.D. diss., Cornell University, 1993), and Thomas Zoumaras, "Path to Pan-Americanism: Eisenhower's Foreign Economic Policy Toward Latin America" (Ph.D. diss., University of Connecticut, 1987).

12. Hoffman, *All You Need Is Love*, 1, 6. In addition, many young people in the United States in those years thought their country had grown "fat, arrogant and materialistic," in the words of an early volunteer, Coates Redmon. Redmon, *Come as You Are: The Peace Corps Story* (San Diego: Harcourt, Brace, Jovanovich, 1986), 3. In the mind of Congressman William F. Ryan, the Peace Corps had a noble mission: to ensure that the world's forgotten could achieve human dignity. Ryan, quoted in Marshall Windmiller, *The Peace Corps and Pax Americana* (Washington, D.C.: Public Affairs Press, 1970), 5.

But was the Peace Corps really for the benefit of the poor in the nonindustrialized world, or mainly for the benefit of the volunteers and their sponsors, the U.S. government and citizenry? Was its primary purpose to soothe the nation's conscience? Important recent studies of the Peace Corps in the 1960s give different assessments. One study has maintained that top Peace Corps officials did not care whether the Peace Corps developed the host nation's economy or not. Only U.S. interests mattered.[13] Other recent commentators have been more positive.[14]

The Peace Corps and Bolivia

In the case of Bolivia, available evidence (from both Peace Corps volunteers and Bolivian nationals working for the Peace Corps) shows that the Peace Corps workers "on the ground" thought that serving the interests of poor *campesinos* (in the 1960s and early 1970s, nearly all volunteers served in the countryside) was important. Although U.S. volunteers received only a few months of training before being sent into the field, for most a relative lack of understanding of the place of assignment proved to be no significant problem.[15] The volunteers learned a great deal in their stints overseas, and their host villages benefited from their work. As it did around the world, the Peace Corps undertook a wide range of activities in Bolivia: helping Bolivians tap their natural resources for economic use, improving health care, and stimulating community development.

The idea of community development proved difficult to define or to agree upon, even by those who conceived of the plan. A good definition of this concept comes from Richard Poston, the first head of the Peace Corps's community development program in Colombia:

> In community development . . . we are trying to reach in to the local community . . . to deal with the community as an entity in itself, or as a social unit. . . . We are trying to help the people fashion themselves into an organized civic body that will make it possible for them

---

13. Glen F. Sheffield, "Peru and the Peace Corps, 1962–1968" (Ph.D. diss., University of Connecticut, 1991), 382.

14. See Hoffman, *All You Need Is Love,* and Jonathan Zimmerman, "Beyond Double Consciousness: Black Peace Corps Volunteers in Africa, 1961–1971," *Journal of American History* 82 (1995): 999–1028.

15. Sheffield has argued that in Peru the lack of training in native languages made it difficult or impossible for the volunteers to be effective in the countryside, where most were

to do things for themselves and enable them to improve their life situation. . . . We are trying to build into the community a set of social skills that will help the community acquire a greater ability to diagnose intelligently and discover its needs . . . [so] they will be able to identify and deal with problems—human problems, social problems, physical problems.[16]

There was an element of social engineering in community development. Historian Thomas F. O'Brien has noted that community development programs "were designed to reverse the dynamics of highly centralized social orders and to prompt villages to identify and solve their own problems with some outside technical assistance."[17] The importance of the community development mission to the Peace Corps was hotly disputed. In its early years some of its top officials did not put much stock in community development. Brent Ashabranner (who held a staff position at the Peace Corps office in Washington) and Charles Peters (director of evaluation, 1961–66) rejected the idea of volunteers trying to teach self-government to poor Latin Americans or getting them to question the rigid social stratification of the region. However, other officials, such as R. Sargent Shriver, the first director, and Frank Mankiewicz, the country director of the Peace Corps in Peru from 1962 to 1964 and the Latin American regional director from 1964 to 1966, argued for the inclusion of community development as an integral part of the Peace Corps's overall agenda. They thought that community development should be nothing short of revolutionary, empowering the people who lived in poor rural regions. Moreover, these two camps clashed over how much discretion Peace Corps volunteers should have in the area of community development. Mankiewicz thought for community development to be effective, the volunteers should have near-total leeway. Other officials who questioned the legitimacy of community development wanted to impose more structure on their activities.[18]

Despite these disagreements, volunteers managed to implement many development projects through improving agricultural production,

---

posted in the 1960s. However, there seems to be little evidence that language barriers were affecting the Bolivian volunteers' performance at this time. Sheffield, "Peru and the Peace Corps," 125.

16. Poston, quoted in Thomas James Nicastro, "Community Development Training in Peace Corps / Latin America: With Special Emphasis on Bolivia" (master's thesis, University of Missouri, 1969), 4.

17. O'Brien, *Making the Americas*, 191.

18. Sheffield, "Peru and the Peace Corps," 246, 259–60, 191.

improving health care, and serving as teachers. Even though the majority of the Peace Corps workers in the early years were inexperienced in the field of enhancing economic growth, Bolivian and U.S. officials, as well as the volunteers themselves, all assessed the Peace Corps's activities as successful. The volunteers seemed by all accounts to have been doing a good job developing Bolivia's vast natural and human resources and promoting public health. Poorer members of Bolivian society were, seemingly, benefiting from Peace Corps's activities.[19] Generally, volunteers did not work in the mining sector, so their efforts proved beneficial in diversifying the Bolivian economy, a key goal of the MNR revolution. With their involvement in agriculture, Peace Corps volunteers helped implement one of the key goals of the revolution, agrarian reform.[20] In turn, the volunteers appreciated the learning experience they received and believed their efforts had a significant effect.[21]

One important reason for the Peace Corps's success in Bolivia was the relaxed yet productive working relationship between the Peace Corps and the Bolivian government. The Peace Corps closely consulted President Víctor Paz Estenssoro regarding Bolivia's needs. The country director of the Peace Corps in Bolivia, Derek Singer, worked well with him in part because Paz Estenssoro was familiar with U.S.-sponsored aid programs, most notably CARE, which operated in Bolivia in the 1950s with Paz Estenssoro's support.[22] Additionally, the Peace Corps worked extensively

19. Lynn Hamilton, former volunteer, interview, March 12, 1997, La Paz; James Cooney, former volunteer, interview, June 25, 1997, Washington D.C.; Nora Lopez, a Bolivian official who worked in the Peace Corps office in Bolivia, interview, April 29, 1997, La Paz; Nora Calderón, a Bolivian official who worked in the Peace Corps office in Bolivia, interview, April 30, 1997, La Paz; Matilde Arze, a Bolivian official who worked in the Peace Corps office in Bolivia, interview, May 15, 1997, La Paz. For more systematic evidence of the volunteers' success in Bolivia, see Richard Griscom, "Bolivia: Impetus Is to East in Land Beset by Geography," *Peace Corps Volunteer* 3 (February 1965): 8–16; Claude Wolfe, *Heifer Project—Peace Corps—Final Report and Evaluation, July 1964, Bolivia II Project, Cochabamba, Bolivia* (Washington, D.C.: Peace Corps, 1962); Carl A. Moore, Contract Overseas Representative, *Bolivia I—Peace Corps—Public Health Group, April 1, 1962—April 1, 1964* (Norman: Extension Division, The University of Oklahoma, 1964); Oficina del Cuerpo de Paz, *Dos Años del Cuerpo de Paz*; Dwight B. Heath, "The Emerging Volunteer Subculture in Bolivia," in *Cultural Frontiers of the Peace Corps*, ed. Robert B. Textor (Cambridge: MIT Press, 1966), 271–97.
20. Donald Schultz, "Heifer Helps Cochabamba," *Peace Corps Volunteer* 3 (February 1965): 4.
21. Lynn Hamilton, former volunteer, interview, March 12, 1997, La Paz; James Cooney, former volunteer, interview, June 25, 1997, Washington D.C.
22. Irwin Rubenstein, foreign service officer who helped set up some early Peace Corps programs in Bolivia, interview, May 22, 1997, Miami; Derek Singer, interview, July 2, 1997, Arlington, Va.

with Bolivia's new Programa Nacional del Desarrollo (National Community Development Program), a project set up by the government to attack rural development problems by teaching *campesinos* technical skills.[23]

Overall, the good working relationship between volunteers and the villagers with whom they worked reflected the generally harmonious U.S.-Bolivian relations in the 1950s and early 1960s. By the late 1960s, however, two important developments strained diplomatic relations and caused the Bolivian government to expel the Peace Corps. First, rising anti-U.S. sentiment swept over the nation. This sentiment was fueled in part by Bolivian opposition to U.S.-sponsored efforts to promote birth control in the nation. Second, and more specifically, a very compelling and artistically innovative movie struck a chord with the Bolivian Left and, more generally, with Bolivian public opinion.

Rising Anti-U.S. Sentiment

The causes of anti-U.S. feeling in Bolivia were multifaceted and complex. Ernesto "Che" Guevara's capture and execution enraged the Bolivian Left. Many Bolivians on the left concluded that the U.S. Central Intelligence Agency (CIA) had killed Guevara. An already anti-U.S. Left grew to hate the United States even more. In addition to the execution of Guevara, another cause of anti-Yankee feeling in the South American nation was the lack of results from the much-heralded Alliance for Progress. U.S. actions in Vietnam and discrimination against African Americans in the United States also fueled resentment.[24] Even middle-of-the-road newspapers in La Paz were publishing anti-U.S. screeds by 1971.[25] But the most important factor behind rising, increasingly virulent, anti-U.S. sentiment in 1960s Bolivia was the controversy that erupted over the Peace Corps's program to provide birth control materials and information to Bolivians.

Few U.S. observers in the mid-1960s thought that birth control would be so controversial.[26] In those years, fears of world overpopulation helped

---

23. G. F. Baumann, "The National Community Development Programme in Bolivia and the Utilization of Peace Corps Volunteers," *Community Development Journal* 5, no. 4 (1970): 191.

24. Daniel Rodríguez, "Goodbye Cuerpo de Paz," *El Diario*, May 23, 1971, 2, and "Exigen una investigación de las actividades del tenebrosos Ku Klux Klan," *El Diario*, April 17, 1971, 7.

25. Siracusa to the Department of State, December 20, 1971, Subject Numeric File POL BOL-US, RG 59, DOS Central Files, NA.

26. Sheffield states that some U.S. officials did understand the political sensitivity of

to forge in the United States a strong bipartisan consensus about the need to reduce the growth of world population through birth control.[27] At the time, the Peace Corps accurately perceived its birth control program to be nonaggressive, small, and voluntary. Moreover, the Peace Corps's family planning activities were sanctioned by the Bolivian Ministry of Health, which had worked out an agreement with the Peace Corps for the distribution of birth control materials.[28] Peace Corps officials and volunteers simply failed to realize the explosive nature of the birth control issue; no one foresaw that it would ultimately contribute to their expulsion. Many Bolivians came to believe that the Peace Corps meant to impose birth control distribution in the nation. But although the Peace Corps had set up a number of clinics in the *campo* (countryside), these same clinics were staffed by Bolivian doctors.[29]

Bolivian attitudes toward contraception were the opposite of those widely held in the United States. Most Bolivians maintained that birth control was not needed in their country, which had a relatively small population of slightly more than three million and plenty of land and resources. In fact, some Bolivians argued that their country was underpopulated and needed more people, to settle its borderlands and protect against foreign encroachment.[30] The Bolivian Left took this argument a step further. It argued that limiting population growth was part of a U.S. conspiracy to reduce what little geopolitical power Bolivia had. Indeed,

---

family planning in 1960s Peru. "Peru and the Peace Corps," 231–37. There is little evidence, however, that U.S. officials working in Bolivia foresaw the political ramifications of the distribution of contraceptives.

27. For example, President Dwight D. Eisenhower, after he left office, sat on the boards of population control agencies (as an ex-officio member). See C. Douglas Dillon, oral history interview by John Luther (New York, 1972), Eisenhower Administration Project, Oral History Collection of Columbia University, New York, N.Y., and Donald T. Critchlow, "Birth Control, Population Control, and Family Planning: An Overview," in *The Politics of Abortion and Birth Control in Historical Perspective*, ed. Critchlow (University Park: Pennsylvania University Press, 1996), 10. A good example of the pro–family planning consensus in the United States, with regard to reducing the future populations of nonindustrialized nations, see William Rich, "Smaller Families Through Social and Economic Progress," in *New Directions in Development: Latin America, Export Credit, Population Growth, and U.S. Attitudes*, ed. Colin I. Bradford et al. (New York: Praeger, 1974), 193–286.

28. Jaime Mendoza, Bolivian head of the Peace Corps office in Bolivia in the 1960s, interview, May 15, 1997, La Paz. The Peace Corps and the Ministry of Public Health worked together in the small birth control programs. Derek Singer corroborated Mendoza's statements in his interview with the author of July 2, 1997.

29. Letter from Ken Rustad, former volunteer in Bolivia, to the author, August 7, 1998. The doctors were Bolivian, but Peace Corps workers staffed the clinics.

30. Ramón Aguilar A., "Necesidad de población," *El Diario*, June 23, 1971, 2; Mariano Baptista Gumucio, *Este País Tan Solo en Su Agonía* (La Paz: Editorial Los Amigos del Libro, 1972), 45–48.

to some on the Bolivian Left, contraception was seen as a form of genocide.[31] One thing that reinforced anticontraceptive attitudes was that family planning had been brought to Bolivia by outsiders, many of whom were white North Americans and Europeans. Many Bolivians of Indian extraction continue to be wary of white foreigners. The Indians have been repelled by the traditionally racist attitudes on the part of whites and *mestizos* toward Indians.

Interestingly, the editors of *El Diario*, Bolivia's oldest and most prominent newspaper, attempted to put the conflict over the use of family planning in historical perspective. In the mid- to late 1960s, editorials in *El Diario* had a leftist slant. The editors argued that U.S. capitalists ("la plutocracia yanqui") were promoting developing-world population control to further their own narrow, economic interests. If Bolivia's population remained stable or fell, the argument held, the Bolivian call to share the wealth generated by foreign investors would be relatively weaker.

A second notable aspect of *El Diario*'s position was its editors' support for the idea of birth control for all in Bolivia *if the family chose it without coercion*. This view ran counter to the widespread Bolivian opposition to all contraception.[32] The editors supported the idea of birth control, but what they disliked was what they saw as outside coercion. They asserted that the Peace Corps, the United States more generally, and the World Bank were pressuring Bolivians to increase the use of contraception beyond what would have been used voluntarily, and that they considered immoral.[33]

---

31. Carlos D. Mesa G., ed., *Cine boliviano: Del realizador al crítico* (La Paz: Editorial Gisbert, 1979), 150; CELADEC (Comisión Evangélica Latinoamericana de Educación Cristiana), *Bolivia: Racismo y anticoncepción* (Lima: CELADEC, 1981), 3. In the forceful words of prominent Uruguayan leftist Eduardo Galeano, it was more convenient for industrialized-world advocates of Third World population control to "kill future guerrillas while still in their mothers' bodies" than after they were born. Galeano, quoted in Alfonso Gumucio Dagron, *Historia del cine en Bolivia* (Cochabamba: Editorial Los Amigos del Libro, 1982), 230.

32. "La madre proletaria," *El Diario*, May 27, 1971, 2; Jorge Sanjinés, one of Bolivia's most prominent filmmakers, interview, April 2, 1997, La Paz; Episcopado Boliviano, quoted in CELADEC, *Bolivia*, 52.

33. Starting in the late 1960s, the United States promoted family planning by means of its foreign assistance programs; in some cases, developing nations' adoption of family planning techniques was mandatory if they wanted to receive aid. For an important historical overview of U.S. foreign policymakers' attempts to promote birth control in developing nations, see John Sharpless, "World Population Growth, Family Planning, and American Foreign Policy," in *The Politics of Abortion and Birth Control in Historical Perspective*, ed. Donald T. Critchlow (University Park: Pennsylvania State University Press, 1996), 87–90. Authors critical of U.S. attempts to prod developing-world nations to increase use of contraception include CELADEC, *Bolivia*, 3, and Jacqueline R. Kasun, *The War Against Population: The Economics and Ideology of World Population Control* (San Francisco: Ignatius Press, 1988), 85–94.

All in all, because it was so small, the Peace Corps's birth control program did little to reduce the size of Bolivia's population. There is no evidence that the Peace Corps wanted to limit population growth to reduce the nation's power. On the contrary, the Peace Corps saw family planning as a means of giving women and families the option of having fewer children, hence freeing more resources for each individual child's economic welfare, thereby offering those children hope for a brighter future.[34] On this point, the Peace Corps and the editors of *El Diario* agreed, but the majority of Bolivians, most of them Catholic, did not.[35] Nonetheless, the Peace Corps continued its program of distributing contraceptives. For the Peace Corps, moral correctness superseded political expediency. This commitment to doing what it thought was morally right—typical of the Peace Corps—may have blinded the Peace Corps volunteers in Bolivia to the political ramifications of their good intentions.[36]

Because most Bolivians did not consider overpopulation a threat in their country, they opposed birth control programs sponsored by foreigners for what they considered to be the "real" reasons for the programs. Many more opposed birth control because it was forbidden by the Catholic Church. However, there were two more reasons, sociocultural ones, why Bolivians opposed population control. First, Bolivia had a high infant mortality rate, especially in the rural areas, which meant that birth control could lead to a family's having few or no children. Since children are a peasant family's main form of wealth, *campesinos* logically feared anything that might reduce the number of their children. Second, Bolivian men feared that birth control would give women too much power over the process of reproduction. Many Bolivian men measure their machismo, virility, and power in terms of the number of children they father. Birth control restricts their authority and hurts their self-image.[37]

In the late 1960s, Bolivia's anticontraception sentiment coincided with rising anti-U.S. feeling. The consequences of the anti-*norteamericano* spirit (exacerbated by the volunteers' pro–birth control policies) were profound. In 1969 the Bolivian government expropriated the holdings of Gulf Oil company. In the late 1960s and early 1970s, student demonstrations against the United States reached a fever pitch. The offices of the Peace

---

34. Jaime Mendoza, Bolivian head of the Peace Corps office in Bolivia in the 1960s, interview, May 15, 1997, La Paz.
35. CELADEC, *Bolivia*, 51–54.
36. Sheffield, "Peru and the Peace Corps," 234.
37. Jaime Mendoza, Bolivian head of the Peace Corps office in Bolivia in the 1960s, interview, May 15, 1997, La Paz; CELADEC, *Bolivia*, 51.

Corps were attacked, and the Centro Boliviano Americano had to be moved from its prominent location near the Universidad Mayor de San Andrés (the center of radicalism in the late 1960s and early 1970s) to a more obscure side street. Allegations that Peace Corps volunteers were CIA agents abounded.[38]

A Compelling Movie Proves the Final Straw

Strained relations provided the context for the expulsion of the Peace Corps. The precipitating incident was the debut of the provocative 1969 film *Yawar Mallku* (in quechua *Blood of the Condor*). The film was, first, a poignant dramatization of how Bolivia's isolated Indians were increasingly caught up in an urbanizing, modernizing Latin America, and second, a powerful anti-imperialist statement.[39] *Yawar Mallku* expressed an indigenist nationalism, holding up Indian culture as the only authentic culture in Bolivia, maintaining that *mestizo* society had only exploited the Indians and therefore the Indians needed to separate themselves from *mestizo* society, which had been taken over by the United States—by violence if necessary.[40] The movie's two goals, in director Jorge Sanjinés's words, were "to denounce the gringos, and to depict one aspect of Bolivia's social reality"— that is, to expose the reality of life for the Indians.[41] The film portrayed Peace Corps volunteers in the *campo* as arrogant, ethnocentric, and narrow-minded imperialists out to destroy Indian culture through the sterilization of Indian women. The power of the movie for many was that Sanjinés's argument went beyond simply contending that the United

---

38. Lynn Hamilton, former volunteer, interview, March 12, 1997, La Paz; "Corpsmen, Out!" *Christian Science Monitor*, June 1, 1971, 3. There were also allegations that the Peace Corps volunteers were using illegal drugs. See Baptista Gumucio, *Este país tan solo en su agonía*, 65–67.

39. The condor was and is a revered animal of the Andean native peoples, and today it is a symbol of their deep sense of a connection with the past. Inca mythology or religion holds that condors transported the souls of the dead to heaven or the underworld.

40. James R. Chamberlain, "Blood of the Condor," in *Latin America: A Filmic Approach*, ed. Leon G. Campbell, Carlos E. Cortés, and Robert Pinger (Riverside: Latin American Studies Program, University of California, 1975), 25–27. Sanjinés as a young man was inspired by the idealism of the 1952 Bolivian revolution. By the 1960s, he had become disillusioned with it—the revolution had not significantly bettered the lives of Bolivia's poor majority. Mesa G., *Cine boliviano*, 138; Jorge Sanjinés, *Theory and Practice of a Cinema with the People*, trans. Richard Schaaf (Willimantic, Conn.: Curbstone Press, 1989), 20.

41. José Carlos Avellar, *A ponte clandestina—Birri, Glauber, Solanas, García Espinosa, Sanjinés, Alea—Teorías de cinema na América Latina* (Rio de Janeiro: Editora 34, 1995), 228.

States aimed to control Bolivia. Instead, the movie argued, the United States, with the collaboration of the whites and *mestizos* of Bolivia, intended the destruction of Indian culture itself.

The movie was immensely popular in Bolivia and gained a following around the world as well. University campuses, art houses, and film festivals showed it to enthusiastic crowds. In Bolivia itself, the movie tapped into a traditional fear of foreign influence. In La Paz, the nation's capital, the movie's popularity increased when the city government, in the first censorship of a film since the 1952 revolution, canceled its opening without explanation. The only statement made by the mayor's office was that "because of instructions from higher up [*instrucciones superiores*], the release of *Yawar Mallku* has been delayed."[42]

Even though the film was meant to dramatize the plight of Bolivia's indigenous people, fascinatingly, and ironically, Indians in the *campo* had a hard time understanding it. In the drama, an Indian family is used to represent the plight of all indigenous peoples in Bolivia. Many Bolivian Indians, however, in contrast to individualistically oriented *mestizos*, Europeans, and North Americans, see themselves first and foremost as part of a specific community, and only second as individuals. This strong community orientation prevented many Indians from comprehending the use of one family to represent the whole indigenous population, a technique used so powerfully in the film.[43]

As to sterilization, Sanjinés claimed that a friend of his, now deceased, had witnessed Peace Corps volunteers sterilizing women in a clinic near Lake Titicaca in northwestern Bolivia.[44] However, Sanjinés also stated that he was not interested in sterilization per se. For him, as an artist, the issue

---

42. Presumably it was censored because of its inflammatory message. The origin of the "instrucciones superiores" is unclear. Jorge Sanjinés, interview, April 2, 1997, La Paz; Gumucio Dagron, *Historia del cine en Bolivia*, 232; Carlos D. Mesa Gisbert, *La aventura del cine boliviano* (La Paz: Editorial Gisbert, 1985), 217.

43. Jorge Sanjinés, interview, April 2, 1997, La Paz. Sanjinés in later films abandoned the use of an individual protagonist. See Michael Chanan, ed., *Twenty-five Years of the New Latin American Cinema* (London: Channel Four Television / BFI Books, 1983), 36. Historian Frederick B. Pike does a superb job exploring how the group-oriented ideology of the native Andean Indians (and Andean culture in general) has clashed with the individualistic culture of North America. This clash goes a long way toward explaining the long history of misunderstanding and mistrust between the two regions. Pike, *The United States and the Andean Republics*.

44. In an interview in 1971 (not conducted by the author), Sanjinés said that a radio station in the late 1960s in La Paz reported that Indian women in Huatajata, a small village on Lake Titicaca in northwestern Bolivia, had been sterilized. He claimed that gynecologists in La Paz had confirmed that a woman had been sterilized at a clinic run by North Americans. Mesa G., *Cine boliviano*, 149–50.

served as a metaphor to make a broader point. The scene on sterilization was to dramatize how U.S. influence, by means of the Peace Corps and the Alliance for Progress, could penetrate the most remote places in Latin America.[45] In symbolic terms, Sanjinés held, North American hegemonic power had sterilized the *mestizo* culture, cutting it off from its Indian roots.[46]

Yet for many Bolivians in the late 1960s and early 1970s, especially left-wing Bolivians, the sterilization issue was anything but a metaphor.[47] To the contrary, it posed an immediate crisis that needed to be resolved—by ending the supposed sterilization program. If that meant the volunteers had to leave, so be it. After all, it was believable that the Peace Corps could be sterilizing women because the Peace Corps in Bolivia was distributing birth control materials, and the United States at that time advocated increased used of birth control measures to reduce overpopulation in nonindustrialized countries. There is no documentary evidence, and the Peace Corps has denied, that the volunteers ever sterilized anyone.[48] Nonetheless, after the release of *Yawar Mallku*, few Bolivians were inclined to listen to the Peace Corps's statements on the policy of contraception.

The Torres Government Sees a Political Opportunity

Stimulated by *Yawar Mallku*, anti-U.S. sentiment grew dramatically, and the Juan José Torres government felt compelled to expel the Peace Corps.[49] Torres himself, a top military leader who came to power in 1970 in a *golpe de estado* (coup d'état), was not virulently anti-*norteamericano*. Nor was he anti–Peace Corps; in fact, he had worked closely with Peace Corps volunteers in El Alto, a suburb of La Paz, in the 1960s. Even so, in May 1971

45. Jorge Sanjinés, interview, April 2, 1997, La Paz. Alfonso Gumucio Dagron makes the same point in his review of the film "Yawar Mallku," in *South American Cinema: A Critical Filmography, 1915–1994*, ed. Timothy Barnard and Peter Rist (Austin: University of Texas Press, 1996), 92–94.
46. Mesa G., *Cine boliviano*, 142; Avellar, *A Ponte Clandestina*, 226.
47. "Expulsión del Cuerpo de Paz," *El Diario*, May 25, 1971, 2.
48. Sheffield, "Peru and the Peace Corps," 235.
49. Former Peace Corps volunteers Ken Rustad and Kevin Healy (who served in Peru but visited La Paz in the late 1960s) emphasized how the movie stimulated anti-*norteamericano* feeling. Ken Rusted to the author, August 7, 1998; conversation with Kevin Healy, Washington, D.C., November 15, 2005.

the Bolivian government announced the Peace Corps was no longer welcome in Bolivia.[50] The Bolivian government's announcement gave a vague reason for the expulsion. The government decided that "deep structural changes" were necessary in Bolivia's relationship with the outside world, most notably the United States. The Torres administration used arguments typical of the Left in the 1960s and 1970s—that foreign economic activity resulted only in dependency for the host nation and would never provide for economic development. Only by dismissing the Peace Corps could Bolivians achieve their goals of "national liberation and popular participation" or implement their concept of "national development."[51]

The Torres government was articulating what scholars refer to as "dependency theory." The crux of dependency theory states that the development of the most dynamic and important sectors of the nonindustrialized world's economy are controlled by the industrialized world for its own benefit. Introduced in the 1960s and especially popular in universities in both Latin and North America in the 1960s and 1970s, the theory has been challenged in recent times.[52] However, the Latin American Left during that time unquestioningly accepted dependency theory as the truth. Leftists

50. According to Mendoza, he successfully managed to convince the Bolivian government that expelling the Peace Corps was too drastic. Torres agreed to curtail the Peace Corps' activities temporarily, but not to break the agreement permitting them to operate in Bolivia; however, the *Washington Post* published an article on the expulsion of the Peace Corps from Bolivia, in a sense forcing Bolivia's hand. Jaime Mendoza, Bolivian head of the Peace Corps office in Bolivia in the 1960s, interview, May 15, 1997, La Paz. As a result, the Peace Corps was forced out and only invited back in 1975 for a brief year. In 1990 a multiyear accord was signed between the Peace Corps and the government of Bolivia.
51. "Bolivia expulsa a Cuerpo de Paz," *El Diario*, May 22, 1971, 1.
52. The classic statement of dependency theory for Latin America is Fernando Henrique Cardoso and Enzo Faletto, *Dependencia y desarrollo en América Latina: Ensayo de interpretación sociológica* (Mexico City: Siglo Veintiuno Editores, 1969); the version in English is Cardoso and Faletto, *Dependency and Development in Latin America*, trans. Marjorie Mattingly Urquidi (Berkeley and Los Angeles: University of California Press, 1979). Another classic statement is Theotonio dos Santos, "The Structure of Dependence," *American Economic Review* 60 (1970): 231–36. Also see Andre Gunder Frank, *Latin America Underdevelopment or Revolution: Essays on the Development or Underdevelopment and the Immediate Enemy* (New York: Monthly Review Press, 1969). Later accounts include Ronald H. Chilcote, ed., *Dependency and Marxism: Toward a Resolution of the Debate* (Westport, Conn.: Greenwood Press, 1982), and Mary Ann Tétreault and Charles Frederick Abel, eds., *Dependency Theory and the Return of High Politics* (New York: Greenwood, 1986). A more recent statement of dependency theory, which emphasizes the psychological need for the developed world to compare itself favorably to the nonindustrialized world is Arturo Escobar, *Encountering Development: The Making and Unmaking of the Third World* (Princeton: Princeton University Press, 1995). A recent challenge to dependency theory is Robert Packenham's *Dependency Movement: Scholarship and Politics in Development Studies* (Cambridge: Harvard University Press, 1992).

therefore argued that the only way Bolivia could develop a vital economy and firmly establish its sovereignty was to eliminate Western influence in Bolivian society—and Peace Corps volunteers were a very visible symbol of that influence.

Although the Bolivian Left pressured the Bolivian government to force out the Peace Corps, the government was not unhappy to see the volunteers leave. One Bolivian official who served as ambassador to the United States in the 1960s and 1970s thought that some members of the Torres government actually feared the Peace Corps. Most Peace Corps volunteers were the cream of the crop of the U.S. educational system, very intelligent and ambitious, and had been doing a good job promoting reforms, such as community development. The Bolivian government (despite its revolutionary rhetoric) feared that the volunteers could empower newly confident Indians so much that the latter might question their subordinate position in society and then rise up to try to change Bolivia's status quo.[53]

The Bolivian government's fears, and the fears of anti-U.S. Bolivians, rose simultaneously. Indeed, as the Peace Corps became more effective at promoting rural development and public health, sentiment against the Peace Corps became more intense. At first the Peace Corps was not very effective in pursuing its mission. However, by the late 1960s it had very much improved its ability to implement its goals. Because the Peace Corps proved itself an effective organization in Bolivia, Peace Corps officials in Washington assigned more volunteers to the Andean nation. According to the country director from 1967 to 1971, Gerold "Gino" Baumann, in 1967 there were too many Peace Corps volunteers in Bolivia for the available postings. In addition, the 1967 volunteers included a number of idealistic rebels—student radicals who at times had few practical skills and were not effective in the field. But by 1971, with a pared-down group of volunteers (about a hundred) and fewer student radicals (many such radicals remained in the United States to protest the Vietnam War and did not apply for the Peace Corps), the Peace Corps was a more effective force.[54]

In the final analysis, the expulsion was a concession to the strong Bolivian Left. A day before Torres issued the fateful order, *El Diario* reported

---

53. Julio Sanjines G. (no relation to Jorge Sanjinés), interview, March 18, 1997, La Paz. Julio Sanjines was the Bolivian ambassador to the United States in the mid- and late 1960s. See also Paul Cowan, *The Making of an Un-American: A Dialogue with Experience* (New York: Viking Press, 1970), 246.

54. G. F. Baumann to the author, personal communication, September 8, 1998.

that two powerful leftist groups, the Central Obrero Boliviano, and the Comité Universitario Boliviano—the nation's largest union and a large organization of academics and students—called for the Peace Corps to be thrown out.[55] Even though Torres forced the Peace Corps to leave, he did not burn all his bridges with the United States. Throwing out the U.S. Agency for International Development or the U.S. military (as some prominent Bolivian leftists demanded) would have proven too costly to the Bolivian economy and too damaging to U.S.-Bolivian relations. The expulsion of the Peace Corps, however, was sufficient to satisfy the anti-U.S. Left. Some even characterized it as a national victory, a "conquista nacional." At the same time, the volunteers' "forced adios" did not excessively damage U.S.-Bolivian relations.[56] In that sense, the Peace Corps was a sacrificial llama.[57]

Although the Left saw the expulsion of the Peace Corps as an important and even necessary move to allow Bolivia to develop to its full potential economically, not all commentators agreed. Writer, journalist, and historian Mariano Baptista Gumucio argued that the Peace Corps was invited in to help smaller, isolated rural communities prosper and to improve the well-being of the poor in the nation. The Peace Corps, he argued, was succeeding in these goals. He also claimed that urban Marxists opposed the Peace Corps because they feared that the Peace Corps's activities would promote capitalism and petit bourgeois attitudes among the poorer *campesinos* and cause the Indians to discard their long-standing traditions and ideas in exchange for the foreign, Western-style way of life of the United States.[58] In fact, in the countryside, many *campesinos* did not want the volunteers to leave. After all, the *norteamericano* idealists were working with the villagers on long-term projects that would be abruptly terminated. In one instance, a volunteer who had worked planting trees in a small town proved to be so well liked that the townspeople put up a roadblock to prevent him from leaving.[59]

55. "ISAL respalda solicitud de expulsión del Cuerpo de Paz," *El Diario*, May 20, 1971, 2; Baumann to the author, September 8, 1998.
56. "Expulsión del Cuerpo de Paz," *El Diario*, May 25, 1971, 2; Juan Lechín Oquendo, a prominent Bolivian leftist and former vice president, demanded that Bolivia sever all contacts with U.S. military and intelligence organizations. Juan de Onís, "Bolivia Yields to Left-Wing Pressure," *New York Times*, July 8, 1971, 4.
57. Many Bolivian Indians sacrifice llamas to their gods to provide for a safe year in the mines, or other requested blessings.
58. Baptista Gumucio, *Este país tan solo en su agonía*, 65–67.
59. Baumann to the author, September 8, 1998.

Ramifications for U.S.-Bolivian Policy

The expulsion of the Peace Corps proved to be a surreal and terrifying experience for some of the volunteers. After the announcement, they were given a very short time (less than three weeks) to exit the country. Anti-U.S. Bolivians took advantage of the volunteers' vulnerability to steal some of their personal possessions. Demonstrators attacked some of the vehicles carrying them to the airport.[60]

The volunteers were given the option of returning to the United States or transferring to Peru, Ecuador, Paraguay, or Costa Rica. Reassignment to the first three countries was guided by geography. Volunteers who had been posted in the Andean regions of Bolivia had developed appropriate skills (for example, sheepherding, *campo* agricultural projects, and rural electrification) and were sent to Peru or Ecuador. Those who had worked in the Bolivian lowlands were offered assignments in neighboring Paraguay.[61] Costa Rica became an option when President José Figueres gave the volunteers an open invitation to work in his country.[62]

In the years since the Peace Corps was expelled, Bolivia and the United States again grew surprisingly close.[63] But though the diplomatic difficulties were repaired, it is important to consider what the expulsion illustrates about the fear many in the nonindustrialized world have of U.S. power and how the Left can galvanize that fear. While perhaps extreme in the case of the Peace Corps, this fear is very real to those people who feel it. Moreover, the events detailed in this chapter show how a compelling visual presentation can sway opinion and create very strong attitudes and beliefs—especially in a culture where many people are illiterate and oral communication is so important. Finally, we learn that when people from one value system ignore deeply held customs of people of a different culture, relations between nations can turn sour very quickly.

The expulsion of the Peace Corps shows that Bolivian leaders, although desirous of U.S. assistance, were not slavishly adhering to U.S. policy in

---

60. Lynn Hamilton, former volunteer, interview, March 12, 1997, La Paz.

61. G. F. Baumann and deputy director of the Peace Corps in Bolivia, Fred Caploe, to all Peace Corps volunteers and staff, May 24, 1971. I would like to thank Baumann for sharing this letter with me.

62. "Cuerpo de Paz en Bolivia agradece a José Figueres," *Ultima Hora*, June 22, 1971, 5; statement by Senator Frank Church of Idaho on June 10, 1971, "Peace Corps Praised and Welcomed in Costa Rica," 92nd Cong., 1st sess., *Congressional Record* 117, pt. 15:19326.

63. This harmony occurred mainly because the general who replaced Torres, Hugo Banzer Suárez, was very pro-U.S., and because during the so-called *banzerato* Bolivia was politically stable. After being ousted in 1978, Banzer was elected president in 1997 and served until he resigned in 2001.

all respects. With anti-U.S. sentiment in Bolivia on the rise in the late 1960s and early 1970s, Bolivian leaders felt more compelled than ever to limit U.S. cultural influence in their nation. Bolivians, fearing that U.S.-sponsored policy which called for distribution of birth control to the Bolivian people would limit Bolivian population growth and ultimately Bolivian power, supported the Torres government's expulsion of the Peace Corps. Many Bolivians saw the expulsion of the Peace Corps as a way of preserving distinctly Bolivian values in the fact of pressure from the United States.

The United States made a tactical retreat in 1971, by largely passively accepting the expulsion of the Peace Corps, but would not relent in its desire to compel Bolivia to accept the U.S.-sponsored Western model of economic development. The facilitation of the entry of U.S. culture, or its way of life, would be more likely to occur when Bolivia accepted the U.S.-backed neoliberal model. Starting in late 1971, more conservative Bolivian regimes were much more amenable to the U.S-sponsored model of economic development. Indeed, with the advent of neoliberal economic and political policies in the 1970s and 1980s, the United States would resume its attempt to promote what it saw was the only proper model of economic development for Bolivia.

THE REVOLUTION'S LONG SHADOW

The Generals and the Indians

In the mid-1980s, Bolivia emerged from two decades of repressive military leadership and constructed a democracy. Bolivia, as it had in the past, proved to be a trailblazer in South America. In the 1980s Bolivia simultaneously embraced neoliberalism (the opening up of markets at home and abroad) and democracy. Much of the rest of South America followed suit by the late 1980s or early 1990s.[1] Because Washington officials advocated neoliberalism as the silver bullet that could solve many of Latin America's problems, one would think that Bolivia's embrace of it would presage harmonious relations between the two nations. However, relations between the United States and Bolivia have been rocky for the last twenty-five years. Because Bolivian interests (naturally) do not always coincide with U.S. interests, the Bolivian leadership and people have challenged, even rejected, U.S. policy toward their nation in significant ways.

In order to understand the twists and turns of U.S.-Bolivian relations in recent decades, it is necessary to take a step back and put these relations in recent historical context. Focusing on the early 1970s as an important turning point proves fruitful. In the early 1970s, two trends emerged that eventually transformed the Bolivian revolution and with it Bolivia's relationship with the United States. First, a string of repressive, right-wing regimes took power. They promoted free-market policies and thus threatened many of the revolutionary initiatives enacted by the MNR during its

---

1. Chile was one of the few South American nations that implemented a thoroughly neoliberal policy before Bolivia; it moved toward democracy only in the late 1980s, after Bolivia. See Peter Kornbluh, *The Pinochet Files: A Declassified Dossier on Atrocity and Accountability* (New York: Free Press, 2003), 423–26.

leadership from 1952 to 1964. These post-1971 regimes in La Paz represented a sharp break with Bolivia's post-1952 revolutionary tradition. Second, a radical Indian movement emerged to challenge the power of the traditional elites in Bolivia.

Right-wing military dictatorships came to power in 1971 and held sway until the early 1980s. The first of these regimes, headed by Hugo Banzer Suárez (1971–78), coupled a repressive political strategy with infrastructure projects aimed at opening up the Oriente to more commerce, including foreign commerce, and economic (in particular agricultural) development. Although General René Barrientos (president from 1964 to 1969) had used force to intimidate some of the more radical miners, Banzer went further. He had radical students and other dissenters—including *campesino* organizers and their followers—killed. For example, the Banzer government's 1974 suppression of a farmers' uprising in Cochabamba protesting price controls on agricultural products resulted in between eighty and two hundred *campesino* deaths.[2] Banzer's repression and right-wing authoritarianism marked an important turning point in recent Bolivian history. Since 1952 the Bolivian state had tried to include the *campesinos* in or at least co-opt them into its governing structure and promoted democracy (at least up to 1969). Banzer's actions were a break with this tradition. Consequently, his repression facilitated *campesino* political organization outside the political boundaries of the state.[3]

When it came to the economy, Banzer reached out to foreign investors by indemnifying some investors whose assets had been nationalized by previous Bolivian governments.[4] The result was increased foreign and domestic investment, which helped the Bolivian economy to diversify. Bolivia accelerated the development of its oil and natural gas reserves in particular. Moreover, the Banzer period saw the beginning of the coca leaf and cocaine booms, which, by the 1980s, had transformed the Bolivian economy. However, Banzer simultaneously ran up the nation's debt, sowing the seeds of future economic crisis, which in turn precipitated the events that led to the advent of neoliberal reforms. Interest payments on the debt reached 30 percent of Bolivia's annual export earnings by the end of his term.[5]

2. Dunkerley, *Rebellion in the Veins*, 206–7, 210–13.
3. Rivera Cusicanqui, "Oppressed but Not Defeated," 122.
4. Raúl Barrios Morón, *Bolivia y los Estados Unidos: Democracia, derechos humanos, y narcotráfico, 1980–1982* (La Paz: HISBOL/FLACSO, 1989), 34.
5. Healy, *Llamas, Weavings, and Organic Chocolate*, 48.

Since the early post–World War II period, Washington leaders had consistently supported noncommunist governments in Latin America. The U.S. government helped to ensure the stability and pro-U.S. orientation of the military governments of the 1970s through increased economic and military assistance.[6] Only with the administration of James Earl (Jimmy) Carter (1977–81) did the generous flow of assistance come to an end. Carter cut off both military and economic assistance to a particularly repressive regime that was reputedly connected with the illegal narcotics trade, that of General Luis García Meza, which came to power in July 1980. To emphasize its dislike of the regime, the U.S. government also withdrew its ambassador, Marvin Weissman, for consultations.[7] President Reagan continued the pressure by also refusing to recognize the García Meza regime. Although it is often difficult to assess the impact of diplomatic events on internal politics, the actions of the Carter and Reagan administrations gave heart to those in Bolivia who desired democracy. By 1982, the groundwork was laid for Bolivia's return to democracy.[8] It is important, however, that even as military authoritarianism crumbled in Bolivia, its legacy of promoting private sector investment, especially foreign private investment, and its fostering of economic diversification in Bolivia (including the production of coca leaf and cocaine) endured.

The second trend in post-1971 Bolivian social and political history mentioned earlier was the emergence of a small but growing ethnically based and politically radical movement of Indians. They called themselves Kataristas, after Tupaj Katari, an Indian rebel leader who led a siege of La Paz in 1781. Although the Indians had been inspired by the hope that the MNR of the 1950s and early 1960s could bring both a better material life and a more just society to Bolivia, by the early 1970s most ethnically based Indian groups had lost faith in the MNR's vision. The Kataristas were in some ways the heirs of the *campesino sindicatos* of the 1950s, some of which were part of the MNR, but by the 1970s the Katarista movement represented an important example of the changing relationship between the Indians and the MNR. The Katarista movement challenged the MNR's ideology of assimilationist nation-building.

6. Barrios, *Bolivia y los Estados Unidos*, 35. The U.S. government quickly gave the incoming Banzer regime $14 million of emergency assistance in late 1971 to help it establish itself. Telegram from the Department of State to the U.S. Embassy in La Paz, March 2, 1972, Subject Numeric File POL BOL-US, RG 59, DOS Central Files, NA.
7. Barrios, *Bolivia y los Estados Unidos*, 67.
8. See Laurence Whitehead, "Bolivia's Failed Democratization, 1977–1980," in *Transitions from Authoritarian Rule: Latin America*, ed. Guillermo O'Donnell, Philippe C. Schmitter, and Laurence Whitehead (Baltimore: Johns Hopkins University Press, 1986), 49–71.

The Katarista movement, however, was interested in doing more than simply criticizing the MNR. For centuries the Western-oriented elites of Bolivia had perceived the Indians, and indigenous culture, as a drag on Western-style "progress." The Katarista movement asserted, first, that the Indians had been historically economically, culturally, and politically repressed and, second, that the Indian majority should be placed at the center of Bolivian history—and present-day experience. Although the Katarista movement began in the Altiplano between La Paz and Lake Titicaca, it spread to Indians in other parts of Bolivia and grew to become a broader movement for social justice for all the Indians of Bolivia.[9] The Katarista's anti-assimilation argument was endorsed by left-wing intellectuals, such as Jorge Sanjinés, the filmmaker who directed *Yawar Mallku* (discussed in the previous chapter). Many Bolivian intellectuals at the time viewed Indian culture as the only authentic culture in Bolivia.

Economic Development and Neoliberalism

Economic development and diversification, on the one hand, and the more vocal radicalism of some Indian groups, on the other, provide two separate road maps to present-day Bolivia. By bringing in more foreign investment and diversifying Bolivia's economy, Banzer further opened up the Bolivian economy and helped pave the way for a Bolivian version of neoliberalism from the 1970s to the present.[10] According to neoliberal economic doctrine, the only way to address the economic problems of the 1980s was through open markets, increased foreign investment, and slimmed-down states, even if in the short run the gap between the wealthy and the poor grew. Neoliberal economic thought assumed that in the long run a "rising tide would lift all boats." The free-market economic reforms of the Latin American governments, then, predated the collapse of communism and the institution of free-market economic systems in the former Eastern bloc.[11] Moreover, Bolivia in the mid-1980s was the first nation with a democratically elected leadership to embrace the tenets of neoliberalism as set

---

9. Albó, "From MNRistas to Kataristas to Katari," 393–95; Healy, *Llamas, Weavings, and Organic Chocolate*, 65–74; Rivera Cusicanqui, "Oppressed but Not Defeated," 117–19; 135.

10. For an overview of neoliberalism, see David Harvey, *A Brief History of Neoliberalism* (Oxford: Oxford University Press, 2005).

11. Eduardo A. Gamarra, "Market-Oriented Reforms and Democratization in Latin America: Challenges of the 1990s," in *Latin American Political Economy in the Age of Neoliberal Reform: Theoretical and Comparative Perspectives for the 1990s*, ed. William C. Smith, Car-

forth in what came to be known in the 1990s as the "Washington Consensus."[12] The Washington Consensus called for Latin American governments to accept "fiscal discipline, public expenditure priorities, tax reform, financial liberalization, unified exchange rates, trade liberalization, foreign direct investment, privatization, deregulation, and respect for property rights."[13]

Why did Bolivia embrace neoliberalism in the late 1980s? The answer lies in the economic legacy of the *banzerato*. In the mid-1980s sharp drops in commodity prices (especially for tin and natural gas), coupled with the printing and distribution of an excess of Bolivian currency, led to a deep economic depression and hyperinflation of the mid-1980s. The result was economic and political crisis—there were eleven separate governments from July 1978 to October 1985.[14] Inflation reached 24,000 percent, threatening the nascent democracy that had emerged after almost twenty years of military dictatorship.[15] Given Bolivia's long history of political instability, few would have been surprised if a military coup had forestalled the return to democracy. However, most Bolivians knew that the military, which was divided, had no quick fix for the hyperinflation problem. In any event, many military leaders desired a return to democracy.[16] Moreover, the repressive García Meza regime (1980–81) had made the very idea of military rule unacceptable to most Bolivians.

Fortunately for Bolivia, the leadership during this crisis proved effective. Víctor Paz Estenssoro came out of retirement to become president again in 1985. In his fourth and final term in office, he virtually dismantled the state mining industry, the Corporación Minero de Bolivia (COMIBOL), which ironically had been formed in his first term in office in 1952, in the early,

---

los H. Acuña, and Eduardo Gamarra (New Brunswick, N.J.: Transaction, 1994), 3. Indeed, proponents of neoliberal policies argue that state entitlements weaken political participation by making citizens dependent on the state. Therefore, the state's functions should be minimized and its role as the guarantor of citizens' rights should be curtailed. Postero, *Now We Are Citizens*, 15.

12. Chile and Argentina implemented neoliberal reforms under military dictatorships in the 1970s. For background, see Harvey, *Brief History of Neoliberalism*, 7–9, 39.

13. Gamarra, "Market-Oriented Reforms," 8.

14. Kenneth P. Jameson, "Austerity Programs Under Conditions of Political Instability and Economic Depression: The Case of Bolivia," in *Paying the Costs of Austerity in Latin America*, ed. Howard Handelman and Werner Baer (Boulder, Colo.: Westview Press, 1989), 90–91.

15. Kenneth Lehman, "A 'Medicine of Death?': U.S. Policy and Political Disarray in Bolivia, 1985–2000," in *Addicted to Failure: U.S. Security Policy in Latin America and the Andean Region*, ed. Brian Loveman (Lanham, Md.: Rowman and Littlefield, 2006), 130.

16. James Dunkerley, "Political Transition and Economic Stabilization: Bolivia, 1982–1989," in *Political Suicide in Latin America*, ed. Dunkerley (London: Verso, 1992), 184, 187.

heady years of the revolution. Interestingly and importantly, one of the main architects of the economic liberalization of the 1980s, Planning Minister Gonzalo Sánchez de Lozada, became president in 1993, deepening the neoliberal reforms initiated by Paz Estenssoro in the previous decade.[17]

During Paz Estenssoro's tenure in office (1984–89), both Bolivia and the United States agreed to economic "shock treatment" for Bolivia. This austerity plan imposed by a team of U.S. and Bolivian economists prescribed, among other things, deep cuts in the government budget, including state-run industries such as COMIBOL. The idea—not a new concept—was that fiscal restraint would create a positive investment climate for businessmen (both foreign and Bolivian) with capital to invest.

In the short run the austerity/stabilization plan was a success. Inflation dropped from stratospheric heights to 16 percent in two years. Major public disturbances were miraculously avoided.[18] Many observers hailed Bolivia as an important case of a poor country that had embraced neoliberal economic reforms even as it experienced fragility with regard to both economic growth and the strengthening of democratic institutions.[19] However, Bolivia still faced economic problems. One author characterized Bolivian economic growth after the 1980s stabilization plan as "the achievement of a mediocre equilibrium 'at the bottom of the well.'"[20] Kenneth Lehman has noted that the 1980s "shock treatment," while streamlining the Bolivian government, did not produce enough economic

17. James Dunkerley sums up Sánchez de Lozada's reforms: "Sánchez de Lozada's prescription for economic recovery was one of orthodox neo-liberalism. Under Decree 21060 (August 1985) he sought to obtain a 'realistic' exchange rate, decrease the public sector wage bill, free almost all prices, and lift most restrictions on financial operations, including those on dollar transactions. Through Decree 21369 (July 1986) he effectively opened up the economy to full external competition by imposing a uniform import tariff of 20 per cent. In March 1986 the government introduced a major tax reform to enhance state revenue. In August of that year (Decree 21377) COMIBOL was 'decentralised' as a first step towards privatisation; in June 1987 the Caja Nacional de Seguro Social (CNSS) was deprived of many of its central welfare functions. In March 1988 the government declared the 'decentralisation' of the Corporación Boliviana de Fomento (CBF) to regional development corporations, and also attempted to devolve responsibility for education to local authorities." "Political Transition and Economic Stabilisation: Bolivia, 1982–1989," in Dunkerley, *Bolivia: Revolution and the Power of History in the Present* (London: Institute for the Study of the Americas, 2007), 149.

18. Dunkerley, "Political Transition and Economic Stabilization," in Dunkerley, *Political Suicide in Latin America*, 173.

19. Eduardo A. Gamarra, *Entre la droga y la democracía: La cooperación entre Estados Unidos–Bolivia y la lucha contra el narcotráfico* (La Paz: El Instituto Latinoamericano de Investigaciones Sociales [ILDIS], 1994), 69–71; Lehman, "Medicine of Death?" 131.

20. Marcelo Cavarozzi, "Politics: A Key for the Long Term in South America," in *Latin American Political Economy in the Age of Neoliberal Reform: Theoretical and Comparative*

growth—or at least not enough benefit for the popular sectors—to offset the political, class, and ethnic tensions that the streamlining exacerbated.[21] What proved to be Bolivia's economic salvation was the rapid growth in the market for cocaine, in which Bolivia served as a key producer of coca leaves, cocaine's raw material. As the Bolivian mining sector contracted and neoliberal policy disproportionally benefited the wealthy, the popular sectors of society increasingly turned to coca production to survive. Miners who had lost their jobs as less productive mines closed increasingly migrated to the Oriente—in particular the Chapare—to become coca farmers. Bolivia's participation in the narco-economy was soon to complicate its relationship with the United States.

Another source of economic problems was that U.S. assistance since the 1950s had not resulted in many tangible benefits for the poor and working class. The U.S.-sponsored projects to improve Bolivian agriculture, for example, did not fit the needs of many Bolivians, in particular the poorer *campesinos*. For example, U.S. technicians introduced insecticides, sprayers, fertilizers, and training schools. Although such innovations could prove useful, they often were not adaptable to the level of agricultural technique in the nation. More seriously, U.S. agricultural experts called on Bolivians to abandon much of their country's diverse base of biological and cultural resources—with long-lasting environmental consequences. Traditional crops, often with high nutritional value, were not promoted by U.S. agricultural experts. In one particular instance, the implementation of Western agricultural techniques in a fragile segment of the Andean ecosystem produced in the words of Kevin Healy, "an ecological disaster zone." In sum, years of U.S. economic assistance had failed to help those who needed it the most.[22]

Perspectives for the 1990s, ed. William C. Smith, Carlos H. Acuña, and Eduardo Gamarra (New Brunswick, N.J.: Transaction, 1994), 138. Juan Antonio Morales goes further in his criticisms of the model of political economy that emerged in the late 1980s. He noted that the neoliberal system that emerged after the 1984–85 crisis had five major problems: a lack of institutional development; insufficient mechanism of democratic participation; a lack of coordination among private economic entities and between them and the government; a lack of effective channels of expression for the most extreme social conflicts; and inadequate preparation for sustained long-term growth. "Democracy, Economic Liberalism, and Structural Reform in Bolivia," in *Democracy, Markets, and Structural Reform in Latin America: Argentina, Bolivia, Brazil, Chile, and Mexico*, ed. William C. Smith, Carlos H. Acuña, and Eduardo Gamarra (New Brunswick, N.J.: Transaction, 1994), 143–44.

21. Lehman, "Medicine of Death?" 130.

22. Healy, *Llamas, Weavings, and Organic Chocolate*, 38. However, in at least one instance, campesinos successfully implemented pre-Conquest agricultural techniques to their benefit. See Clark Erickson, "Prehistoric Landscape Management in the Andean Highlands:

The Cold War Ends and Coca Production Increases

Considering the widespread poverty in the *campo*, it was not surprising that many poorer *campesinos*, when they discovered a potentially lucrative crop, coca leaves, started producing it in large amounts. Interestingly, both the trend toward neoliberalism and the Indian movement intersected in one of the most important aspects of recent U.S.-Bolivian relations: the "drug war." Although coca leaves have been chewed by indigenous Bolivians for centuries, some Indians began to produce coca for a distinctly different purpose: for sale to international drug dealers for the production of cocaine. The *cocaleros* (coca leaf farmers), most of whom were of Indian background, were taking a page from the neoliberal book in that they wanted to maximize their profits by participating in the global marketplace. They were making quite a bit of money from exports of coca (and later on coca paste and cocaine). The only problem was that it was illegal. Coca leaf is produced in Bolivia for both illegal and legal purposes. Legal production of coca, in particular for chewing and for tea, accounts for less than one-fifth of the acreage employed to grow coca leaves, and less than one-tenth of the total harvest.[23]

The *cocaleros* represented a challenge to the prevailing, tacitly understood rules of U.S.-Bolivian relations. They challenged the dogma embraced by a number of Bolivian elites—that for Bolivia to prosper it must act in accordance how the United States wants it to develop economically. The *cocaleros* formed organizations to protest the Bolivian government's attempts—spurred by the United States—to interdict the flow of coca leaves to processing plants in other Andean countries and to eradicate the production of coca for making cocaine.

But a wider lens is needed to understand recent U.S.-Bolivian relations. The drug war was not the only dynamic in this relationship. Changes in worldwide ideological trends also proved critically important. Latin America's relationship with the United States transformed as the cold war came to an abrupt end. During the cold war, U.S.–Latin American relations were focused on preventing communism, in particular Soviet-sponsored communism, from extending its reach to the Western Hemisphere. To achieve

---

Raised-Field Agriculture and Its Environmental Impact," *Population and Environment* 13, no. 4 (1992): 285–300; cited in Brian Fagan, *Time Detectives* (New York: Simon and Schuster, 1995), chap. 11 (the entire chapter is about Bolivia)

23. Felipe E. MacGregor, *Coca and Cocaine: An Andean Perspective*, trans. Jonathan Cavanagh and Rosemary Underhay (Westport, Conn.: Greenwood Press, 1993), 3, 9.

that end, the United States operated as a paternalistic leader of the hemisphere, ensuring that the Soviet threat would not imperil Latin America. The United States had worked hand-in-hand in multilateral fashion with Latin American countries against communism; the 1947 Rio Pact and the 1948 creation of the Organization of American States are two early examples of this effort. However, once the cold war ended, this U.S. paternalist-multilateral system for containing communism was totally transformed. Instead of the sole focus being on communism, a multiplicity of factors emerged that framed the U.S.–Latin American relationship: environmental issues, Latin America's access to technology, the problems their external debt poses for economic development, the trade in illegal narcotics, and social justice.[24]

With the end of the cold war, some (cynical) observers have concluded that the United States replaced its obsession with eliminating communism from the hemisphere with an obsession with seeking economic opportunity south of the border. In the words of two Latin American academics: "The relationship between the United States and Latin America can be summed up in three words: business, business, business."[25]

But the choices facing the United States with regard to its Latin American policy are more complex. Indeed, U.S. policy toward Latin America was at a crossroads. One option was for Washington to give up its desire for hegemony in the Western Hemisphere. Or, given that it no longer needed to allocate resources to a global cold war against the Soviet Union and its proxies, it could choose to attempt to strengthen its hegemony in the region. From the perspective of some Latin American scholars, it chose the second option. In the words of Luis Verdesoto and Gloria Ardaya Salinas, the United States "intensified its pressure for a strategic vision of a new international order in which it would solidify its hegemonic power." What that meant, the two concluded, was, first, a new emphasis on neoliberal economics and free trade between North America and Latin America; and second, an intensification of the war on drugs.[26] The concept of the

24. Luis Verdesoto and Gloria Ardaya Salinas, eds., *Entre la presión y el consenso: Escenarios y previsiones para la relación Bolivia–Estados Unidos* (La Paz, Bolivia: UDAPEX [Unidad de Análisis de Política Exterior] and Instituto Latinoamericano de Investigaciones Sociales [ILDIS], 1993), 6–7; 4.

25. Angulo and Correa, "La política exterior norteamericana en América Latina," 407.

26. Verdesoto and Ardaya Salinas, *Entre la presión y el consenso*, 3–4; my translation. For a left-wing perspective by a North American, see Greg Grandin, *Empire's Workshop: Latin America, the United States, and the Rise of a New Imperialism* (New York: Metropolitan Books / Holt Paperbacks, 2006), 215–22.

"war on drugs" went back to the presidency of Richard M. Nixon, when he used the phrase in the 1968 electoral campaign to refer to his plans, if elected, to reduce consumption of illegal narcotics in the United States. But it was the presidency of Ronald Reagan (1981–89) that revived the phrase for the international side of the narcotics-control effort—and decided that U.S. military assistance to Bolivia to fight the drug war was the best technique for doing so.[27]

But just because the United States wanted more influence over Latin America did not mean that Latin Americans would let it have it. Indeed, even as the United States aimed to solidify its power in the Western Hemisphere, some Bolivians challenged the power of the United States by growing coca. An important aspect of the U.S.-Bolivian patron-client relationship was that if the Bolivians played by U.S. rules, the United States would reciprocate with economic assistance. But some nonelite Bolivians—the *cocaleros*—chose to opt out of the traditional patron-client relationship. Even as U.S. leaders and some Bolivian officials (often responding to U.S. pressure) teamed up to attempt to suppress the production of coca leaves destined for the factories that produced cocaine, Bolivian *cocaleros* persisted in participating in the illegal, yet lucrative, production.[28]

From the point of view of Bolivian *campesinos*, coca was a nearly perfect crop. One plot of even marginal land can produce multiple coca harvests per season with little up-front investment or maintenance. Coca itself is easy to store and transport. These factors added up to significantly increased profits when compared to other, more perishable products.[29] Consequently, the *cocaleros* had no intention of giving up their lucrative trade without a fight. Yet participating in the international illegal narcotics market proved dangerous. As one Bolivian observer noted with some bitterness, "If anything eats away at and distorts our [the Bolivian] economy, it is the trafficking in narcotics. If anything creates tension between different groups in society, and threatens the democratic system, it is drug trafficking. If anything hurts Bolivia's relationship with the United States, hurts

27. Adam Isacson, "The U.S. Military in the War on Drugs," in *Drugs and Democracy in Latin America: The Impact of U.S. Policy*, ed. Coletta A Youngers and Eileen Rosin (Boulder, Colo.: Lynne Rienner, 2005), 19, 22.
28. Gamarra asserts that the principle reason Bolivian officials adopted anti-narcotrafficking policies was U.S. government pressure, and that some Bolivian officials supported the efforts of the *cocaleros*. Gamarra, *Entre la droga y la democracía*, 3–4.
29. Lehman, "Medicine of Death?" 133.

Bolivian sovereignty, and inhibits economic development, it is the trafficking in narcotics."[30]

For the United States and Bolivia after the cold war, three issues dominated the agenda: democracy, drugs, and development. Of these three, the issue of drugs was the primary sticking point. The issue of development took a back seat to the anti-narco-trafficking efforts. Washington's militarization of the drug war eroded Bolivian democracy—although the nation remains democratic. From the early 1980s to the present, narco-trafficking dominated the agenda of U.S.-Bolivian relations.

Since the 1980s, the center of cocaine manufacturing in Bolivia has been the Chapare and Isiboro regions. The Chapare, located on the western edge of the vast Amazonian lowlands, is the second biggest coca-producing area in the world (only the Huallaga Valley in Peru produces more coca). About 80–90 percent of the *cocaleros* produce both coca leaf and coca paste, the first stage of cocaine production. The refinement of the paste into cocaine, which takes place in secretive and isolated regions in Bolivia, is a capital-intensive process, requiring electricity, special presses, ether, acetone, and ceramic corrosion-resistant containers. Then the cocaine is transported to Colombia or Brazil for sale on the international market.[31]

"They say that you North Americans can do anything. If that's the case, why don't you produce your own cocaine, so we can abandon our coca fields here in the Chapare and return to our homes, so we can spend more time with our families?"[32] This lament of a *campesino* touches on the problematic effects of coca production in Bolivia. Before the coca boom of the 1980s, the Chapare was relatively uninhabited and ecologically diverse. Growing world demand for cocaine generated a demand for Bolivian coca leaves, which poor *campesinos* quickly filled.

Two key factors facilitated the coca boom in Bolivia: the migration of laborers from the highlands to the lowlands and the collapse of the price of cotton in the late 1970s.[33] The migration of the highland Indians was triggered in large part by the low price of tin in the 1970s and 1980s; and low tin prices translated into closed mines, which meant rising unemployment among the working class. Even as highland residents complained

---

30. Marc Meinardus, quoted in Gamarra, *Entre la droga y la democracia*, vii.
31. Jaime Malamud-Goti, *Smoke and Mirrors: The Paradox of the Drug Wars* (Boulder, Colo.: Westview Press, 1992), 2.
32. The unidentified campesino is quoted in Jack M. Weatherford, *Narcoticos en Bolivia y los Estados Unidos* (La Paz: Editorial Los Amigos del Libro, 1987), 9; my translation.
33. Malamud-Goti, *Smoke and Mirrors*, 10.

about having to live a long distance from their homeland, dire economic circumstances forced them to search for opportunity, finding it in the Amazon lowlands. Along with economic opportunity came depopulation (in particular of males) of a number of regions in the highlands. Nonetheless, because of the strong connection the Indians of the Andes have for the villages and lands their ancestors inhabited for centuries, the highland Indians return to their depopulated and increasingly impoverished villages from time to time.[34] The capital required to finance this boom came from wealthy *cruceños* (residents of Santa Cruz), who were abandoning the faltering cotton market in favor of a more lucrative investment.[35]

With inexpensive labor and investment capital, the cocaine industry in Bolivia was off and running by the mid-1980s. Although estimates vary, according to one assessment, by 1986, this segment of the underground economy accounted for about 40 percent of Bolivia's gross domestic product.[36] In more concrete terms, the coca/cocaine trade produced around $2.5 billion of income per year, accounted for about one-half of agricultural production, and 20–25 percent of total employment.[37] However, it should be noted that the revenue from cocaine comes with high social costs, as noted above. The cocaine trade has degraded the Bolivian citizenry's faith (limited though it is) in its country's leadership. Regarding the broader civic costs of the drug trade, wealthy and powerful Bolivians who run the illicit trade use their profits to influence Bolivian politicians. Consequently, Bolivian citizens grow more and more cynical as candidates running for office denounce the drug trade; but once in office, because of financial and other types of ties to Bolivians who have grown wealthy from the cocaine trade, do little or nothing to stop it.[38]

In addition, the human costs are significant. Many of these costs are borne by those who work to convert coca leaves into coca paste, the first step toward refinement into cocaine. Paste is created by pressing, usually

34. Weatherford, *Narco'ticos*, 12–13.
35. Malmud-Goti, *Smoke and Mirrors*, 10.
36. Weatherford, *Narco'ticos*, 89, 50.
37. Melvin Burke, "Visiones e ilusiones del trafico ilícito de drogas y la guerra contra las drogas en el siglo XX," in *Visiones de fin de siglo: Bolivia y América Latina en el siglo XX*, ed. Dora Cajías, Magdalena Cajías, Carmen Johnson, and Iris Villegas (La Paz: Institut Français d'Études Andines, Embajada española en Bolivia, Coordinadora de Historia, 2001), 508.
38. A friend of mine who taught at the Calvert (American) School in La Paz's Zona Sur, its wealthiest neighborhood, once joked with me, "As I look at the students in my classes, I've noticed that about half are the sons and daughters of wealthy Bolivians in the narcotics trade; and the other half are the sons and daughters of politicians. But the two [narcotraffickers and politicians] are really the same thing."

with one's feet while standing in a large vat, a mixture of chemicals, including a combination that could include kerosene with added salts, acetone, and sulfuric acid, and coca leaves. Because the corrosive mixture destroys shoes and boots so rapidly, poorer peasants, normally younger men or even boys, press the mixture with their feet, losing layers of skin in the process and greatly damaging their feet. Some Bolivians smoke cigarettes made of the paste, which, due to its chemical content, causes low-level but permanent brain damage.[39] In addition, *cocaleros* in the Chapare have been injured or killed as they have resisted military forces entering the region to suppress coca production or interdict the transport of coca leaves, paste, or cocaine.

Repression and U.S.-Bolivian Relations

As the cocaine trade in the Oriente picked up steam, U.S. and Bolivian efforts to combat it increased in intensity. Although in 1961 Bolivia, Peru, and the United States signed, and in 1973 Bolivia ratified, the Single Convention on Narcotic Drugs, in which the participant nations pledged to prevent illegal narcotics from reaching world markets,[40] it was not until the 1980s that the coca and cocaine trades in Bolivia reached significant proportions. In 1974, however, the U.S. government financed an $8 million pilot project to determine the feasibility of a long-tem coca-reduction policy. Each year during the 1977–79 period, Bolivia and the United States signed bilateral antidrug agreements.[41] In 1983, a new special antidrug police corps, the Unidad Mobil de Patrullaje Rural (Mobile Rural Patrol Unit, UMOPAR), was created, and in 1984 the military took control of part of the Chapare on orders from President Hernán Siles-Suazo.[42] Since that time, although leaders have come and gone, and the level of funding of the drug war has risen and fallen, the tactics and strategy remained largely the same until the election of Evo Morales in 2006.

An analysis of early U.S. efforts to curtail coca production in the Oriente reveals the myriad problems inherent in the antidrug effort. First, some UMOPAR officials proved corruptible. Even though UMOPAR was formed

---

39. Weatherford, *Narco'ticos*, 19–24.
40. Waltraud Q. Morales, "Political Economy of Bolivia's Foreign Policy," *Bolivian Studies Journal* 9 (2001): 113.
41. MacGregor, *Coca and Cocaine*, 17.
42. Malamud-Goti, *Smoke and Mirrors*, 13.

to combat the production of coca and to interdict cocaine flows, some UMOPAR officials joined some military officers—allegedly involved in the drug trade—in a failed coup attempt in June 1984.[43] A second problem is deeper. U.S. officials did not seem to understand (or at least did not publicly articulate any such understanding) that the militarization of the drug war, by increasing the institutional power of the military, could threaten democratic rule.[44]

Indeed, a lack of U.S. understanding of how Bolivian institutions actually operate continually undermined U.S. antidrug efforts. Failing, or not even seriously trying, to build consensus for U.S.-backed antinarcotics efforts, Washington's policy damaged U.S.-Bolivian relations. U.S. efforts to eradicate coca leaves and to interdict cocaine flows began in earnest with Operation Blast Furnace in 1986. The Bolivian Congress was not officially informed of the effort until four years later—although information had leaked out in the interim.[45] Working directly with the Bolivian executive branch, Blast Furnace enhanced its power. As information about Blast Furnace's activities leaked out, the Bolivian Congress became more and more disillusioned with the drug war. Not surprisingly, some members of Congress, as well as members of the international press, criticized this example of U.S. intervention. Further, since the aircraft employed in Blast Furnace were easily identifiable, drug traffickers simply hid or moved their operations. In addition, U.S. forces, the U.S. Drug Enforcement Agency (DEA), and UMOPAR disagreed over to how to implement the plan, and this lack of coordination further reduced Blast Furnace's effectiveness. In the end, Blast Furnace (which was implemented for only one year) was a failure: no major drug dealer was arrested, and no large laboratories were shut down by the operation.[46]

In 1988, President Paz Estenssoro agreed to the implementation of the Coca and Controlled Substances Law (Law 1008), which has guided U.S. antidrug policy in Bolivia ever since. U.S. legal officials reportedly helped Bolivian leaders draft the law.[47] Although the judicial mechanism dictated

43. Ibid., *Smoke and Mirrors*, 28.
44. MacGregor, *Coca and Cocaine*, 28.
45. Kathryn Ledebur, "Bolivia: Clear Consequences," in *Drugs and Democracy in Latin America*, ed. Coletta A. Youngers and Eileen Rosin (Boulder, Colo.: Lynne Rienner, 2005), 145. The precedent for secrecy was set. In May 1990, President Jaime Paz Zamora signed a secret agreement with the United States that formalized the Bolivian military's role in counternarcotics policy. Ledebur, "Bolivia: Clear Consequences," 150.
46. Malamud-Goti, *Smoke and Mirrors*, 30–31.
47. Ledebur, "Bolivia: Clear Consequences," 153.

by Law 1008 has meted out harsh penalties, especially on members of the poorer socioeconomic groups, in some ways it is more carrot than stick, unlike Operation Blast Furnace.[48] It calls for gradual eradication of the production of coca, coupled with indemnification for *cocaleros* who give up coca growing. The law recognizes the cultural significance of coca—indeed, some religious leaders in the Indian groups in the highlands use coca leaves to divine the future. Moreover, the law set apart twelve thousand hectares in the Yungas region of Bolivia for the legal production of coca. The Yungas traditionally has produced a type of coca good for chewing, making tea, and other purposes, but not for processing into cocaine.[49]

By 1990, the Bolivian government had agreed, under the provisions of article 3 of the Treaty of Cooperation of 1990, to give the U.S. government the right to station U.S. military forces in Bolivia to fight the drug war. This was almost certainly due to the fear of cuts in U.S. aid.[50]

The years 1988 through 1992 saw a significant turn in U.S. antinarcotics policy in Bolivia and, thus, in U.S.-Bolivian relations. As the cold war came to a close, the primary motive of U.S. policymakers in Bolivia shifted from anticommunism to stemming the flow of narcotics from Bolivia to the industrialized world. Bolivia became a laboratory (as it was for U.S. assistance policy in the 1950s) for how U.S. officials in the future would pursue their antinarcotics agenda in other Latin American nations.

A manifestation of the George H. W. Bush administration's intensified interest in the drug war was the 1991 Andean Strategy. As announced to Congress, it outlined four principal objectives of the newly intensified war on drugs. First, the U.S. government would, through assistance and training, promote increased political will and institutional development on the part of the governments of Colombia, Peru, and Bolivia to more efficiently implement antidrug policy. Second, the U.S. government would help the police and military organizations in the three governments improve their intelligence networks. Third, the U.S. government would work to improve the coordination of antidrug policy among civil and military offices in the three governments. Fourth, the U.S. government would grant $2.2 billion

---

48. In her "Social Impacts Associated with Antidrug Law 1008," in *Coca, Cocaine, and the Bolivian Reality*, ed. Madeline Barbara Léons and Harry Sanabria (Albany: State University of New York Press, 1997), Linda Farthing investigates the harshly punitive aspects of the law. See 264–66.

49. Lehman, "Medicine of Death?" 130. In recent years, some *cocaleros* in the Yungas have begun to produce coca for cocaine production.

50. Verdesoto and Ardaya Salinas, *Entre la presión y el consenso*, 41.

of economic assistance to the governments, if they successfully implemented the antidrug policy.[51]

Eduardo Gamarra has aptly summed up the conflict between U.S. and Bolivian officials regarding antidrug efforts. For the United States, the illegal drug trade represents a threat to the national security of the United States. The Bolivians do not see the drug trade as a national security issue. Instead, they perceive the United States as taking advantage of its superpower status while infringing on Bolivia's sovereignty.[52] The Bolivian government works with the United States to quell the narcotics trade in order to stay on good terms with its giant "neighbor" in North America in order to maintain the flow of U.S. assistance—a goal of Bolivian foreign policy going back to the 1950s.

Resistance to the Militarization of the Drug War

As U.S. government efforts to militarize the drug war escalated, *campesinos* and *cocaleros* organized to counter the militarization. As *cocaleros* (many of them Indians) defended their economic interests, they used traditional ethnic ties to solidify their organizations.[53] The different Indian groups had collective experiences spanning centuries to draw upon. Indians in Bolivia had faced injustice going back to the Spanish conquest. The 1992 quincentennial of Columbus's voyage provided an opportunity for Indians to publicize the history of how *mestizos* and whites in Bolivia and other parts of the continent had historically treated the Indians unjustly. The 1992 commemoration provided opportunities to organize against and resist such treatment. As is common in Latin American history, social change begot political change. This rapid transformation in civil society in Bolivia caused a political earthquake by the early twenty-first century, with profound ramifications for Bolivia's relationship with the United States. Left-wing political parties, as they increased in power, resisted U.S. initiatives in Bolivia.[54]

---

51. Gamarra, *Entre la droga y la democracía*, 97–100; Sewall H. Menzel, *Fire in the Andes: U.S. Foreign Policy and Cocaine Politics in Bolivia and Peru* (Lanham, Md.: University Press of America, 1996).

52. Eduardo A. Gamarra, "Fighting Drugs in Bolivia: United States and Bolivian Perceptions at Odds," in *Coca, Cocaine, and the Bolivian Reality*, ed. Madeline Barbara Léons and Harry Sanabria (Albany: State University of New York Press, 1997), 246–47, 248–49.

53. Gamarra, *Entre la droga y la democracia*, 111.

54. Dunkerley, "Political Transition and Economic Stabilization," 236. A good overview of the growing power of the Left in Bolivia from the 1990s to the present, as well as of the increasing power of left-wing Indian movements, can be found in James Dunkerley, "Evo

What is fascinating and key to any understanding of recent Bolivian political and social change is how the *cocalero* movement and the Indian movement began to overlap and merge in the 1980s. The Indian movement started out with the Katarista movement mentioned at the beginning of this chapter and grew quickly to include a diverse coalition of Indians.[55] The connection between the two movements is logical. After all, many Indians had chewed coca for centuries, for medicinal and spiritual purposes. Since many Indian *campesinos* were benefiting from coca exports, the Bolivian government's attempt to curtail these exports seemed to the Indians but one more example in a long list stretching back centuries of Bolivian government injustices against the Indians.

Considering the large allocation of resources in the 1990s to antidrug efforts, the victories in this drug war have been rare and minor. Two trends explain the program's ineffectiveness. Since the onset of the drug war, demand for cocaine in the industrialized world has remained strong, and to meet that demand, *cocaleros* have produced more and more coca. With interdiction, not surprisingly, as supply falls, the price of cocaine rises, which only offers more of an incentive for coca farmers to produce more of the leaf for export to cocaine processing plants. But more broadly, the techniques for fighting the drug war have not proven effective at interdicting coca leaves bound for cocaine plants. Even as UMOPAR's role in fighting the drug war has become more important, it has become less efficient, for many reasons, among them the lack of communications equipment and adequate weaponry and its inability to pay its officers a decent wage.[56] Jaime Malamud-Goti has observed that whereas nearly all who study the drug war roundly criticize it on the grounds of economics, civil liberties, and international relations, U.S. politicians remain undeterred. Even though the drug war has done no good and much harm, and cannot be won using the techniques the U.S. government is using, Washington leaders insist on continuing it.[57] Bolivian leaders have "played along" in order to maintain the flow of U.S. assistance.

The effect of the coca industry on the Bolivian economy is profound. First, it crowds out forms of enterprise that could allow for significant

---

Morales, Álvaro García Linera and the Third Bolivian Revolution," in Dunkerley, *Bolivia: Revolution and the Power of History in the Present* (London: Institute for the Study of the Americas, 2007), 1–56.

55. Xavier Albó, "And from Kataristas to MNRistas? The Surprising Alliance Between Aymaras and Neoliberals in Bolivia," in *Indigenous Peoples and Democracy in Latin America*, ed. Donna Lee Van Cott (New York: St. Martin's Press, 1994), 55–81.

56. Malamud-Goti, *Smoke and Mirrors*, 64.

57. Ibid., 3.

investment in the Bolivian economy; only a small portion of the tremendous profits of the drug trade find their way back to Bolivia. Second, if Bolivian resources were directed toward a legal activity, government taxation could direct resources to economic development that would benefit a large proportion of the Bolivian people. In addition, the cocaine trade contaminates the official bureaucracy with drug money.

The cocaine trade erodes the power of an already weak Bolivian state.[58] U.S. policy challenges the power of the Bolivian state in a number of ways. First, U.S. military assistance increases the power of the Bolivian military at the expense of the civilian state institutions.[59] Second, U.S. policy represents intervention in Bolivian affairs. U.S. law has required that Bolivia set up special drug tribunals, and Washington policymakers have threatened to cut economic assistance unless Bolivian officials use them to prosecute those accused of participating in the cocaine trade. Bowing to the economic pressure, Bolivian leaders have complied.[60]

The very nature of the war on drugs is inconsistent with a definition, much less the possibility, of victory. This would not be the case if the officials in Washington in charge of pursuing the drug war were actually seeking a significant reduction in drug use in the industrialized world and not just more funding for their particular enforcement agencies. By using difficult-to-verify estimates of the size and growing danger of the trade in illegal drugs, these officials ensure their own long-term employment.[61] Similarly, by assuring Washington that further allocations of assistance will eventually lead to "victory" on the drug front, their Bolivian counterparts ensure that the flow of U.S. aid is not interrupted.

Jeffrey Sachs, one of the U.S. architects of Bolivia's economic "shock treatment" in the 1980s, which paved the way for about fifteen years of economic growth, finds it ironic that the U.S. government sponsors violence against the nation's most enterprising entrepreneurs. In 1993 Gonzalo Sánchez de Lozada proposed the legalization and regulation of cocaine, a position he quietly repudiated after he became president that same year.[62]

58. Ibid., 92.
59. Since 2001, the Bolivian government has begun to transfer jurisdiction of high-profile human rights cases to its military court, despite stipulations in the Bolivian constitution and in international law requiring such cases be tried in civil courts. In military courts, there are no laws requiring transparency in the proceedings. Ledebur, "Bolivia: Clear Consequences," 169.
60. Ibid., 150–51.
61. Gamarra, *Entre la droga y la democracia*, 192–93.
62. Lehman, "Medicine of Death?" 132.

Resistance to Neoliberalism Reaches the Presidency of Bolivia

Although the trade in coca and cocaine continues, the U.S. and Bolivian governments' efforts to suppress it did reduce the income of *cocaleros,* and as a result, reduced the share of national income earned by Bolivian *campesinos.* Simultaneously, by the early twenty-first century, the neoliberal reforms stopped producing solid economic growth. Critics noted that neoliberal policies were benefiting only the wealthiest members of society.[63] Because a majority of Bolivians have given up on neoliberalism, coca production remains a viable economic enterprise. Because U.S. officials seem loath to question the efficacy of the war on drugs, the drug war will continue much as it has for nearly three decades. President Evo Morales, who took power in 2006 and became Bolivia's first president to openly acknowledge his indigenous roots, cut his political teeth as an organizer of the *cocaleros.*[64] Not surprisingly, his campaign literature featured coca leaves and discussed the leaf's historic importance to Bolivia's indigenous population.

One of Morales's predecessors, President Carlos Mesa, in October 2004, introduced some innovative ideas to curtail the production of coca for cocaine, such as allowing growers to use sixteen hundred square meters of their property to grow coca for legitimate purposes, provided they registered this production with the government. Morales has continued this program. As a former organizer of *cocalero* unions, he has understandably criticized the militarization of the drug war.[65] Yet the basic features of the "war on drugs" remain in place.[66] And as a consequence, the raising of coca for the production of cocaine still complicates U.S.-Bolivian relations.

In 2002 an incident revealed how clumsy attempts to influence Bolivian politics could stimulate nationalism in Bolivia, causing Bolivians to support a leader who challenged U.S. hegemony. On the eve of a presidential election in which Evo Morales was running a strong campaign, U.S. Ambassador to Bolivia Manuel Rocha tried to threaten the Bolivian people

---

63. Ricardo Ffrench-Davis, *Reforming the Reforms in Latin America* (Oxford: Macmillan, 2000), 1–2.

64. Martín Sivak, *Jefazo: Retrato íntimo de Evo Morales* (Santa Cruz, Bolivia: El Pais, 2008), 125.

65. Benjamin Dangl, *The Price of Fire: Resource Wars and Social Movements in Bolivia* (Oakland, Calif.: AK Press, 2007), 207.

66. Kathryn Ledebur and Coletta A. Youngers, "Balancing Act: Bolivia's Drug Control Advances and Challenges," May 2008, 2, http://www.wola.org/media/AIN-WOLA%20Balancing%20Act%205-23-08.pdf (accessed June 25, 2008)

to vote against Morales by stating his ascension to power would result in the loss of U.S. assistance and markets for Bolivian textile exports. Voters flocked to Morales's campaign, which now wore the mantle of Bolivian nationalism. Morales lost by only 1.5 percent, laying the groundwork for his eventual election in December 2005.[67]

---

67. Sivak, *Jefazo*, 137, 141.

CONCLUSION:
ANOTHER ROUND OF TENSION

A recent U.S. film helps us to understand why some Bolivians often see themselves as powerless in the face of international groups that aim to manipulate Bolivian politics and policy. In the 2008 James Bond movie *Quantum of Solace,* a Bolivian military officer accepts a large bribe from a wealthy international businessman. The businessman offers the bribe in exchange for the officer's promise to stage a coup, after which he is to transfer generous land and water rights to the businessman. At first the officer balks—he complains that the transfer of land and water rights to the businessman will result in higher water costs for the average Bolivian. The businessman coolly responds that if the officer does not accept the offer, the businessman will find another rebellious military officer willing to accept the bargain. Realizing that the businessman controls the situation, the officer signs an agreement to transfer the land and water rights. The film portrays Bolivians as having no choice but to consent to the demand of powerful foreigners. The reality, however, is that the Bolivian state, and its citizenry, have found means of getting powerful international actors to respond, at times, to Bolivia's needs.

Indeed, an example from recent history about the controversial issue of the access to water—and the price Bolivian citizens pay for it—provides an example. In 1999, a foreign company, Aguas de Tunari, purchased the rights to dispense water in Cochabamba. The company, in exchange for a promise of improving the infrastructure of water delivery in Cochabamba, sharply raised the price of water. Public protests, in which four protestors died, forced the Cochabamba government to terminate the contract. When the water-distribution system was return to the public sector, the water bills for *cochabambinos* correspondingly fell.[1]

It is true that the decision to privatize Cochabamba's water-distribution system came (at least in part) because of outside pressure—the World Bank informed Bolivia that a failure to privatize the water system would hold up $600 million in needed debt relief.[2] Many Bolivians, however, have resisted such outside pressure—at times successfully. Decisions by the neoliberal government of Gonzalo Sánchez de Lozada (Goni) in 2002 and 2003 to raise taxes and sell natural gas to Chile, a traditional enemy of Bolivia, resulted in protests that the Bolivian government forcefully—and bloodily—suppressed.[3] But Bolivia, as a nation, was not intimidated by Goni's use of force. Indeed, his administration was so discredited that he resigned, paving the way for the presidency of Carlos Mesa and, ultimately, Evo Morales, who would—like the 2003 protestors—resist neoliberal policies.

According to Benjamin Kohl and Linda Farthing, on October 21, 2003, as Carlos Mesa was settling into his presidency, the U.S. ambassador informed him that "any reversion of neoliberalism and coca eradication could threaten U.S. support."[4] But unlike the military officer in the film *Quantum of Solace* discussed above, the Bolivians decided not to capitulate. A time-honored pattern was repeating itself—U.S. pressure, followed by a Bolivian resistance to that pressure. The resistance would come a little more than two years later with the election of Morales to Bolivia's presidency.

Resistance to the policies of outsiders, of course, has deep roots in Bolivian history.[5] In the cosmology of some Aymara Indians, who reside in northwestern Bolivia, the past, according to their doctrine, mentally coincides with the present. Another way of stating it is that because the past is so relevant to today's issues and problems, past and present coexist in the minds of many Aymara. Therefore, in that light, the past as explored in this book is extremely relevant to the unfolding present in Bolivia. Perhaps the Aymara cosmology is even more important for understanding the worldview of Bolivia's leaders in the early twenty-first century because the current president of Bolivia, Morales, is of Aymara extraction.

1. Sivak, *Jefazo*, 130–31.
2. Dangl, *Price of Fire*, 59.
3. Ibid., 87. As Dangl notes (*Price of Fire*, 121), the roots of the 2003 "Gas War" go back to the mid-1990s.
4. Benjamin Kohl and Linda Farthing, *Impasse in Bolivia: Neoliberal Hegemony and Popular Resistance* (London: Zed Books, 2006), 179.
5. Postero, *Now We Are Citizens*, 217.

Morales's rise coincided with an important turning point in the history of U.S. foreign policy—and U.S.-Bolivian relations. From the perspective of the recent history of U.S.-Bolivian relations, U.S. motivations in its policy toward Bolivia changed as much with the end of the cold war. During the cold war, the primary motive of Washington leaders was firm support of anticommunist leaders. As the cold war wound down, and the post–cold war world emerged, preventing exports of narcotics became the highest priority.[6] Some themes, however, remained constant in U.S. policy toward Bolivia: the promotion of security, stability, expanded trade, and democracy (probably in that order of importance).[7]

Bolivia's goals vis-à-vis the United States are to influence U.S. policy toward Bolivia as much as possible without straining its (essentially patron-client) relationship with the United States too much. The *cocaleros* and the Indian ethnic movements challenged U.S. policy; the two merged in Morales's presidency. In addition, the growing gap in income between the wealthy and nonelites caused many in Bolivia to question the neoliberal orthodoxy—especially with regard to higher prices for water, higher taxes, and high rates of return on investment for foreign natural gas holdings. As opposition to neoliberal policies grew, so did support for Morales's movement.[8] Despite billions of dollars of U.S. assistance and years of neoliberal "reform" that would supposedly lead the nation out of poverty, the poverty rate hovers around 85 percent.[9] Another factor that helped Morales win the presidency was widespread dissatisfaction with the traditional political parties.[10]

Morales's vision is clear. He stated, "I'm convinced that capitalism is the worst enemy of humanity and the environment, the enemy of the entire planet."[11] His anticapitalist stance is not surprising. After all, Bolivia's

6. Verdesoto and Ardaya Salinas, *Entre la presión y el consenso*, 6–7; 35–43.
7. Mark Eric Williams, "U.S. Policy in the Andes: Commitments and Commitment Traps," in *The Andes in Focus: Security, Democracy, and Economic Reform*, ed. Russell Crandall, Guadalupe Paz, and Riordan Roett (Boulder, Colo.: Lynne Rienner, 2005), 151–72.
8. A good review of how nonelite Bolivians have contested neoliberal policy since the late 1990s can be found in Kohl and Farthing, *Impasse in Bolivia*, 149–296. For a discussion of how recent threats to Bolivia's economic stability, democracy, and national security have produced profound changes in recent Bolivian history, including the rise of Morales, see Ramiro Orias Arredondo, "Bolivia: Democracy Under Pressure," in *The Andes in Focus: Security, Democracy, and Economic Reform*, ed. Russell Crandall, Guadalupe Paz, and Riordan Roett (Boulder, Colo.: Lynne Rienner, 2005), 45–65.
9. Orias Arredondo, "Bolivia: Democracy Under Pressure," 60.
10. Ledebur, "Bolivia: Clear Consequences," 175.
11. Evo Morales, quoted in William Powers, *Whispering in the Giant's Ear: A Frontline Chronicle from Bolivia's War on Globalization* (New York: Bloomsbury, 2006), 133.

experience with neoliberalism has been bitter: the average Bolivian has not benefited from over twenty years of neoliberalism.[12] Even as the poverty rate for poor *mestizos* fell in the late 1990s, it did not for indigenous people. A World Bank report noted that in 2005 over half of the indigenous population lived in poverty.[13] This pent-up anger, along with the indignities suffered by Indians in Bolivia because of discrimination against them by the white and *mestizo* elite and middle class, helps to explain the strength of the Indian movements in Bolivia in the early twenty-first century—indeed, they proved strong enough, with their non-Indian supporters, to oust two of Bolivia's presidents between 2003 and 2005, laying the groundwork for Morales's 2006 electoral victory.[14]

But another, deeper issue helps to explain Morales's policies and the conflict between the United States and Bolivia during his time in office. Morales perceptively realized that many Bolivians feared that neoliberalism meant that outside groups would control Bolivia's natural resources. A number of Bolivians began to link in their minds the desire to retain control over their natural resources and Bolivian resistance to the "war on drugs." Indeed, the *cocaleros*' resistance against the "war on drugs" was an example, of which Bolivian history is rife, of an attempt to maintain control over how Bolivia used a crucial resource—its fertile land in the eastern lowlands. Resisting the attempts of outsiders to control how natural resources were used has been a persistent theme in Bolivia's recent history. From 1953 to 1996, Bolivia built upon its 1937 nationalization of its oil-and-gas industry by nationalizing the holdings of the three largest (and all foreign-owned) mining companies to ensure national control over what many considered national patrimony.

Morales, as a *cocalero* leader, had proven he was willing to fight outside forces that wanted to eradicate coca production in the Chapare, and thus had proven he was willing to fight for Bolivia to regain control over its natural resources, which had to some extent been lost with Bolivia's decision to implement neoliberal policies.[15] President Gonzalo Sánchez de Lozada's decision to sell Bolivian gas to world markets through Chile focused Bolivians' attention on how neoliberal policies could lead to the Bolivian nation's losing control over how its raw materials would be used. Many Bolivians feared that agreements to ship gas through their traditional

12. Ibid., 228.
13. Postero, *Now We Are Citizens*, 3.
14. Powers, *Whispering in the Giant's Ear*, 295.
15. Sivak, *Jefazo*, 131.

enemy, Chile, at lower-than-world prices, would mean Bolivia's precious (and nonrenewable) resources would be frittered away. Protests over the issue led to, according to some estimates, seventy-seven deaths and a larger number injured. Sánchez de Lozada resigned the presidency because of the controversy.[16] The protests represented an important turning point in the history of opposition movements in Bolivia. No longer were opposition movements seen as simply supporting their own (narrow) interests; they were objecting to Bolivian policy on behalf of "the Bolivian people."[17]

Morales's presidency, in a sense, mirrors the period from 1969 to 1971, when left-wing leaders in Bolivia instituted social and political changes that displeased U.S. officials. From 1970 to 1971, President Torres established the Popular Assembly to include more groups in the governing of Bolivia; Morales, similarly, is calling a constituent assembly that will include, he claims, traditionally marginalized groups. But Morales's rise was the result of a deeper historical force. As an Indian, Morales's career in politics would have been impossible but for the Bolivian revolution, which extended the suffrage to Indians. More significantly, the revolutionaries viewed the Indians as full-fledged citizens, a viewpoint not shared by Bolivia's elite up to that point. A comparison of the Bolivian revolution of the 1950s and Morales's own "revolution" of the twenty-first century is instructive. Morales's rise to power is similar to that of the MNR in 1952 in some ways, and different from it in others. The MNR was a tenuous coalition of leftists and moderates. Similarly, Morales's Movimiento a Socialismo (MAS, Movement Toward Socialism) is comprised of a variety of groups. Some members of the MAS coalition are mainly concerned with economic issues. Others, in particular Indian groups, see racial and ethnic issues as primary. Further, Morales's rise to power has accentuated divisions within Bolivia society, just as the MNR's rise to power in 1952 did.

However, in the first decade of the twenty-first century, the primary social and political divisions are between the political "ins" (Morales's MAS), on the one hand, and the political "outs" (many of the *mestizos* in the Oriente who dislike Morales), on the other. An example is the dispute over land reform. As I discussed in chapter 2, by the end of the 1950s elites in some parts of the Oriente had put a stop to the 1953 Agrarian Reform. Morales, however, has indicated that he intends to bring land

16. Ibid., 154–56.
17. Postero, *Now We Are Citizens*, 4.

reform to the Oriente, which angers the large landholders there, who are not part of his coalition.

With respect to U.S.-Bolivian relations, Morales, when he first entered office, seemed ready to challenge what the United States sees as the proper economic policy for Bolivia—neoliberalism—and to implement reforms that would threaten social harmony. In addition, he may push through reforms—such as land reform—that might exacerbate already existing social and economic divisions in Bolivia. U.S. officials are wary of reforms that may threaten stability in Bolivia—an unstable Bolivia might lay the groundwork for an anti-U.S. leadership in the nation in the future. Ultimately, how the United States responds will have a large impact on future U.S.-Bolivian relations.

Morales, along with other left-of-center South American leaders, such as Hugo Chávez of Venezuela, has headed up a coalition of anti-U.S. groups that oppose the deepening of neoliberal policies in the region. Morales has condemned the Free Trade Area of the Americas (FTAA), a U.S.-supported effort to free up trade and investment throughout the hemisphere, as "a neocolonial project" and "a policy of economic genocide."[18] Perhaps U.S.-Bolivian relations have reverted back to the condition they were in during the late 1960s and early 1970s.

Indeed, U.S. officials have accused Morales of working with revolutionary groups in the region, such as the Fuerzas Armadas de Revolucionarias de Colombia (FARC), and with Libya, and have even compared him with the Taliban.[19] For his part, Morales has expelled U.S. diplomats who he claims were fomenting opposition movements in Bolivia. Thus, the prospects of a U.S.-Bolivian entente in the short run appear slim. However, perhaps the historical precedent of U.S.-Bolivian relations in the 1950s is a better historical analogy for understanding how the Morales phenomenon will affect those relations. Even as Evo (as he is commonly known) challenges U.S. policy in some aspects, however, the United States and Bolivia, as in the 1950s, have forged a generally harmonious relationship. Admittedly, the crystal ball for determining the future of U.S.-Bolivian relations is murky. Although Morales, to the chagrin of Washington leaders, challenged neoliberalism by raising taxes on foreign oil and gas concessions, he seems to have indicated that he will work with the United States—as Paz Estenssoro did in the 1950s and early 1960s. For example,

18. Morales, quoted in Alan McPherson, "Introduction," in *Anti-Americanism*, 24.
19. Sivak, *Jefazo*, 134, 136.

Morales states that he will work with the United States with regard to the war on drugs. In Morales's Bolivia, coca production for the production of cocaine remains illegal. (He is trying to develop more non-cocaine uses for coca leaves, beyond chewing the leaves and using them to make tea.) More broadly, he has not questioned key aspects of the U.S.-Bolivian relationship, such as the patron-client model, which has been in place since the nineteenth century. Morales wants to ensure that Bolivia will continue to enjoy preferential trade agreements with the United States and, more important, large flows of U.S. economic assistance. One traditional aspect of the patron-client relationship (that Morales implicitly accepts) is that Bolivia must pay for favorable trade agreements for Bolivian exports to the big U.S. market and U.S. assistance by continuing to fight the drug war.[20]

A wild card in the U.S.-Bolivian relationship is the degree to which Morales will work with anti-U.S. groups—in particular Venezuela's Hugo Chávez—to form an anti-U.S. bloc in South America. At present, it is too difficult to tell whether Chávez can form an anti-U.S. bloc in South America and if Bolivia will actively participate. If Bolivia chooses active participation in such a bloc, it will most certainly damage its relations with the United States. But it will represent another example of Bolivia resisting U.S. policy, carving out its own political "space" in its relationship with its giant "neighbor" to the north.

Just as Bolivia had been a trailblazer with regard to Latin American economic nationalism in the 1930s (its expropriation of Standard Oil presaged Mexico's expropriation of its foreign oil industry), and just as it had proved a trailblazer with its U.S. economic aid program in the 1950s (presaging the Alliance for Progress), it proved a trailblazer in the 1980s as well. The economic shock therapy of that period, administered with the assistance of U.S. advisers, helped usher in the neoliberal era in Latin America. But Bolivia's trailblazer role does not end there. At the dawn of the twenty-first century, Morales, with his anti-neoliberal policies, is

---

20. Global Exchange Web site, http://www.globalexchange.org/campaigns/afta/3980.html (accessed June 25, 2008). The Andean Trade Preference Act of 1991 allows the Andean nations to export some products duty-free into the United States. The most commonly exported items include cut flowers, leather goods, and handbags. U.S. Department of Commerce, *Guidebook to the Andean Trade Preference Act* (Washington, D.C.: U.S. Government Printing Office, 1992), 4, 27. An extension of the act was passed in 2001. In addition, in 1991, the United States enacted the Andean Trade Promotion and Drug Eradication Act. For information on how access by the Andean nations to the U.S. market is tied to their performance when it comes to fighting the drug war, see http://www.salon.com/tech/htww/2006/06/22/drugs_and_free_trade/print.html (accessed June 25, 2008).

spearheading a continent-wide questioning of the U.S.-backed neoliberal prescription. Whether the current upsurge in left-tinged nationalism in the region proves permanent or not, Bolivia has once again shown the continent that what happens in Bolivia is a window looking onto what will happen throughout the region.

APPENDIX: U.S. ECONOMIC ASSISTANCE TO BOLIVIA

From 1946 to 1959, U.S. economic assistance to Bolivia grew from US$0.4 million to US$24.0 million. During the same period, military assistance grew at a similar rate, from US$0.4 million to US$25.2 million.[1] The following table summarizes U.S. assistance to Bolivia from 1960 to 1972.

---

1. See U.S. Agency for International Development, *U.S. Overseas Loans and Grants,* http://qesdb.usaid.gov/cgi-bin/broker.exe (accessed October 16, 2007).

Table A-1. U.S. assistance to Bolivia, 1960–72 (in millions of U.S. dollars)

Program or account	1960	1961	1962	1963	1964	1965	1966	1967	1968	1969	1970	1971	1972
USAID and predecessor agencies													
USAID loans	0.0	7.3	7.9	18.5	42.7	0.6	22.0	11.0	4.5	7.1	0.0	0.0	50.0
USAID grants	14.8	20.6	24.4	17.3	17.8	8.8	6.4	4.5	4.1	3.5	3.0	3.7	5.6
Total	14.8	27.9	32.3	35.8	60.5	9.4	28.4	15.5	8.6	10.6	3.0	3.7	55.6
Department of Agriculture													
PL 480 program account (title I)	0.0	2.4	2.5	12.2	7.1	2.9	5.5	0.6	7.4	8.2	0.0	5.1	0.0
PL 480 grants (title II)	0.2	0.4	0.9	3.9	6.3	1.0	0.8	0.9	0.9	1.2	3.6	1.8	4.4
Total	0.2	2.8	3.4	16.1	13.4	3.9	6.3	1.5	8.3	9.4	3.6	6.9	4.4
Other economic assistance													
Peace Corps	n.a.	n.a.	0.9	0.7	2.5	2.2	2.6	2.2	1.7	1.5	1.4	1.1	0.0
Social Progress Trust Fund (loans)	0.0	0.0	0.0	10.4	0.8	3.3	0.0	0.0	0.0	0.0	0.0	0.0	0.0
Total	0.0	0.0	0.9	11.1	3.3	5.5	2.6	2.2	1.7	1.5	1.4	1.1	0.0
Total economic assistance	15.0	30.7	36.6	63.0	77.2	18.8	37.3	19.2	18.6	21.5	8.0	11.7	60.0
Total military assistance	0.3	1.8	2.4	5.0	2.9	2.5	2.9	3.7	2.4	2.0	1.5	2.5	6.0

Source: U.S. Agency for International Development, *U.S. Overseas Loans and Grants (Greenbook)*, http://gbk.eads.usaidallnet.gov/query/do (accessed July 29, 2010).

BIBLIOGRAPHY

Unpublished Primary Sources

Papers and Records in U.S. and British Archives

Bolivian Pamphlets Collection (Pittsburgh Pamphlets). University of Pittsburgh Library.
U.S. National Archives and Records Administration. Archives II. College Park, Md. Department of State Records, Record Group 59.
Dwight D. Eisenhower Presidential Library, Abilene, Kans. Papers as President.
John F. Kennedy Presidential Library, Boston, Mass. National Security Files.
Lyndon B. Johnson Presidential Library, Austin, Tex. National Security Files.
Richard Nixon Presidential Library, Yorba Linda, Calif. National Security Council Files.
Rockefeller Archive Center, Tarrytown, N.Y. Nelson A. Rockefeller Files.
National Archive, Kew Gardens, Richmond, Surry, United Kingdom. Records of the Foreign Office.

Papers and Records in Bolivian Archives

Archivo de Relaciones Exteriores y Culto (ARE), La Paz, Bolivia.
Sistema de Documentación e Información Sindical (SIDIS), La Paz, Bolivia.
Archivo Nacional de Bolivia, Sucre, Bolivia.
Archivo de La Paz, La Paz, Bolivia. Papers of Col. Ballivan Saracho. Coleción de Corporación Boliviana de Fomento.

Published Primary Sources

Andrade Uzquiano, Víctor. *Bolivia: Problems and Promise*. Washington, D.C.: Embassy of Bolivia, 1956.
———. *My Missions for Revolutionary Bolivia, 1944–1962*. Pittsburgh: University of Pittsburgh Press, 1976.
———. *La revolución boliviana y los Estados Unidos, 1944–1962*. La Paz: Editorial Gisbert, 1979.
Antezana Paz, Franklin. *La política monetaría de Bolivia*. La Paz: Banco Central de Bolivia, 1954. Pittsburgh Pamphlets.
Barrios de Chungara, Domitila. *Let Me Speak! Testimony of Domitila, a Woman of the Bolivian Mines*. New York: Monthly Review Press, 1978.
Baumann, G. F. "The National Community Development Programme in Bolivia and the Utilization of Peace Corps Volunteers." *Community Development Journal* 5, no. 4 (1970): 191–96.

Central Obrero Boliviano (COB). *Programa ideológico y estatutos de la C.O.B. aprobados por el Congreso Nacional de Trabajadores.* La Paz: COB, October 31, 1954. Pittsburgh Pamphlets.
Congressional Record. 92nd Cong., 1st sess., June 10, 1971. Vol. 117, pt. 15:19326.
Corporación Boliviana de Fomento, La. *La Corporación Boliviana de Fomento: Sus origenes, organización y actividad.* La Paz: n.p., 1943.
Eder, George Jackson. *Inflation and Development in Latin America: A Case History of Inflation and Stabilization in Bolivia.* Ann Arbor: Graduate School of Business Administration, University of Michigan, 1968.
Eisenhower, Milton. *Report to the President: United States–Latin American Relations.* November 18, 1953. Washington, D.C.: Department of State, 1953.
———. *The Wine Is Bitter: The United States and Latin America.* Garden City, N.Y.: Doubleday, 1963.
Frei, Edwardo Montalva. "The Alliance That Lost Its Way." *Foreign Affairs* 45, no. 3 (1967): 437–48.
Gallardo Lozada, Jorge. *De Torres a Banzer: Diez meses de emergencia en Bolivia.* Buenos Aires: Ediciones Periferia, 1972.
Gueiler Tejada, Lydia. *La mujer y la revolución.* La Paz: Editorial Los Amigos del Libro, 1983.
Guevara, Che. *Guerrilla Warfare.* Edited by Brian Loveman and Thomas M. Davies Jr. Wilmington, Del.: Scholarly Resources, 1997.
Guevera Arze, Walter. *Plan inmediato de política económica del gobierno de la revolución nacional.* La Paz: Ministerio de Relaciones Exteriores y Culto, 1955.
———. *Planteamientos de la revolución nacional en la décima conferencia inter-americano.* La Paz: Ministerio de Relaciones Exteriores y Culto, Departamento de Prensa y Publicaciones, 1954. Pittsburgh Pamphlets.
Moore, Carl A. *Bolivia I—Peace Corps—Public Health Group, April 1, 1962–April 1, 1964.* Norman: Extension Division, The University of Oklahoma, 1964.
Oficina del Cuerpo de Paz. *Dos años del Cuerpo de Paz en Bolivia, 10 July 1964.* La Paz: Cuerpo de Paz, 1964.
Ostria Gutierrez, Alberto. *The Tragedy of Bolivia: A People Crucified.* New York: Devin-Adair, 1958.
Paz, Néstor. *My Life for My Friends: The Guerrilla Journal of Néstor Paz, Christian.* Edited and translated by Ed García and John Eagleson. Maryknoll, N.Y.: Orbis, 1975.
Prado Salmón, Gary. *The Defeat of Che Guevara: Military Response to Guerrilla Challenge in Bolivia.* Translated by John Deredita. New York: Praeger, 1987.
———. *Poder y fuerzas armadas, 1949–1982.* La Paz: Editorial Los Amigos del Libro, 1987.
Public Papers of the Presidents of the United States: Dwight David Eisenhower, 1953. Washington, D.C.: U.S. Government Printing Office, 1954.
Public Papers of the Presidents of the United States: John Fitzgerald Kennedy, 1961. Washington, D.C.: U.S. Government Printing Office, 1962.
Public Relations Office, Office of the Ministry of Foreign Affairs. *Bolivia's Struggle.* La Paz: Public Relations Office, Office of the Ministry of Foreign Affairs, 1956. Pittsburgh Pamphlets.
República de Bolivia, Ministerio de Hacienda y Estadística, Direccion General de Estadística y Censos. *Censo Demografico, 1950.* La Paz: Dirección General de Estadística y Censos, 1955.

República de Bolivia, Ministerio de Hacienda, Dirección General de Estadística y Censos. *Boletín Estadístico* 89 (1964).
Rodríguez, Felix I., and John Weisman. *Shadow Warrior*. New York: Simon and Schuster, 1989.
Saldaña, Rodolfo. *Fertile Ground—Che Guevara and Bolivia: A Firsthand Account by Rodolfo Saldaña*. New York: Pathfinder, 2001.
Sanjinés, Jorge. *Theory and Practice of a Cinema with the People*. Translated by Richard Schaaf. Willimantic, Conn.: Curbstone Press, 1989.
U.N. Economic and Social Council, Economic Commission for Latin America. *Development of Agriculture in Bolivia*. E/CN-12/218/Add.2. New York: United Nations, 1951.
U.S. Agency for International Development, Statistics and Reports Division, Office of Programs and Policy Coordination. *U.S. Overseas Loans and Grants: Obligations and Loan Authorizations* Washington, D.C.: U.S. Government Printing Office, 1985. http://qesdb.usaid.gov/cgi-bin/broker.exe.
U.S. Department of Commerce. *Guidebook to the Andean Trade Preference Act*. Washington, D.C.: U.S. Government Printing Office, 1992.
U.S. Department of State. *Foreign Relations of the United States, 1906*. Vol. 2. Washington, D.C.: U.S. Government Printing Office, 1906.
———. *Foreign Relations of the United States, 1941*. Vol. 6, American Republics. Washington, D.C.: U.S. Government Printing Office, 1941.
———. *Foreign Relations of the United States, 1942*. Vol. 5, American Republics. Washington, D.C.: U.S. Government Printing Office, 1942.
———. *Foreign Relations of the United States, 1947*. Vol. 8, American Republics. Washington, D.C.: U.S. Government Printing Office, 1947.
———. *Foreign Relations of the United States, 1948*. Vol. 9, American Republics. Washington, D.C.: U.S. Government Printing Office, 1948.
———. *Foreign Relations of the United States, 1961–1963*. Vol. 33, Southeast Asia. Washington, D.C.: U.S. Government Printing Office, 1996.
———. *Foreign Relations of the United States, 1964–1968*. Vol. 31, American Republics: Central and South America; Mexico*. Washington, D.C.: U.S. Government Printing Office, 2004.
U.S. Office of Inter-American Affairs. *Activities of the Coordinator of Inter-American Affairs in Bolivia*. Washington, D.C.: U.S. Government Printing Office, 1943.
U.S. Peace Corps. *Peace Corps Seventh Annual Report*. Washington, D.C.: U.S. Government Printing Office, June 30, 1968.
Villegas, Harry Tamayo (Pombo). *Pombo: A Man of Che's Guerrilla: With Che Guevara in Bolivia, 1966–1968*. New York: Pathfinder, 1997.
Wolfe, Claude. *Heifer Project—Peace Corps—Final Report and Evaluation, July 1964, Bolivia II Project, Cochabamba Bolivia*. Washington, D.C.: U.S. Government Printing Office, 1962.

Interviews by the Author and Oral Histories

Lupe Andrade Salmón. La Paz, Bolivia. April 15, 1997.
Matilde Arze. La Paz, Bolivia. May 15, 1997.
Sinforoso Cabrera. La Paz, Bolivia. August 4, 1999.
Nora Calderón. La Paz, Bolivia. April 30, 1997.

James Cooney. Washington, D.C. June 25, 1997.
Lynn Hamilton. La Paz, Bolivia. March 12, 1997.
Juan Lechin Oquiendo. La Paz, Bolivia. February 20, 1997.
Nora Lopez. La Paz, Bolivia. April 29, 1997.
Jaime Mendoza. La Paz, Bolivia. May 15, 1997.
Irwin Rubenstein. Plantation, Fla. May 22, 1997.
Jorge Sanjinés. La Paz, Bolivia. April 2, 1997.
Julio Sanjines Goitia. La Paz, Bolivia. March 18, 1997.
Derek Singer. Arlington, Va. July 2, 1997.
C. Douglas Dillon. Oral history interview by John Luther (New York, 1972), Eisenhower Administration Project, Oral History Collection of Columbia University, New York, N.Y.

Secondary Sources

Abendroth, Hans Huber, et al. *La deuda externa de Bolivia: 125 años de renegociaciones y ¿cuántos más?* La Paz: Centro de Estudios para el Desarrollo Laboral y Agrario, 2001.
Adams, Francis. *Dollar Diplomacy: United States Economic Assistance to Latin America*. Aldershot, England: Ashgate, 2000.
Aguilar A., Ramon. "Necesidad de población." *El Diario*, June 23, 1971, 2.
Albó, Xavier. "And from Kataristas to MNRistas? The Surprising Alliance Between Aymaras and Neoliberals in Bolivia." In *Indigenous Peoples and Democracy in Latin America*, ed. Donna Lee Van Cott, 55–81. New York: St. Martin's Press, 1994.
———. "Etnias y pueblos originarios: Diversidad étnica, cultural y lingüística." In *Bolivia en el siglo XX*, ed. Fernando Campero Prudencia, 451–82. La Paz: Harvard Club of Bolivia, 1999.
———."From MNRistas to Kataristas to Katari." In *Resistance, Rebellion, and Consciousness in the Andean Peasant World, 18th to 20th Centuries*, ed. Steve Stern, 385–86. Madison: University of Wisconsin Press, 1987.
Alexander, Robert. *The Bolivian National Revolution*. New Brunswick: Rutgers University Press, 1958.
Ameringer, Charles D. *The Democratic Left in Exile: The Antidictatorial Struggle in the Caribbean, 1945–1949*. Coral Gables: University of Miami Press, 1974.
Anderson, Jon Lee. *Che Guevara: A Revolutionary Life*. New York: Grove Press, 1997.
Anglade, Christian, and Carlos Fortin, eds. *The State and Capital Accumulation in Latin America*. Vol. 2. Pittsburgh: University of Pittsburgh Press, 1990.
Angulo, Salvador, and Loreto Correa. "La política exterior norteamericana en América Latina: Los casos de Chile y Bolivia, 1960–1980." In *Visiones de fin de siglo: Bolivia y América Latina en el siglo XX*, ed. Dora Cajías, Magdalena Cajías, Carmen Johnson, and Iris Villegas, 402–31. La Paz: IFEA / Coordinadora de Historia, Embajada de España en Bolivia, 2001.
Antezana Ergueta, Luis. *La clase media y la clase obrera en la revolución nacional del MNR*. N.p.: n.p., 1987.
———. *Historia secreta del a Moviemiento Nacionalista Revolucionario*. 8 vols. La Paz: Librería Editorial, 1986.

Arnade, Charles. "The United States and the Ultimate Roots of the Bolivian Revolution." *Historia: Publicación Bianual del Capítulo Beta Delta de la Sociedad Nacional Honoraria de Historia, Phi Alpha Theta* 1, no. 1 (January 1962): 35–49.
Arze Z., René Danilo. *Guerra y conflictos sociales: El caso rural boliviano durante la campaña del Chaco*. La Paz: Centro de Estudios de la Realidad Economica y Social, Ediciones CERES, 1987.
Avellar, José Carlos. *A ponte clandestina—Birri, Glauber, Solanas, García Espinosa, Sanjinés, Alea—Teorías de cinema na América Latina*. Rio de Janeiro: Editora 34, 1995.
Baily, Samuel L. *The United States and the Development of South America, 1945–1975*. New York: New Viewpoints, 1976.
Baptista Gumucio, Mariano. *Este país tan solo en su agonía*. La Paz: Editorial Los Amigos del Libro, 1972.
Barnet, Richard J. *The Alliance: America, Europe, Japan—Makers of the Postwar World*. New York: Touchstone, 1983.
Barrios Morón, Raul. *Bolivia y Estados Unidos: Democracia, derechos humanos, y narcotráfico, 1980–1982*. La Paz: HISBOL/FLACSO, 1989.
———. *Ejercito y revolución en Bolivia, 1952–1960*. Investigación inédita realizada con el apoyo de CLACSO y FLACSO-Bolivia, Parte IV. La Paz: CLACSO y FLACSO-Bolivia, 1986.
Bassett, Lawrence J., and Stephen E. Pelz. "The Failed Search for Victory: Vietnam and the Politics of War." In *Kennedy's Quest for Victory: American Foreign Policy, 1961–1963*, ed. Thomas G. Paterson, 223–52. New York: Oxford University Press, 1989:
Bethell, Leslie. "From the Second World War to the Cold War, 1944–1954." In *Exporting Democracy: The United States and Latin America: Themes and Issues*, ed. Abraham F. Lowenthal. Baltimore: Johns Hopkins University Press, 1991.
Bethell, Leslie, and Ian Roxborough. *Latin America Between the Second World War and the Cold War, 1944–1948*. Cambridge: Cambridge University Press, 1992.
Blasier, Cole. *The Giant's Rival: The USSR and Latin America*. Rev. ed. Pittsburgh: University of Pittsburgh Press, 1987.
———. *The Hovering Giant: U.S. Response to Revolutionary Change in Latin America, 1910–1985*. 2nd ed. Pittsburgh: University of Pittsburgh Press, 1986.
Blight, James G., and Philip Brenner. *Sad and Luminous Days: Cuba's Struggle with the Superpowers After the Missile Crisis*. Lanham, Md.: Rowman and Littlefield, 2002.
Boeger, Andrew. "Struggling for Emancipation: Tungsten Miners and the Bolivian Revolution." In *Workers' Control in Latin America, 1930–1979*, ed. Jonathan Brown. Chapel Hill: University of North Carolina Press, 1997.
"Bolivia expulsa a Cuerpo de Paz." *El Diario*, May 22, 1971, 1.
"Bolivia." *Hispanic American Report: An Analysis of Developments in Spain, Portugal, and Latin America* 11, no. 1 (1958): 40–41.
Borstelmann, Thomas. *The Cold War and the Color Line: American Race Relations in the Global Arena*. Cambridge: Harvard University Press, 2001.
———. "'Hedging Our Bets and Buying Time': John Kennedy and Racial Revolutions in the American South and Southern Africa." *Diplomatic History* 24, no. 3 (Summer 2000): 435–63.

Bowie, Robert R., and Richard H. Immerman. *Waging Peace: How Eisenhower Shaped an Enduring Cold War Strategy*. New York: Oxford University Press, 1998.
Bradford, Colin I., Jr., et al., eds. *New Directions in Development: Latin America, Export Credit, Population Growth, and U.S. Attitudes*. New York: Praeger, 1974.
Brands, H. W. *The Specter of Neutralism: The United States and the Emergence of the Third World, 1947–1960*. New York: Columbia University Press, 1989.
Brill, William H. *Military Intervention in Bolivia: The Overthrow of Paz Estenssoro and the MNR*. Washington, D.C.: Institute for the Comparative Study of Political Systems, 1967.
Burke, Melvin. *The Corporación Minera de Bolivia (COMIBOL) and the Triangular Plan: A Case Study in Dependency*. Meadville, Pa.: Allegheny College, 1987.
———. "Does 'Food for Peace' Assistance Damage the Bolivian Economy?" *Inter-American Economic Affairs* 25, no. 1 (Summer 1971): 3–21.
———. "Visiones e ilusiones del tráfico ilícito de drogas y la guerra contra las drogas en el siglo XX." In *Visiones de fin de siglo: Bolivia y América Latina en el siglo XX*, ed. Dora Cajías, Magdalena Cajías, Carmen Johnson, and Iris Villegas, 508. La Paz: IFEA / Coordinadora de Historia, Embajada de España en Bolivia, 2001.
Calderon Gutierrez, Fernando. "Actores sociales: Un siglo de luchas sociales." In *Bolivia en el siglo XX*, ed. Fernando Campero Prudencia. La Paz: Harvard Club of Bolivia, 1999.
Cardoso, Fernando, and Enzo Faletto. *Dependency and Development in Latin America*. Translated by Marjorie Mattingly Urquidi. Berkeley and Los Angeles: University of California Press, 1979.
Casanovas, Winston Moore. "Capital Accumulation and Revolutionary Nationalism in Bolivia, 1952–1985." In *The State and Capital Accumulation in Latin America*, ed. Christian Anglade and Carlos Fortin, vol. 2. Pittsburgh: University of Pittsburgh Press, 1990.
Castañeda, Jorge. *Compañero: The Life and Times of Che Guevara*. New York: Knopf, 1997.
Castro, Daniel, ed. *Revolution and Revolutionaries: Guerrilla Movements in Latin America*. Wilmington, Del.: Scholarly Resources, 1999.
Cavarozzi, Marcelo. "Politics: A Key for the Long Term in South America." In *Latin American Political Economy in the Age of Neoliberal Reform: Theoretical and Comparative Perspectives for the 1990s*, ed. William C. Smith, Carlos H. Acuña, and Eduardo Gamarra, 138–52. New Brunswick: Transaction, 1994.
CELADEC (Comisión Evangélica Latinoamericana de Educación Cristiana). *Bolivia: Racismo y anticoncepción*. Lima: CELADEC, 1981.
Chamberlain, James R. "Blood of the Condor." In *Latin America: A Filmic Approach*, ed. Leon G. Campbell, Carlos E. Cortés, and Robert Pinger, 25–45. Riverside: Latin American Studies Program, University of California, 1975.
Chanan, Michael, ed. *Twenty-five Years of the New Latin American Cinema*. London: Channel Four Television / BFI Books, 1983.
Chilcote, Ronald H., ed. *Dependency and Marxism: Toward a Resolution of the Debate*. Boulder, Colo.: Westview Press, 1982.
Cobbs, Elizabeth A. "Decolonization, the Cold War, and the Foreign Policy of the Peace Corps." *Diplomatic History* 20, no. 2 (Winter 1996): 80.

Collier, Simon, and William R. Sater. *History of Chile 1880–2002*. 2nd ed. Cambridge: Cambridge University Press, 2004.
Conaghan, Catherine M. "Reconsidering Jeffery Sachs and the Bolivian Economic Experiment." In *Money Doctors, Foreign Debts, and Economic Reforms in Latin America: From the 1890s to the Present*, ed. Paul W. Drake, 236–66. Wilmington, Del.: Scholarly Resources, 1994.
Contreras C., Manuel E. *The Bolivian Tin Mining Industry in the First Half of the 20th Century*. London: Institute of Latin American Studies, University of London, 1993.
Cook, Blance Wiesen. *The Declassified Eisenhower: A Divided Legacy*. Garden City, N.Y.: Doubleday, 1981.
"Corpsmen, Out!" *Christian Science Monitor*. June 1, 1971, 3.
Cottam, Martha L. *Images and Intervention: U.S. Policies in Latin America*. Pittsburgh: University of Pittsburgh Press, 1994.
Cowan, Paul. *The Making of an Un-American: A Dialogue with Experience*. New York: Viking, 1970.
Critchlow, Donald T. "Birth Control, Population Control, and Family Planning: An Overview." In *The Politics of Abortion and Birth Control in Historical Perspective*, ed. Donald T. Critchlow, 1–20. University Park: Pennsylvania State University Press, 1996.
"Cuerpo de Paz en Bolivia agradece a José Figueres." *Ultima Hora*, June 22, 1971, 5.
Cullather, Nick. "'Fuel for the Good Dragon': The United States and Industrial Policy in Taiwan, 1950–1965." In *Empire and Revolution: the United States and the Third World Since 1945*, ed. Peter Hahn and Mary Ann Heiss, 242–68. Columbus: Ohio State University Press, 2001.
Cumings, Bruce. *Origins of the Korean War*. 2 vols. Ithaca: Cornell University Press, 2004.
———. *The Roaring of the Cataract, 1947–1950*. Princeton: Princeton University Press, 1990.
Dandler, Jorge, and Juan Torrico A. "From the National Indigenous Congress to the Ayopaya Rebellion: Bolivia, 1945–1947." In *Resistance, Rebellion, and Consciousness in the Andean Peasant World: 18th to 20th Centuries*, ed. Steve J. Stern, 334–78. Madison: University of Wisconsin Press, 1987.
Dangl, Benjamin. *The Price of Fire: Resource Wars and Social Movements in Bolivia*. Oakland, Calif.: AK Press, 2007.
"Diplomacia a la moderna: Un embajador tiene que ser más campechano que cortesano." *Visión: Revista Internacional*, September 27, 1957, 24–27.
Dosal, Paul J. *Comandante Che: Guerrilla Soldier, Commander, and Strategist, 1956–1967*. University Park: Pennsylvania State University Press, 2003.
Dozer, Donald M. *Are We Good Neighbors? Three Decades of Inter-American Relations, 1930–1960*. Gainesville: University of Florida Press, 1959.
Dudziak, Mary L. *Cold War Civil Rights: Race and the Image of American Democracy* Princeton: Princeton University Press, 2000.
Dujovne, Carlos. *Trabajo y salarios en la revolución nacional*. La Paz: Subsecretaria de Prensa, Informaciones y Cultura, 1955. Pittsburgh Pamphlets.
Dunkerley, James. *Americana: The Americas in the World Around 1850 (or "Seeing the Elephant" as the Theme for an Imaginary Western)*. London: Verso, 2000.
———. "Evo Morales, Álvaro García Linera, and the Third Bolivian Revolution." In James Dunkerley, *Bolivia: Revolution and the Power of History in the Present*, 1–56. London: Institute for the Study of the Americas, 2007.

———. "The Origins of the Bolivian Revolution in the Twentieth Century: Some Reflections." In *Proclaiming Revolution: Bolivia in Comparative Perspective*, ed. Merilee S. Grindle and Pilar Dominguez, 135–63. Cambridge: David Rockefeller Center for Latin American Studies, Harvard University Press, 2003.

———. "Political Transition and Economic Stabilisation: Bolivia, 1982–1989." In James Dunkerley, *Bolivia: Revolution and the Power of History in the Present*, 49–89. London: Institute for the Study of the Americas, 2007.

———."Political Transition and Economic Stabilization: Bolivia, 1982–1989." In *Political Suicide in Latin America*, ed. Dunkerly. London: Verso, 1992.

———. *Rebellion in the Veins: Political Struggle in Bolivia, 1952–1982*. London: Verso, 1984.

———. "The United States and Latin America in the Long Run (1800–1945)." In *The United States and Latin America: The New Agenda*, ed. Victor Bulmer-Thomas and James Dunkerley, 3–32. Cambridge: David Rockefeller Center for Latin American Studies, Harvard University Press, 1999.

Dwyer, John J. "Diplomatic Weapons of the Weak: Mexican Policymaking During the U.S.–Mexican Agrarian Dispute, 1934–1941." *Diplomatic History* 26, no. 3 (Summer 2002): 375–95.

Eckstein, Susan. *Impact of Revolution: A Comparative Analysis of Mexico and Bolivia*. London: Sage Publications, 1976.

Economic Commission for Latin America (ECLA). "Economic Policy of Bolivia in 1952–64." *Economic Bulletin for Latin America* 12, no. 2 (October 1967): 61–90.

Edgerton, Russell. *Sub-Cabinet Politics and Policy Commitment: The Birth of the Development Loan Fund*. Syracuse: Inter-University Case Program, 1970.

Eichengreen, Barry. "House Calls of the Money Doctor: The Kemmerer Missions to Latin America, 1917–1931." In *Money Doctors, Foreign Debts, and Economic Reforms in Latin America from the 1890s to the Present*, ed. Paul Drake, 110–31. Wilmington, Del.: Scholarly Resources, 1994.

Escobar, Arturo. *Encountering Development: The Making and Unmaking of the Third World*. Princeton: Princeton University Press, 1995.

"Expulsión del Cuerpo de Paz." *El Diario*, May 25, 1971, 2.

Fagan, Brian. *Time Detectives*. New York: Simon and Schuster, 1995.

Farcau, Bruce W. *The Chaco War: Bolivia and Paraguay, 1932–1935*. New York: Praeger, 1996.

Farthing, Linda. "Social Impacts Associated with Antidrug Law 1008." In *Coca, Cocaine, and the Bolivian Reality*, ed. Madeline Barbara Léons and Harry Sanabria, 253–73. Albany: State University of New York Press, 1997.

Ffrench-Davis, Ricardo. *Reforming the Reforms in Latin America*. Oxford: Macmillan, 2000.

Fifer, J. Valerie. *Bolivia: Land, Location, and Politics Since 1825*. Cambridge: Cambridge University Press, 1972.

Franco Guachalla, Alfredo. *Acotaciones para la doctrina del partido*. La Paz: Editorial "Casegural," 1961. Pittsburgh Pamphlets.

Frank, Andre Gunder. *Latin America: Underdevelopment or Revolution*. New York: Monthly Review Press, 1969.

Fraser, Cary. "An American Dilemma: Race and Realpolitik in the American Response to the Bandung Conference, 1955." In *Window on Freedom: Race, Civil Rights, and Foreign Affairs, 1945–1988*, ed. Brenda Gayle Plummer, 115–40. Chapel Hill: University of North Carolina Press, 2003.

Friedman, Max Paul. *Nazis and Good Neighbors: The United States Campaign Against the Germans of Latin America During World War II*. New York: Cambridge University Press, 2003.

———. "Retiring the Puppets, Bringing Latin America Back In: Recent Scholarship on United States–Latin American Relations." *Diplomatic History* 27, no. 5 (November 2003): 621–36.

Frontaura Argandoña, Manuel. *La revolución nacional*. La Paz: Editorial Los Amigos del Libro, 1974.

Galarza, Ernesto. "Debts, Dictatorship, and Revolution in Bolivia and Peru." *Foreign Policy Reports*, May 13, 1931, 101–18.

Gamarra, Eduardo A. *Entre la droga y la democracía: La cooperación entre Estados Unidos–Bolivia y la lucha contra el narcotráfico*. La Paz: El Instituto Latinoamericano de Investigaciones Sociales [ILDIS], 1994.

———. "Fighting Drugs in Bolivia: United States and Bolivian Perceptions at Odds." In *Coca, Cocaine, and the Bolivian Reality*, ed. Madeline Barbara Léons and Harry Sanabria. Albany: State University of New York Press, 1997.

———. "Market-Oriented Reforms and Democratization in Latin America: Challenges of the 1990s." In *Latin American Political Economy in the Age of Neoliberal Reform: Theoretical and Comparative Perspectives for the 1990s*, ed. William C. Smith, Carlos H. Acuña, and Eduardo Gamarra, 85–126. New Brunswick, N.J.: Transaction, 1994.

———. "The United States and Bolivia: Fighting the Drug War." In *The United States and Latin America: The New Agenda*, ed. Victor Bulmar-Thomas and James Dunkerley, 177–206. Cambridge: David Rockefeller Center for Latin American Studies, Harvard University Press, 1999.

Gamboa Rocabado, Franco. *Itinerario de la esperanza y el desconcierto: Ensayos sobre política, sociedad y democracia en Bolivia*. La Paz: Muela del Diablo Editores, 2001.

Gilderhus, Mark T. "An Emerging Synthesis? U.S.–Latin American Relations Since the Second World War." *Diplomatic History* 16 (Summer 1992): 429–52.

———. *The Second Century: U.S.–Latin American Relations Since 1889*. Wilmington, Del.: Scholarly Resources, 2000.

Gildner, Matthew. "Revolution, Recognition, and Reconciliation: Bolivia, the United States, and the Alliance for Progress, 1961–1964." Unpublished paper in possession of the author. N.d.

Gleijeses, Piero. *Conflicting Missions: Havana, Washington, and Africa, 1959–1976*. Chapel Hill: University of North Carolina Press, 2002.

———. *The Dominican Crisis: The 1965 Constitutionalist Revolt and American Intervention*. Baltimore: Johns Hopkins University Press, 1978.

Goodman, Walter. "ABC on the Trail of Cocaine Traffickers in Bolivia." *New York Times*, December 28, 1992, C16.

Gordillo, José M. *Arando en la historia: La experiencia política campesina en Cochabamba*. La Paz: Universidad Mayor de San Simón, Plural Editores Centro de Estudio de la Realidad Económica y Social, 1998.

———. *Campesinos revolucionarios en Bolivia: Identidad, territorio y sexualidad en el Valle Alto de Cochabamba, 1952–1964*. La Paz: Promec, 1999.

Gotkowitz, Laura. *A Revolution for Our Rights: Indigenous Struggles for Land and Justice in Bolivia, 1880–1952*. Durham: Duke University Press, 2007.

———. "'Under the Dominion of the Indian': Rural Mobilization, the Law, and Revolutionary Nationalism in Bolivia in the 1940s." In *Political Cultures in the Andes, 1750–1950*, ed. Nils Jacobsen and Cristóbal Aljovín de Losada, 137–58. Durham: Duke University Press, 2005.
Grandin, Greg. *Empire's Workshop: Latin America, the United States, and the Rise of a New Imperialism*. New York: Metropolitan Books / Holt Paperbacks, 2007.
Green, David. *The Containment of Latin America*. Chicago: Quadrangle, 1971.
Grindle, Merilee S. "1952 and All That: The Bolivian Revolution in Comparative Perspective." In *Proclaiming Revolution: Bolivia in Comparative Perspective*, ed. Merilee S. Grindle and Pilar Dominguez, 1–21. Cambridge: David Rockefeller Center for Latin American Studies, Harvard University Press, 2003.
Griscom, Richard. "Bolivia: Impetus Is to East in Land Beset by Geography." *Peace Corps Volunteer* 3 (February 1965): 8–16.
Gumucio Dagron, Alfonso. *Historia del cine en Bolivia* La Paz: Editorial Los Amigos del Libro, 1982.
———. "Yawar Mallku." In *South American Cinema: A Critical Filmography, 1915–1994*, ed. Timothy Barnard and Peter Rist, 92–94. Austin: University of Texas Press, 1996.
Harris, Richard. *Death of a Revolutionary*. New York: W. W. Norton, 2000.
Harrison, Lawrence. *Underdevelopment Is a State of Mind: The Case of Latin America*. Cambridge: Harvard University Press, 1985.
Hartz, Louis. *The Liberal Tradition in America*. New York: Harcourt Brace, 1955.
Harvey, David. *A Brief History of Neoliberalism*. Oxford: Oxford University Press, 2005.
Healy, Kevin. *Caciques y patrones, una experiencia de desarrollo rural en el sud de Bolivia*. Cochabamba: Ediciones El Buitre, 1983.
———. *Llamas, Weavings, and Organic Chocolate: Multicultural Grassroots Development in the Andes and Amazon of Bolivia*. Notre Dame: University of Notre Dame Press, 2001.
Heath, Dwight B. "The Emerging Volunteer Subculture in Bolivia." In *Cultural Frontiers of the Peace Corps*, ed. Robert B. Textor and Lambros Comitas, 271–97. Cambridge: MIT Press, 1966.
Heath, Dwight B., Charles J. Erasmus, and Hans C. Buechler. *Land Reform and Social Revolution in Bolivia*. New York: F. A. Praeger, 1969.
Heller, Jack, and Miguel S. Wionczek. "The Assumptions of the Alliance." In *The Alliance for Progress: A Retrospective*, ed. L. Ronald Scheman, 131–38. New York: Praeger, 1988.
Hersh, Seymour M. *The Price of Power: Kissinger in the Nixon White House*. New York: Summit, 1983.
Hoffman, Elizabeth Cobbs. *All You Need is Love: The Peace Corps and the Spirit of the 1960s*. Cambridge: Harvard University Press, 1998.
Hofstadter, Richard. *The American Political Tradition*. New York: Vintage, 1948.
Holland, Emmett James. *A Historical Study of Bolivian Foreign Relations, 1935–1946*. Ph.D. diss., American University, 1967.
Humphreys, R. A. *Latin America and the Second World War*. Vol. 1, *1939–1942*. London: Athlone, 1981.
Immerman, Richard. *The CIA in Guatemala*. Austin: University of Texas Press, 1982.
Ingram, George M. *Expropriation of U.S. Property in South America: Nationalization of Oil and Copper Companies in Peru, Bolivia, and Chile*. New York: Praeger, 1974.

Isacson, Adam. "The U.S. Military in the War on Drugs." In *Drugs and Democracy in Latin America: The Impact of U.S. Policy*, ed. Coletta A. Youngers and Eileen Rosin, 19–47. Boulder, Colo.: Lynne Rienner, 2005.
"ISAL respalda solicitud de expulsión del Cuerpo de Paz." *El Diario*, May 20, 1971, 2.
James, Daniel. "Introduction." In Che Guevara, *The Complete Bolivian Diaries of Che Guevara and Other Captured Documents*, 11–69. New York: Cooper Square Press, 2000.
Jameson, Kenneth P. "Austerity Programs Under Conditions of Political Instability and Economic Depression: The Case of Bolivia." In *Paying the Costs of Austerity in Latin America*, ed. Howard Handelman and Werner Baer, 90–91. Boulder, Colo.: Westview Press, 1989.
Jáuregui, Juan H. "Pucarani: Apuntes para una historia regional." *Historia: Revista de la Carrera de Historia* 23 (1998): 105–21.
Joseph, Gilbert M., and Daniel Nugent, eds., *Revolution and the Negotiation of Rule in Modern Mexico*. Durham: Duke University Press, 1999.
Kahin, George McTurnan. *Intervention: The United States and Vietnam*. New York: Knopf, 1986.
Kamimura, Naoki. "Liberal America and Revolution: U.S. Cold War Policy and the Bolivian Revolution of 1952." Paper prepared for presentation at the 1997 Society of Historians of American Foreign Policy Annual Conference, Georgetown University, June 19–22, 1997.
Karabell, Zachary. *Architects of Intervention: The United States, the Third World, and the Cold War, 1946–1962*. Baton Rouge: Louisiana State University Press, 1999.
Kasun, Jacqueline R. *The War Against Population: The Economics and Ideology of World Population Control*. San Francisco: Ignatius Press, 1988.
Kaufman, Burton I. *Trade Not Aid: Eisenhower's Foreign Economic Policy*. Baltimore: Johns Hopkins University Press, 1982.
Keen, Benjamin, and Keith Haynes. *A History of Latin America*. 6th ed. Boston: Houghton Mifflin, 2000.
Kelley, Jonathan, and Herbert S. Klein. *Revolution and the Rebirth of Inequality*. Berkeley and Los Angeles: University of California Press, 1981.
Kenworthy, Eldon. *America/Américas: Myth in the Making of U.S. Policy Toward Latin America*. University Park: Pennsylvania State University Press, 1995.
Kirkland, Robert O. *Observing Our Hermanos de Armas: U.S. Military Attachés in Guatemala, Cuba, and Bolivia, 1950–1964*. New York: Routledge, 2003.
Klarén, Peter F. "Lost Promise: Explaining Latin American Development." In *Promise of Development*, ed. Peter F. Klarén and Thomas J. Bossert, 3–33. Boulder, Colo.: Westview Press, 1987.
Klein, Herbert S. *Bolivia: The Evolution of a Multi-ethnic Society*. 2nd ed. New York: Oxford University Press, 1992.
———. *A Concise History of Bolivia*. Cambridge: Cambridge University Press, 2003.
———. *Orígenes de la revolución nacional boliviana: La crisis de la generación del Chaco*. Translated by Rodolfo Medrano. La Paz: Editorial Juventud, 1968. Microfilm.
———. *Parties and Political Change in Bolivia, 1880–1952*. New York: Cambridge University Press, 1969.

Kohl, Benjamin, and Linda Farthing. *Impasse in Bolivia: Neoliberal Hegemony and Popular Resistance.* London: Zed Books, 2006.
Kohl, James V. "National Revolution to Revolution of Restoration: Arms and Factional Politics in Bolivia." *Inter-American Economic Affairs* 39, no. 1 (Summer 1985): 3–30.
Kolko, Gabriel. *Confronting the Third World: United States Foreign Policy, 1945–1980.* New York: Pantheon Books, 1988.
Kornbluh, Peter. *The Pinochet Files: A Declassified Dossier on Atrocity and Accountability.* New York: Free Press, 2003.
Krenn, Michael. *Black Diplomacy: African Americans in the State Department, 1945–1966.* Armonk, N.Y.: M. E. Sharpe, 1999.
———. *Economic Nationalism in Latin America.* Wilmington, Del.: Scholarly Resources, 1990.
Kruijt, Dirk. *Revolution by Decree: Peru, 1968–1975.* Amsterdam: Thela, 1994.
Kryzanek, Michael J. *U.S.–Latin American Relations.* 2nd ed. Westport, Conn.: Praeger, 1990.
LaFeber, Walter. "The Alliances for Progress." In *Bordering on Trouble: Resources and Politics in Latin America,* ed. Andrew Maguire and Janet Welsh Brown, 337–99. Bethesda, Md.: Adler and Adler, 1986.
———. *The American Age: U.S. Foreign Policy at Home and Abroad.* 2nd ed. 2 volumes in 1. New York: W. W. Norton, 1994.
———. "The Evolution of the Monroe Doctrine from Monroe to Reagan." In *Redefining the Past: Essays in Diplomatic History in Honor of William Appleman Williams,* ed. Lloyd C. Gardner, 121–45. Corvallis: Oregon State University Press, 1986.
———. *Inevitable Revolutions: The United States in Central America.* 2nd ed. New York: W. W. Norton, 1993.
———. "Thomas C. Mann and the Devolution of Latin American Policy: From the Good Neighbor to Military Intervention." In *Behind the Throne: Servants of Power to Imperial Presidents, 1898–1968,* ed. Thomas J. McCormick and Walter LaFeber, 166–203. Madison: University of Wisconsin Press, 1993.
"La madre proletaria." *El Diario,* May 27, 1971, 2.
Langer, Erick D. "Andean Rituals of Revolt: The Chayanta Rebellion of 1927." *Ethnohistory* 37 (1990): 227–53.
———. *Economic Change and Rural Resistance in Southern Bolivia.* Stanford: Stanford University Press, 1989.
Latham, Michael. *Modernization as Ideology: American Social Science and "Nation Building" in the Kennedy Era.* Chapel Hill: University of North Carolina Press, 2000.
Ledebur, Kathryn. "Bolivia: Clear Consequences." In *Drugs and Democracy in Latin America,* ed. Coletta A. Youngers and Eileen Rosin, 145–71. Boulder, Colo.: Lynne Rienner, 2005.
Ledebur, Kathryn, and Coletta A. Youngers. "Balancing Act: Bolivia's Drug Control Advances and Challenges." May 2008, 2. http://www.wola.org/media/AIN-WOLA%20Balancing%20Act%205-23-08.pdf (accessed June 25, 2008).
Lehman, Kenneth. *Bolivia and the United States: A Limited Partnership.* Athens: University of Georgia Press, 1999.

———. "Braked but Not Broken: Mexico and Bolivia; Factoring the United States into the Revolutionary Equation." In *Proclaiming Revolution: Bolivia in Comparative Perspective*, ed. Merilee S. Grindle and Pilar Domingo, 91–113. Cambridge: David Rockefeller Center for Latin American Studies, Harvard University Press, 2003.

———. "A 'Medicine of Death'? U.S. Policy and Political Disarray in Bolivia, 1985–2000." In *Addicted to Failure: U.S. Security Policy in Latin America and the Andean Region*, ed. Brian Loveman, 130–68. Lanham, Md.: Rowman and Littlefield, 2006.

———. "Revolutions and Attributions: Making Sense of Eisenhower Administration Policies in Bolivia and Guatemala." *Diplomatic History* 21 (Spring 1997): 185–213.

———. "U.S. Foreign Aid and Revolutionary Nationalism in Bolivia, 1952–1964: The Pragmatics of a Patron-Client Relationship." Ph.D. diss., University of Texas, 1992.

Lerdau, Enrique. "The Alliance for Progress: The Learning Experience." In *The Alliance for Progress: A Retrospective*, ed. L. Ronald Scheman, 165–84. New York: Praeger, 1988.

Levinson, Jerome, and Juan de Onís. *The Alliance That Lost Its Way*. Chicago: Quadrangle, 1970.

Loayza, Matthew. "An 'Aladdin's Lamp' for Free Enterprise: Eisenhower, Fiscal Conservatism, and Latin American Nationalism, 1953–61." *Diplomacy and Statecraft* 14 (September 2003): 83–105.

Longley, Kyle. *In the Eagle's Shadow: The United States and Latin America*. Wheeling, Ill.: Harlan Davidson, 2002.

———. *The Sparrow and the Hawk: Costa Rica and the United States During the Rise of José Figueres*. Tuscaloosa: University of Alabama Press, 1997.

Lora, Guillermo. *A History of the Bolivian Labour Movement, 1848–1971*. Edited by Lawrence Whitehead. Translated by Christine Whitehead. Cambridge: Cambridge University Press, 1977.

Loveman, Brian. *Chile: A History of Hispanic Capitalism*. 3rd ed. New York: Oxford University Press, 2001.

Lowenthal, Abraham. *The Dominican Intervention*. 2nd ed. Baltimore: Johns Hopkins University Press, 1995.

———. "'Liberal,' 'Radical,' and 'Bureaucratic' Perspectives on U.S. Latin American Policy: The Case of the Alliance for Progress." In *Latin America and the United States: Changing Relations*, ed. Julio Cotler and Richard Fagen, 212–38. Stanford: Stanford University Press, 1974.

Lowther, Kevin, and C. Payne Lucas. *Keeping Kennedy's Promise: The Peace Corps and the Unmet Hope of the New Frontier*. Boulder, Colo.: Westview Press, 1978.

MacGregor, Felipe E. *Coca and Cocaine: An Andean Perspective*. Translated by Jonathan Cavanagh and Rosemary Underhay. Westport, Conn.: Greenwood Press, 1993.

MacLeod, Murdo J. "The Bolivian Novel, the Chaco War, and the Revolution." In *Beyond the Revolution: Bolivia Since 1952*, ed. James M. Malloy and Richard S. Thorn, 341–65. Pittsburgh: University of Pittsburgh Press, 1971.

Malamud-Goti, Jaime. *Smoke and Mirrors: The Paradox of the Drug Wars*. Boulder, Colo.: Westview Press, 1992.

Mallon, Florencia. *Peasant and Nation: The Making of Postcolonial Mexico and Peru.* Berkeley and Los Angeles: University of California Press, 1995.
Malloy, James M. *Bolivia: The Uncompleted Revolution.* Pittsburgh: University of Pittsburgh Press, 1970.
———. "Revolutionary Politics." In *Beyond the Revolution: Bolivia Since 1952,* ed. James M. Malloy and Richard Thorn, 111–56. Pittsburgh: University of Pittsburgh Press, 1971.
Marsh, Margaret A. *Bankers in Bolivia: A Study of Foreign Investment.* 1928. Reprint, New York: Vanguard Press, 1970.
Martin, Edwin McCammon. *Kennedy and Latin America.* Lanham, Md.: University Press of America, 1994.
Martin, Lois Deicke. "Bolivia in 1956: An Analysis of Political and Economic Events." *Hispanic American Report: An Analysis of Developments in Spain, Portugal, and Latin America* 11, no. 1 (1958): 20–21.
May, Gary. "Passing the Torch and Lighting Fires: The Peace Corps." In *Kennedy's Quest for Victory: American Foreign Policy, 1961–1963,* ed. Thomas G. Paterson, 284–315. New York: Oxford, 1989.
McMahon, Robert J. "Introduction." In *Empire and Revolution: The United States and the Third World Since 1945,* ed. Peter Hahn and Mary Ann Heiss. Columbus: Ohio State University Press, 2001.
———. *The Limits of Empire: The United States and Southeast Asia Since World War II.* New York: Columbia University Press, 1999.
McPherson, Alan, ed. *Anti-Americanism in Latin America and the Caribbean.* New York: Berghahn Books, 2006.
Menzel, Sewall H. *Fire in the Andes: U.S. Foreign Policy and Cocaine Politics in Bolivia and Peru.* Lanham, Md.: University Press of America, 1996.
Mesa Gisbert, Carlos D. *La aventura del cine boliviano, 1952–1985.* La Paz: Editorial Gisbert, 1985.
———. *Cine boliviano: Del realizador al crítico.* La Paz: Editorial Gisbert, 1979.
Mitchell, Christopher. *The Legacy of Populism in Bolivia: from the MNR to Military Rule.* New York: Praeger, 1977.
Montenegro, Carlos. *Nacionalismo y coloniaje, su expresión histórica en la prensa de Bolivia.* La Paz: Ediciones Autonomía, 1943.
Morales, Juan Antonio. "Democracy, Economic Liberalism, and Structural Reform in Bolivia." In *Democracy, Markets, and Structural Reform in Latin America: Argentina, Bolivia, Brazil, Chile, and Mexico,* ed. William C. Smith, Carlos H. Acuña, and Eduardo Gamarra, 143–64. New Brunswick, N.J.: Transaction, 1994.
Morales, Waltraud Q. "Political Economy of Bolivia's Foreign Policy." *Bolivian Studies Journal* 9 (2001): 113–237.
Navia Ribera, Carlos. *Los Estados Unidos y la revolución nacional: Entre el pragmatismo y el sometimiento.* Cochabamba: Centro de Información y Documentación para el Desarrollo Regional, 1984.
Nicastro, Thomas James. "Community Development Training in Peace Corps / Latin America: With Special Emphasis on Bolivia." Master's thesis, University of Missouri, 1969.
Nieto, Clara. *Masters of War: Latin America and United States Aggression from the Cuban Revolution Through the Clinton Years.* Translated by Chris Brandt. New York: Seven Stories Press, 2003.

Nugent, David. *Modernity at the Edge of Empire: State, Individual, and Nation in the Northern Peruvian Andes, 1885–1935.* Stanford: Stanford University Press, 1997.

O'Brien, Thomas F. *The Century of U.S. Capitalism in Latin America.* Albuquerque: University of New Mexico Press, 1999.

———. *Making the Americas: The United States and Latin America from the Age of Revolutions to the Era of Globalization.* Albuquerque: University of New Mexico Press, 2007.

O'Donnell, Guillermo. "Towards an Alternative Conceptualization of South American Politics." In *Promise of Development: Theories of Change in Latin America,* ed. Peter F. Klarén and Thomas J. Bossert, 239–75. Boulder, Colo.: Westview Press, 1987.

Onís, Juan de. "Bolivia Yields to Left-Wing Pressure." *New York Times,* July 8, 1971, 4.

Orias Arredondo, Ramiro. "Bolivia: Democracy Under Pressure." In *The Andes in Focus: Security, Democracy, and Economic Reform,* ed. Russell Crandall, Guadalupe Paz, and Riordan Roett. Boulder, Colo.: Lynne Rienner, 2005.

Orias Luna, Guido, et al., eds. *16 personajes paceños.* La Paz: Ediciones Casa de la Cultura, 1988.

Packenham, Robert. *Dependency Movement: Scholarship and Politics in Development Studies.* Cambridge: Harvard University Press, 1992.

———. *Liberal America and the Third World.* Princeton: Princeton University Press, 1973.

Park, James William. *Latin American Underdevelopment: A History of Perspectives in the United States, 1970–1965.* Baton Rouge: Louisiana State University Press, 1995.

Parker, Jason. "Small Victory, Missed Chance: The Eisenhower Administration, the Bandung Conference, and the Turning of the Cold War." In *The Eisenhower Administration, the Third World, and the Globalization of the Cold War,* ed. Kathryn C. Statler and Andrew L. Johns, 153–74. Lanham, Md.: Rowman and Littlefield, 2006.

Paterson, Thomas G., J. Garry Clifford, and Kenneth J. Hagan. *American Foreign Relations: A History Since 1895.* Vol. 2. 5th ed. Boston: Houghton Mifflin, 2000.

Pentland, Joseph Barclay. "Report on Bolivia, 1827." *Camden Miscellany,* vol. 25. Camden Fourth Series, vol. 13, ed. J. Valerie Fifer, 169–267. London: Royal Historical Society, 1974.

Pike, Frederick B. *The United States and the Andean Republics: Peru, Bolivia, and Ecuador.* Cambridge: Harvard University Press, 1977.

Plummer, Brenda Gayle. *Rising Wind: Black Americans and U.S. Foreign Affairs, 1935–1960.* Chapel Hill: University of North Carolina Press, 1996.

———. *Window on Freedom: Race, Civil Rights, and Foreign Affairs, 1945–1988.* Chapel Hill: University of North Carolina Press, 2003.

Postero, Nancy Grey. *Now We Are Citizens: Indigenous Politics in Postmulticultural Bolivia.* Stanford: Stanford University Press, 2007.

Powers, William. *Whispering in the Giant's Ear: A Frontline Chronicle from Bolivia's War on Globalization.* New York: Bloomsbury, 2006.

Purnell, Jennie. *Popular Movements and State Formation in Revolutionary Mexico: The Agraristas and Cristeros of Michoacán.* Durham: Duke University Press, 1999.

Quebracho [Libario Justo]. *Bolivia: La Revolución Derrotada*. Cochabamba: n.p., 1967.
Querejazu Calvo, Roberto. *Historia de la Guerra del Chaco*. La Paz: Librería Editorial "Juventud," 1990.
Quintana T., Juan Ramón. "El servicio militar obligatorio en América Latina y Bolivia: Una aproximación al estado de la cuestión afin de siglo." In *Visiones de fin de siglo: Bolivia y América Latina en el siglo XX*, ed. Dora Cajías, Madalena Cajías, Carmen Johnson, and Iris Villegas, 223–45. La Paz: IFEA / Coordinadora de Historia, Embajada de España en Bolivia, 2001.
Rabe, Stephen G. "Controlling Revolutions: Latin America, the Alliance for Progress, and Cold War Anti-communism." In *Kennedy's Quest for Victory: American Foreign Policy, 1961–1963*, ed. Thomas G. Paterson, 105–22. New York: Oxford University Press, 1989.
———. *Eisenhower and Latin America: The Foreign Policy of Anticommunism*. Chapel Hill: University of North Carolina Press, 1988.
———. "Marching Ahead (Slowly): The Historiography of Inter-American Relations." *Diplomatic History* 13 (Summer 1989): 300–20.
———. *The Most Dangerous Area of the World: John F. Kennedy Confronts Communist Revolution in Latin America*. Chapel Hill: University of North Carolina Press, 1999.
Radu, Michael. "A Matter of Identity: The Anti-Americanism of Latin American Intellectuals." In *Understanding Anti-Americanism: Its Origins and Impact at Home and Abroad*, ed. Paul Hollander, 144–64. Chicago: Ivan R. Dee, 2004.
Redmon, Coates. *Come As You Are: The Peace Corps Story*. San Diego: Harcourt Brace Jovanovich, 1986.
Rice, Gerard T. *Twenty Years of the Peace Corps*. Washington, D.C.: Peace Corps, U.S. Government Printing Office, 1981.
Rich, William. "Smaller Families Through Social and Economic Progress." In *New Directions in Development: Latin America, Export Credit, Population Growth, and U.S. Attitudes*, ed. Colin I. Bradford et al., 193–286. New York: Praeger, 1974.
Rivas, Darlene. "Like Boxing with Joe Louis: Nelson Rockefeller in Venezuela, 1945–1948." In *Empire and Revolution: The United States and the Third World Since 1945*, ed. Peter Hahn and Mary Ann Heiss, 217–41. Columbus: Ohio State University Press, 2001.
Rivera Cusicanqui, Silvia. *"Oppressed but Not Defeated": Peasant Struggles Among the Aymara and Qhechwa in Bolivia, 1900–1980*. Geneva: U.N. Research Institute for Social Development, 1987.
Rodríguez, Daniel. "Exigen una investigación de las actividades del tenebrosos Ku Klux Klan." *El Diario*. April 17, 1971, 7.
———. "Goodbye Cuerpo de Paz." *El Diario*, May 23, 1971, 2.
Rodríguez Ostria, Gustavo. "Bolivia en el ciclo guerrillero, 1963–1970: Continuidades y diferencias," *La Prensa*, July 17, 2005, 3.
———. *Sin tiempo para las palabras: Teoponte, la otra guerrilla guevarista en Bolivia*. La Paz: Grupo Editorial Kipus, 2006.
———. *El Socavón y el sindicato: Ensayos historicos sobre los trabajadores mineros, siglos XIX–XX*. La Paz: Instituto Latinoamericano de Investigaciones Sociales (ILDIS), 1991.
———. "Teoponte: La otra guerrilla guevarista en Bolivia." *La Prensa*, July 17, 2005, 3–6.

Ronning, C. Neale, and Albert P. Vannucci. *Ambassadors in Foreign Policy: The Influence of Individuals on U.S.–Latin American Policy.* New York: Praeger, 1987.
Roque Bacarreza, Francisco. *Los años del condor: Sesenta crónicas del triunfo revolucionario boliviano en plena Guerra Fría.* La Paz: Mundy Color, 1996.
Rosenberg, Emily S. *Financial Missionaries to the World: The Politics and Culture of Dollar Diplomacy, 1900–1930.* Cambridge: Harvard University Press, 1999.
——— . *Spreading the American Dream: Economic and Cultural Expansion, 1890–1945.* New York: Hill and Wang, 1982.
Rosenberg, Emily S., and Norman L. Rosenberg. "From Colonialism to Professionalism: The Public Private Dynamic in United States Foreign Financial Advising, 1898–1929." In *Money Doctors, Foreign Debts, and Economic Reforms in Latin America from the 1890s to the Present,* ed. Paul Drake, 59–83. Wilmington, Del.: Scholarly Resources, 1994.
Rosenberg, Robin L. "OAS and Summit of the Americas: Coexistence or Integration of Forces for Multilateralism?" *Latin American Politics and Society* 43 (Spring 2001): 83–109.
Rotchin, Glen. *The Clientelist State and International Patronage: The Case of Revolutionary Bolivia, 1952–1964.* Master's thesis, Institut Universitaire de Hautes Études Internationales (Geneva), 1994.
Rowland, Donald W. *History of the Office of the Coordinator of Inter-American Affairs.* Washington, D.C.: Government Printing Office, 1947.
Ryan, Henry Butterfield. *The Fall of Che Guevara: A Story of Soldiers, Spies, and Diplomats.* New York: Oxford University Press, 1998.
Sanders, G. Earl. "The Quiet Experiment in U.S Foreign Policy." *The Americas* 33 (Spring 1976): 25–49.
Sanjines Goitia, Julio. *148 años de las relaciones diplomáticas Bolivia–Estados Unidos.* La Paz: Centro Boliviano Americano, 1996.
Santos, Theotonio dos. "The Structure of Dependence." *American Economic Review* 60 (1970): 231–36.
Schlesinger, Stephen, and Stephen Kinzer. *Bitter Fruit: The Story of the American Coup in Guatemala.* Rev. and expanded ed. Cambridge: David Rockefeller Center for Latin American Studies, Harvard University Press, 2005.
Schultz, Donald. "Heifer Helps Cochabamba." *Peace Corps Volunteer* 3 (February 1965): 3–6.
Scobari de Querejazu, Laura. *Historia de la industria molinera boliviana.* La Paz: Asociación de Industriales Molineros, 1987.
Scott, James C. *Domination and the Arts of Resistance: Hidden Transcripts.* New Haven: Yale University Press, 1990.
——— . *Weapons of the Weak: Everyday Forms of Peasant Resistance.* New Haven: Yale University Press, 1985.
Seidel, Robert N. "American Reformers Abroad: The Kemmerer Missions in South America, 1923–1931." In *Money Doctors, Foreign Debts, and Economic Reforms in Latin America from the 1890s to the Present,* ed. Paul Drake, 85–109. Wilmington, Del.: Scholarly Resources, 1994.
Shafer, D. Michael. *Deadly Paradigms: The Failure of U.S. Counterinsurgency Policy.* Princeton: Princeton University Press, 1988.
Sharpless, John. "World Population Growth, Family Planning, and American Foreign Policy." In *The Politics of Abortion and Birth Control in Historical Perspective,* ed. Donald T. Critchlow, 72–102. University Park: Pennsylvania State University Press, 1996.

Sheffield, Glen F. "Peru and the Peace Corps, 1962–1968." Ph.D. diss., University of Connecticut, 1991.
Siekmeier, James F. *Aid, Nationalism, and Inter-American Relations: Guatemala, Bolivia, and the United States, 1945–1961*. Lewiston, N.Y.: Edwin Mellen Press, 1999.
———. "Fighting Economic Nationalism: United States Economic Aid and Development Policy Toward Latin America, 1952–1961." Ph.D. diss., Cornell University, 1993.
———. "Responding to Nationalism: The Bolivian Movimiento Nacionalista Revolucionario and the United States, 1952–1956." *Journal of American and Canadian Studies* 15 (Spring 1998): 39–58.
———. "'[T]he most generous assistance': U.S. Economic Aid to Guatemala and Bolivia, 1944–1959." *Journal of American and Canadian Studies* 11 (Spring 1994): 1–44.
———. "Trailblazer Diplomat: Víctor Andrade Uzquiano's Efforts to Influence U.S. Policy Towards Bolivia, 1944–1962." *Diplomatic History* 28, no. 3 (June 2004): 385–406.
Sivak, Martín. *Jefazo: Retrato íntimo de Evo Morales*. Santa Cruz, Bolivia: El Pais, 2008.
Skidmore, Thomas, and Peter H. Smith. *Modern Latin America*. 5th ed. New York: Oxford University Press, 2001.
Smith, Joseph. *The United States and Latin America: A History of American Diplomacy, 1776–2000*. New York: Routledge, 2005.
Smith, Robert Freeman. *The United States and Revolutionary Nationalism in Mexico, 1916–1932*. Chicago: University of Chicago Press, 1972.
Spedding, Alison L. "The Coca Field as Total Social Fact." In *Coca, Cocaine, and the Bolivian Reality*, ed. Madeline Barbara Leóns and Harry Sanabria, 47–70. Albany: State University of New York Press, 1997.
Spenser, Daniela. "The Caribbean Crisis: Catalyst for Soviet Projection into Latin America." In *In from the Cold: Latin America's New Encounter with the Cold War*, ed. Gilbert M. Joseph and Daniela Spenser, 77–111. Durham: Duke University Press, 2008.
Swansbrough, Robert H. *The Embattled Colossus: Economic Nationalism and United States Investors in Latin America*. Gainesville: University of Florida Press, 1976.
Taffett, Jeffrey F. *Foreign Aid as Foreign Policy: The Alliance for Progress in Latin America*. New York: Routledge, 2007.
Tancer, Shoshana B. *Economic Nationalism in Latin America: The Quest for Economic Independence*. New York: Praeger, 1976.
Tétreault, Mary Ann, and Charles Frederick Abel, eds. *Dependency Theory and the Return of High Politics*. Westport, Conn.: Greenwood Press, 1986.
Thorn, Richard S. "The Economic Transformation." In *Beyond the Revolution: Bolivia Since 1952*, ed. James M. Malloy and Richard S. Thorn, 157–216. Pittsburgh: University of Pittsburgh Press, 1971.
Torinia, Irma. *El nacionalismo en Bolivia de la pre y posguerra del Chaco, 1910–1945*. La Paz: Plural Editores, 2006.
Torres Calleja, Mario. *Ayuda Americana: Una experiencia frustrada*. La Paz: Federación Sindical de Trabajadores Mineros de Bolivia, 1962.
Tulchin, Joseph S. "The Promise of Progress: U.S. Relations with Latin America During the Administration of Lyndon B. Johnson." In *Lyndon Johnson Confronts the World: American Foreign Policy, 1963–1968*, ed. Warren I. Cohen

and Nancy Bernkopf Tucker, 211–44. New York: Cambridge University Press, 1994.
Vargas Llosa, Alvaro. "The Killing Machine: Che Guevara, from Communist Firebrand to Capitalist Brand." *New Republic*, July 11–18, 2005, 25–30.
Verdesoto, Luis, and Gloria Ardaya Salinas. *Entre la presión y el consenso: Escenarios y previsiones para la relación Bolivia– Estados Unidos*. La Paz: Unidad de Análisis de Política Exterior / Instituto Latinoamericano de Investigaciones Sociales, 1993.
Volk, Steve. "Tin and Imperialism." *NACLA's Latin America and Empire Report* 8, no. 2 (February 1974): 12–18.
Von Eschen, Penny M. *Race Against Empire: Black Americans and Anticolonialism, 1937–1957*. Ithaca: Cornell University Press, 1997.
Wallerstein, Immanuel. *The Modern World-System: Capitalist Agriculture and the Origins of the European World-Economy in the Sixteenth Century*. New York: Academic Press, 1976.
Weatherford, Jack M. *Narco'ticos en Bolivia y Los Estados Unidos*. La Paz: Editorial Los Amigos del Libro, 1987.
Whitehead, Laurence. "The Bolivian National Revolution: A Twenty-first-Century Perspective." In *Proclaiming Revolution: Bolivia in Comparative Perspective*, ed. Merilee S. Grindle and Pilar Dominguez, 25–47. Cambridge: David Rockefeller Center for Latin American Studies, Harvard University Press, 2003.
———. "Bolivia's Failed Democratization, 1977–1980." In *Transitions from Authoritarian Rule: Latin America*, ed. Guillermo O'Donnell, Philippe C. Schmitter, and Laurence Whitehead, 49–71. Baltimore: Johns Hopkins University Press, 1986.
———. *The United States and Bolivia: A Case of Neo-colonialism*. Oxford: Haslemere Group, 1969.
Wiarda, Howard J. "Corporatism and Development in the Iberic-Latin World: Persistent Strains and New Variations." In *The New Corporatism: Social-Political Structures in the Iberian World*, ed. Frederick B. Pike and Thomas Stritch, 3–36. Notre Dame: University of Notre Dame Press, 1974.
———. "Did the Alliance 'Lose its Way,' or Were Its Assumptions All Wrong from the Beginning and Are Those Assumptions Still with Us?" In *The Alliance for Progress: A Retrospective*, ed. L. Ronald Scheman, 95–118. New York: Praeger, 1988.
Wickham-Crowley, Timothy P. *Guerrillas and Revolution in Latin America: A Comparative Study of Insurgents and Regimes Since 1956*. Princeton: Princeton University Press, 1992.
———. "Terror and Guerrilla Warfare in Latin America, 1956–1970." *Comparative Studies in Society and History* 32 (April 1990): 201–37.
Wilkie, James W. "Bolivia: Ironies in the National Revolutionary Process, 1952–86." *Statistical Abstract of Latin America (SALA)* 25, ed. James W. Wilkie and David Lorey (1987): 911–28.
———. *Bolivian Foreign Trade: Historical Problems and MNR Revolutionary Policy, 1952–64*. Buffalo: Council on International Studies, State University of New York at Buffalo, 1971.
———. *The Bolivian Revolution and U.S. Aid Since 1952*. Los Angeles: Latin American Center, University of California, 1969.

———. "U.S. Foreign Policy and Economic Assistance in Bolivia, 1948–1976." In *Modern-Day Bolivia*, ed. Jerry R. Ladman, 83–121. Tempe: Arizona State University Press, 1982.
Williams, Mark Eric. "U.S. Policy in the Andes: Commitments and Commitment Traps," In *The Andes in Focus: Security, Democracy, and Economic Reform*, ed. Russell Crandall, Guadalupe Paz, and Riordan Roett. Boulder, Colo.: Lynne Rienner, 2005.
Windmiller, Marshall. *The Peace Corps and Pax Americana*. Washington, D.C.: Public Affairs Press, 1970.
Wittner, Lawrence S. *American Intervention in Greece, 1943–1947*. New York: Columbia University Press, 1982.
Wood, Bryce. *The Dismantling of the Good Neighbor Policy*. Austin: University of Texas Press, 1985.
———. *The Making of the Good Neighbor Policy*. New York: Columbia University Press, 1961.
Wright, Thomas C. *Latin America in the Era of the Cuban Revolution*. Rev. ed. New York: Praeger, 2001.
Zavaleta Mercado, René. *La caída del MNR y la conjuración de noviembre: Historia del golpe militar del 4 de noviembre de 1964 en Bolivia*. Cochabamba: Editorial Los Amigos del Libro, 1995.
Zheng, Guoqiang. "The Invisible Hand: The United States and the Aftermath of the Tibetan Revolt, 1959–1960." *American Review of China Studies: Journal of the Association of Chinese Professors of Social Sciences in the U.S.* 4 (Spring 2003): 49–64.
Zieger, Robert. *The CIO, 1935–1955*. Chapel Hill: University of North Carolina Press, 1995.
Zimmerman, Jonathan. "Beyond Double Consciousness: Black Peace Corps Volunteers in Africa, 1961–1971." *Journal of American History* 82 (1995): 999–1028.
Zorrilla, Jose Gamarra. *Liberalismo y neoliberalismo: Breve intrerpretación de la historia política de Bolivia (1879–1993)*. La Paz: Editorial Los Amigos del Libro, 1993.
Zoumaras, Thomas. "Path to Pan-Americanism: Eisenhower's Foreign Economic Policy Toward Latin America." Ph.D. diss., University of Connecticut, 1987.
Zunes, John Stephen. "Decisions on Intervention: United States Responses to Third World Revolutionary Movements." Ph.D. diss., Department of Government, Cornell University, 1990.
———. "The United States and Bolivia: The Taming of a Revolution, 1952–1957." *Latin American Perspectives* 28 (September 2001): 33–49.

INDEX

Acción Democrática (AD, Venezuela), 44–45, 69n141
African Americans, 140
agriculture, Bolivian, 23, 24, 42
  undermined by U.S. policies, 52, 158
Aguas de Tunari, 172
Ajacopa, José M., 30
Allende Gossens, Salvador, 104–5, 121, 122–23
Alliance for Progress, 86, 97, 100, 106
  anticommunist goal of, 91, 104, 136
  Bolivia and, 85, 93–94
  failure of, 88–89, 140
  as U.S. foreign policy centerpiece, 87
Andean Strategy, 166–67
Andrade Uzquiano, Víctor, 77–78
  as advocate for MNR moderates, 56, 64, 71, 72
  anticommunist assurances of, 46–47, 63
  on Bolivia as test case for aid, 55, 69–70
  on Bolivia's tin, 36–37, 53, 67
  cajoles aid from U.S., 8, 48, 61, 62–63, 69
  career of, 8, 37, 55, 56n84
  cultivates U.S. contacts, 56, 66, 68
  defends against tin barons, 62, 69–70n142, 72
  on Economic Stabilization Plan, 71, 75
  as educator about Bolivia, 8, 67, 68–69
  Indian background of, 57–58
  key role of, 8, 55, 83
  use of U.S. media by, 62, 67
  at World Labor Conference, 59–60
anti-Americanism, 9, 10, 11, 121, 128, 131
  attacks on U.S. offices, 77–78, 128
  and Peace Corps, 140, 143–44, 146, 151
  resentment against "colossus of the North," 1, 3
Appleton, John, 13
Arbenz Guzmán, Jacobo, 47
Ardaya Salinas, Gloria, 160
Argentina, 79, 105, 122
Arguedas, Antonio, 120
Arze Murillo, José Antonio, 96n10
Ashabranner, Brent, 138
Aymara Indians, 58, 173

Balcázar, J. M., 33n77
Bandung Conference (1955), 57
Banzer Suárez, Hugo, 11, 131, 150n63, 153, 155
Baptista Gumucio, Mariano, 149
Barrientos Ortuño, René, 86, 153
  biographical information, 110, 126
  and *campesinos*, 83, 101
  and Che Guevara, 114, 117
  coup by, 86, 100, 109
  popularity of, 101, 110
  and U.S., 100–101, 126, 128–29
Batista, Rubén Fulgencio, 87n60, 109
Baumann, Gerold "Gino," 148
Belzú, Manuel, 6
Bernbaum, Maurice, 81
Betancourt, Rómulo, 69n141
birth control and contraception, 11, 140–43, 151
Blasier, Cole, 25, 39n3
Bledsoe, Sam B., 65
Bloque Reestructuradora del COB, 78
Bohan Mission, 8, 22–23, 27, 43
Bolivia Development Corporation. *See* Corporación Boliviana de Fomento (CBF)
Bolivian Oil Company, 127
Bolivian revolution
  April 12, 1952, insurrection, 43
  Che Guevara on, 108
  economic and social measures of, 4, 46, 61–62, 90, 92
  as part of world decolonization movement, 4, 39–40, 57
  persistence into 1970s, 2, 85–86, 101, 109–10
  radical dimension of, 5, 42
  retreat of, 3, 71, 73–74, 153
  semifeudal relations prior to, 4, 22, 31, 101
  as spur to political participation, 85
  transformed Bolivia's relations with world, 20, 39
  as turning point in Bolivian history, 1, 85
  U.S. recognition of, 6, 47, 59, 70n142
  See also Movimiento Nacionalista Revolucionario (MNR)

Bonsal, Philip, 76
Brazil, 105, 125
Briggs, William T., 73
Britain, 14, 15, 25
Brubeck, William H., 96
Buchanan, James, 13
Bundy, McGeorge, 100
Busch, Germán, 34
Bush, George H. W., 166–67

Calvo, Carlos, 18
campesinos
  and Che Guevara effort, 111, 112–13, 115
  coalition with military, 79, 82–83, 110–11
  and coca leaf, 158, 161
  discontent and protests by, 28, 30–31, 32, 36, 59
  and land reform, 4, 101
  and MNR, 27, 31–32, 78–79
  and Peace Corps, 149
  repression of, 153
  unions of, 85, 154
  See also agriculture; land reform
Carter, James Earl (Jimmy), 154
Castro, Fidel, 80, 87, 97, 103–4
  and Che Guevara, 115, 116
Catavi massacre (1942), 32–33, 35, 65
Central Intelligence Agency (CIA), 113, 120, 140
Central Obrera Bolivian (COB), 43, 149
Centro Boliviano Americano, 133, 144
Chaco War, 19, 29
  Bolivian military in, 59, 112
  impact of, 16–17, 28, 30, 59
Chapare, 158, 162, 175
Chávez, Hugo, 177, 178
children, 11, 143
Childs, Marquis, 67
Chile, 152n1, 175–76
  Allende victory in, 122–23, 125
  U.S. and, 104–5, 124, 125, 130
civic action programs, 82, 94, 112, 119
Clayton, William, 61n107
Coca and Controlled Substances Law (Law 1008), 165–66
coca leaf and cocaine
  and Bolivian economy, 153, 154, 163, 168–69
  boom in production of, 153, 162–63
  campesinos and, 158, 161
  cocalero movement around, 161, 168, 174, 175
  legal production of coca, 159, 170, 178
  and narcotics trafficking, 161–62

  social and human costs of, 163–64
  traditional use of, 159, 166
  world demand for, 158, 168
  See also drug war
Cochabamba, 133, 172–73
cold war
  Bolivian loyalty to U.S. during, 53
  covert actions during, 136
  fear of communism as U.S. motive during, 9–10, 49, 61, 91, 136, 159–60, 174
  as ideological struggle, 54–55n76
  U.S.-Latin American relations during, 40–41, 159–60
Colombia, 123
Comité Universitario Boliviano, 149
communism
  as catchall term, 40–41
  MNR assurances to U.S. about, 47, 49, 63
  Peace Corps in fight against, 135, 136
  used by Bolivia to increase aid, 5, 10, 64
  as U.S. policy centerpiece, 9–10, 39, 40–41, 49, 61, 91, 92, 100, 136, 159–60, 174
Communist Party. *See* Partido Comunista Boliviano
Condori, Apolinario, 31
Congress of Industrial Organizations (CIO), 60, 65
constitution, Bolivian, 99, 110n30
Corporación Boliviana de Fomento (CBF), 20, 22, 23–24, 26
Corporación Minera de Bolivia (COMIBOL), 74, 85
  austerity cuts by, 76, 93, 157
  creation of, 6, 46, 156–57
corporatism, 119
Costa Rica, 45n36, 69n141, 150
counterinsurgency, 86n53, 104, 119n72
  U.S. training in, 82, 113–14, 115, 117
coup d'états
  1943, 25
  1946, 36, 60
  1951, 43
  1956 (aborted), 70
  1964, 3, 9, 74n2, 86, 99–100, 109, 123
  1970, 130
  1971, 131
  U.S. and, 96–97, 105
Crowley, Leo, 61n107
Cuba
  Batista regime in, 87n60, 109
  and Bolivian Communist Party, 98
  and Latin America guerrilla movements, 118, 124
  relations with Soviet Union, 116–17, 124
  support for Che Guevara by, 115, 116

Cuban Missile Crisis, 98
Cuban revolution, 1, 5, 80, 97
  as inspiration for Left, 78, 118, 123, 129
  as model, 108
  U.S. efforts to avert repeat of, 91, 96
  See also Castro, Fidel; Guevara, Ernesto "Che"

decolonization movement, 39–40, 57
democracy
  Bolivia's return to, 154, 156
  drug war as threat to, 162, 165
  U.S. lack of concern for, 99, 100
dependency theory, 147–48
Diario, El, 142, 143, 148–49
Dillon, Clarence D., 80, 93
Dominican Republic, 105, 136
Dosal, Paul J., 108
Drug Enforcement Agency (DEA), 165
drug war
  corruption in, 164–65
  Evo Morales and, 164, 170, 178
  impact on U.S.-Bolivian relations of, 159, 165
  ineffectiveness of, 168
  militarization of, 164–65, 166, 168, 169
  origins of, 160–61, 164
  resistance to militarization of, 167–68, 175
  as threat to democracy, 162, 165
  See also coca leaf and cocaine
Dunkerley, James, 74n2, 157n17

economic aid to Bolivia, U.S.
  amount of, 37, 48, 56n82, 69, 98n90, 181–82
  assists moderate wing of MNR, 75, 81, 83, 91
  during Banzer regime, 131, 154n6
  Bolivian agency in obtaining, 1, 5, 10, 83, 92, 95, 97, 167
  Bolivia's dependency on, 75, 77, 81, 91, 120
  and Bolivia's stability, 10, 81
  cuts in, 120–21, 127, 128, 154
  and economic diversification, 22, 60, 81
  food aid, 50, 51–52, 54
  forms of, 21, 50
  as method for fighting communism, 5, 10, 39, 64, 136
  as method for fighting economic nationalism, 9, 21–22, 41
  seen as investment capital, 62–63, 94
  strings attached to, 8, 20–21, 71
  as test case for Latin America, 54–55, 69–70, 84–85, 92, 178
  Triangular Plan for, 93–94
  as U.S. leverage instrument, 1, 5, 6, 7, 12, 38–39, 41–42, 49, 91
  See also economy, Bolivian; military aid, U.S.
economic diversification, 4n11, 42, 154
  Bohan Mission report on, 22–23
  Bolivian attempts at, 9, 20
  and economic nationalism, 17
  and foreign investment, 11, 153
  as MNR goal, 43, 54
  thwarted by U.S. food aid, 52, 54
  U.S. economic aid and, 22, 60, 81
economic nationalism, 37
  defined, 17
  in Latin America, 17–18
  MNR advocacy of, 42–43
  during 1930 and '40s, 19–21, 24, 25, 178
  U.S. opposition to, 6, 18–19, 22, 25, 39, 41, 63–64
Economic Stabilization Plan
  impact on MNR, 76–77, 83, 85
  resistance to, 71, 76, 77
  U.S. as architects of, 8, 71, 73, 75–76
economy, Bolivian
  coca and, 153, 154, 163, 168–69
  dependency of, 4–5, 9, 12, 42, 70–71, 77, 94
  exchange rates, 74–75, 76
  foreign debt, 15, 153
  foreign investments, 11, 15, 50–51, 61n107, 153
  impact of tin on, 4–5, 9, 14, 74, 94
  infrastructure, 15, 16, 23, 43
  printing of currency, 71, 156
  U.S. control over, 8, 9, 12, 39
  See also mines and mining; neoliberalism; oil and oil industry; tin
Eder, George Jackson, 71n148, 75n10
Edgerton, Glen E., 54
Egger, Roland, 93
Eisenhower, Dwight D., 48, 68, 83–84, 141
Eisenhower, Milton, 6, 64–65
  and U.S. aid to Bolivia, 39n3, 49, 50, 65–66
Ejército de Liberación Nacional (Bolivia), 129–31
Ejército de Liberación Nacional (Colombia), 123
Ejército de Liberación Nacional (Peru), 123
exchange rates, 74–75, 76
Export-Import Bank, 20, 23, 26

Falange Socialista Boliviana (FSB), 110
Farthing, Linda, 173
fascism and Nazism, 25–26, 59
Feder, Ernest, 111n35
Federación Sindical de Trabajadores Mineros de Bolivia (FSTMB)
    creation of, 34
    goals of, 34, 35n94
    and MNR, 35, 36, 78
    Trotskyites in, 34, 47
Figueres, José "Pepe," 69n141, 150
Flanders, Ralph, 65n110
foco theory, 129
foreign debt, 15, 153
foreign investments, 11, 15, 50–51, 61n107, 153
Foreign Ministry, Bolivian, 71, 78
    on fight against Che Guevara, 117–18
Free Trade Area of the Americas (FTAA), 1, 177
Frei, Eduardo, 104–5
Fuerzas Armadas Revolucionarias de Colombia (FARC), 123, 177

Galarza, Ernesto, 65n118
Galeano, Eduardo, 142n31
Gamarra, Eduardo, 3, 161n28, 167
García Meza, Luis, 154, 156
Garrastazu Medici, Emilio, 125
gas, natural, 156, 175–76
Germany, Federal Republic of, 93
Gibbon, Lardner, 14
Gildner, R. Matt, 100
Good Neighbor policy, 5, 26, 61, 66
Great Depression, 19, 58
Greece, 114–15, 48
Green, David, 25
Guatemala, 5, 47, 84, 136
guerrilla movements
    in Bolivia, 123–24, 129–31. *See also* Guevara, Ernesto "Che"
    Cuban inspiration for, 123, 129
    in Latin America, 123, 130
Guevara, Ernesto "Che," 102
    in Africa, 107, 108n22, 116
    Bolivian diary of, 120
    causes of defeat of, 115
    as divisive icon, 103
    execution of, 115, 117–18, 119, 140
    goal of world socialist revolution, 103, 107
    significance of defeat of, 118
    strategic perspective of, 106–7
    view of Bolivia by, 108, 109
    view of United States by, 106, 109

Guevara, José Rosa, 78–79
Guevara Arze, Walter, 43n22, 44, 60
Gulf Oil, 10, 126–28, 143

Hanson's Latin American Letter, 62n111
Healy, Kevin, 146n49, 158
Heath, Dwight B., 101
Henderson, Douglas, 113, 115, 120
highway, Cochabamba to Santa Cruz, 23–24
Hoffman, Elizabeth Cobbs, 133
Hofstadter, Richard, 14n3
Hoover, Herbert, 26
Huallaga Valley, 162
Hull, Cordell, 25
Humphrey, George, 54
Humphreys, R. A., 25

income distribution, 4, 92, 118, 174
indigenous people
    Andrade and, 58
    Bolivian revolution and, 4, 43
    and contraception, 142
    cosmology of, 173
    debt peonage of, 22, 31, 101
    emergence of radical movement of, 153, 154–55, 167, 168, 174
    Evo Morales and, 173, 176
    as majority in Bolivia, 27
    racism toward, 14, 58n93, 155
    social conditions of, 4, 30, 175
    Sociedad República de Kolasuyo, 29–30
    suffrage extended to, 4, 43, 57
    Yawar Malku depiction of, 145
infant mortality rate, 143
inflation, 8, 71, 74, 156, 157
International Monetary Fund (IMF), 8, 71
Iran, 50–51
Isiboro, 162

Jackson, Gardner, 64
Jennings, Peter, 38
Johnson, Lyndon B., 10, 100, 104–5

Katari, Tupaj, 154
Kataristas, 154–55, 168
Kelly, Jonathan, 101
Kemmerer, Edwin, 16
Kennedy, John F., 10, 98n92
    and Alliance for Progress, 86, 87, 100, 104
    interest in Bolivia of, 96
    and Peace Corps, 134
    and U.S. anticommunist efforts, 91–92, 93
Kenworthy, Eldon, 66n127

Khrushchev, Nikita, 87, 98
Kissinger, Henry A., 124
Klein, Herbert S., 101
Kohl, Benjamin, 173
Krock, Arthur, 67

labor unions, 43, 91
  history of in Bolivia, 29, 32–33
  from U.S., 59–60, 65
  See also Federación Sindical de Trabajadores Mineros de Bolivia (FSTMB)
land reform, 76, 85
  assurances to U.S. about, 47, 64, 68
  Barrientos and, 101
  Bolivian revolution's measures for, 45, 46, 90
  Evo Morales and, 176–77
  impact on Che Guevara effort, 111
  MNR calls for, 32, 43
Lanusse, Alejandro Agustín, 122
Laos, 114–15
La Paz, 29, 128, 145
Latin America
  and Alliance for Progress, 86–89
  anti-Americanism in, 11, 125
  anti-U.S. bloc in, 177, 178
  Bolivia as test case and trailblazer for, 55, 85, 69–70, 84–85, 92, 97, 152, 155–56, 178
  corporatist political culture in, 119
  economic nationalism in, 17–18
  guerrilla movements in, 123, 130
  leftward lurch during 1960s and '70s, 122–23
  military coups in, 9–10, 36, 105, 106
  revolutions in, 1, 5, 64
  Soviet Union and, 79, 97–98
  during World War II, 21n30, 25–26, 35–36, 58
Latin America policy, U.S.
  averting "another Cuba," 91, 96, 105
  under Carter and Reagan administrations, 154
  combating economic nationalism, 18–19, 21–22
  communism fear as cold war centerpiece, 9–10, 40–41, 61, 100, 105, 159–60
  drug war as, 160, 166–67
  under George H. W. Bush administration, 166–67
  history of, 13–14
  under Johnson administration, 10, 104–5
  under Kennedy administration, 10, 86, 87, 91–92, 100, 104

military and covert interventionism, 5, 47, 84, 105, 136
military assistance, 10, 125
  1967 as turning point in, 106–7, 118
  under Nixon administration, 121, 122, 124–25
  nonrecognition as tool of, 26
  Peace Corps as part of, 136
  promoting economic and political reforms, 14, 16, 18, 66, 73, 76, 87, 92
  role of individual leaders in, 56–57
  support for military coups, 3, 9–10, 105, 106
  U.S. lack of understanding about Latin America, 10, 11, 90, 106, 124
  See also U.S.-Bolivian relations
Lausche, Frank, 68
Lechín Oquendo, Juan
  as leader of MNR Left, 63n113, 78, 79, 110
  as minister of mines, 43–44
  on U.S. intervention in Bolivia, 75, 149n45
Lechín Suárez, Juan, 96–97
Lehman, Kenneth, 15n8, 39n3, 157–58
Levingston, Roberto, 122
Liberation Theology, 125
Lippman, Walter, 67
Lleras Restrepo, Carlos, 135
Lloyd, John, 15n6

Macomber, William B., Jr., 113n47
Malamud-Goti, Jaime, 168
Mankiewicz, Frank, 138
Mann, Thomas, 72, 82, 93, 105
Matthews, Herbert, 67
McCarthy, Joseph, 39n3
McMahon, Robert, 45
Mendoza, Jaime, 141n28, 147n50
Mesa, Carlos, 170, 173
Mexico, 1, 5, 19, 79
middle class, 42, 58, 81, 94, 175
  and Bolivian revolution, 42
  in Latin America, 58, 88–89, 90
migration, internal, 162–63
military, Bolivian
  alliance with campesinos, 79, 82–83, 110–11
  and Bolivian revolution, 43, 50, 112
  in Chaco War, 59, 112
  and Che Guevara, 109, 112
  civic action programs of, 82, 94, 112, 119
  increasing power of, 77, 169
  and MNR, 9, 77, 110, 119–20
  See also coup d'états

military aid, U.S., 10, 77, 94, 113
  Alliance for Progress and, 86
  for civic action programs, 82
  in counterinsurgency training, 82, 113–14, 115, 117
  origins of, 81
  providing counterintelligence, 113
  through Military Assistance Plan, 112, 130
milling industry, 52
miners
  and Che Guevara guerrilla effort, 108
  militias of, 43
  and MNR, 35, 36
  political weight of, 32, 33
  unionization of, 33, 34
  See also Federación Sindical de Trabajadores Mineros de Bolivia (FSTMB)
mines and mining
  Bolivia's dependence on, 33
  under Economic Stabilization Plan, 71, 76
  nationalization of by revolution, 4, 6, 43, 46, 47–48, 61–62, 64, 90
  neoliberalism's impact on, 158, 162
  See also tin
Mining Code, 35
modernization theory, 41, 54–55
Monje Molina, Mario, 108–9, 116
Monroe Doctrine, 13, 15
Montes, Ismael, 15
Morales, Evo
  anticapitalist stance of, 174–75
  as *cocalero* leader, 170, 175
  and Hugo Chávez, 177, 178
  Indian extraction of, 173, 176
  and land reform, 176–77
  resists neoliberalism, 173, 174, 177, 178–79
  and U.S.-Bolivian relations, 1, 3, 174–75, 177–78
  and U.S. drug war, 164, 170, 178
  U.S. efforts to prevent election of, 170–71
Morales, Juan Antonio, 158n20
Morse, Wayne, 68
Movimiento al Socialismo (MAS), 176
Movimiento de Izquierda Revolucionaria (Peru), 123
Movimiento Nacionalista Revolucionario (MNR)
  anticommunist assurances by, 47, 49, 63
  branded as fascist and pro-Nazi, 25, 62
  campesinos and, 27, 31–32, 78–79
  economic objectives of, 42–43, 44–45, 54
  and Economic Stabilization Plan, 76–77, 83, 85

Evo Morales movement compared to, 176
  fragmentation into moderate and left wings, 7, 43, 76, 81, 85, 176
  loss of revolutionary legitimacy by, 123
  McCarthyite concern about, 39n3
  and military, 9, 77, 110, 119–20
  and miners union, 35, 36
  moderate wing ascendency in, 8, 71, 76, 81, 85
  origins of, 6, 25
  pro-U.S. stance of, 6, 7, 10, 44, 45–46, 47
  Soviet feelers by, 79, 80
  stability of, 70, 93–94
  taking of power by, 43
  tin barons' propaganda against, 62, 70n142
  U.S. recognition and support of, 6, 7, 92
  U.S. support for moderates in, 49, 63, 75, 91
  in Villarroel government, 25, 31, 35
  working class and, 27
  See also Bolivian revolution
Movimiento Nacionalista Revolucionario (MNR) Left
  conservative ascendency over, 8, 71, 76, 81, 85
  goals of, 7, 44, 45
  labor movement as base of, 43, 47, 78
  split within, 78
  U.S. opposition to, 45, 46, 63, 75
Movimiento Revolucionario Autentico, 43n22

nationalism, 28, 120, 170–71. See also anti-Americanism; economic nationalism
nationalization
  of Gulf Oil, 10, 126–28, 143
  of Standard Oil, 10, 19, 20–21, 50
  of tin mines, 4, 6, 43, 46, 47–48, 61–62, 64, 90
neoliberalism
  benefits wealthy, 158, 170, 174
  Bolivia's embrace of, 151, 152, 155–56, 178
  Evo Morales on, 173, 174, 177, 178–79
  popular resistance to, 172–73, 174, 175–76, 179–80
  results of, 157–58
  U.S. view of, 152
  working class and poor under, 158, 175
Nicaragua, 1, 5
Nixon, Richard M., 121, 122, 124–25, 132, 161

O'Brien, Thomas F., 138
oil and oil industry
  foreign investment in, 15

oil and oil industry (*continued*)
  Gulf Oil nationalization, 10, 126–28, 143
  MNR on, 44, 54
  Standard Oil nationalization, 10, 19, 20–21, 50
  U.S. interests in, 23, 24, 50–51
Open Door Policy, 67
Operation Blast Furnace, 165
Organization of American States, 160
Ovando Candia, Alfredo, 114n52, 127, 129–30

Packenham, Robert A., 89
Panama Canal Zone, 86n53
Paraguay, 16–17
Paredes, Pedro, 31
Park, James William, 55n77
Partido Comunista Boliviano (PCB), 47, 98
  and Che Guevara, 108, 115–16
Partido Obrero Revolucionario, 34
Partido Revolucionario de la Izquierda Nacional (PRIN), 110
Paz Estenssoro, Víctor, 43, 48, 70n147, 79, 91, 110–11
  assurances to U.S. by, 45–46, 47, 64, 92
  erosion of support for, 99–100
  ousted by 1964 coup, 100, 109
  and Peace Corps, 139
  and Perón, 45
  plays Soviet card, 79, 80, 97
  as president in 1980s, 156–57, 165
  U.S. recognition and support for, 47, 59, 91, 99
Paz Zamora, Jaime, 38, 165n45
Peace Corps
  birth control materials provided by, 140–43
  Bolivia's expulsion of, 10–11, 126, 133, 146–47, 148–49, 150–51
  community development program of, 137–39
  establishment of, 134
  idealistic youth in, 134–35, 136, 149
  Left view of, 149
  popular hostility to in Bolivia, 133, 143–44, 148
  portrayal in *Yawar Malku*, 144–46
  relationship to Bolivian government, 139–40
  U.S. goals for, 135–36
Pearson, Drew, 67
Pentland, J. B., 14
Perón, Juan, 45

Peru, 123, 162
  Velasco regime in, 122, 124, 130
Peters, Charles, 138
Petroleum Code, 51, 126
Pike, Frederick B., 145n43
Pillericol, Israel, 30
Popular Assembly, 122, 176
population of Bolivia, 27, 134n4
Poston, Richard, 137–38
poverty rate, 174–75
Prado Salmón, Gary, 104n4, 112n41, 114n50, 119
  on Che Guevara execution, 118
privatization, 156
  of oil industry, 51, 83
  of water, 172–73
Programa Nacional del Desarrollo, 140
Punta del Este, Uruguay, 106

Quantum of Solace, 172

Rabe, Stephen G., 39n3
railroads, 15
Razón de Patria (RADEPA), 112
Read, Benjamin H., 100
Reagan, Ronald, 154, 161
Reconstruction Finance Corporation (RFC), 52–53, 66–67, 69
Reston, James "Scotty," 106
Rio Pact, 160
Rivas, Darlene, 44–45
Rocha, Manuel, 170–71
Rockefeller, Nelson, 61n107, 66
Rodríguez, Felix I., 104n4
Romualdi, Serafino, 60n102
Roosevelt, Franklin, 26
Rostow, Walt W., 105, 114n51, 116n62
Rotchin, Glen, 119
rubber, 24–25
Rubottom, Roy R., 73
Rusk, Dean, 99n95, 114–15
Rustad, Ken, 146n49
Ryan, William F., 136

Sachs, Jeffrey, 169
Sánchez de Lozada, Gonzalo, 157, 169, 173, 175, 176
Sanjinés, Jorge, 144–46, 155
Sanjines Goitia, Julio, 127
Scheffield, Glen F., 137–38n15
Schlesinger, Arthur, Jr., 96
shock therapy, 157, 169, 178
Shriver, R. Sargent, 138
Siles Salinas, Luis Adolfo, 114

INDEX 209

Siles Suazo, Hernán, 43, 78
Singer, Derek, 134nn5–6, 139
Single Convention on Narcotic Drugs, 164
Siracusa, Ernest, 131
Sociedad República de Kolasuyo, 29–30
Soviet Union
  Bolivian government feelers to, 5, 40, 79–80, 97–98
  relations with Cuba, 116–17, 124
  U.S. ideological struggle with, 54–55n76
  See also communism
Special Group for Counterinsurgency, 114
Standard Oil, 18
  nationalization of, 10, 19, 20–21, 50
Stephansky, Benjamin, 92
sterilization, 11, 145–46
Stettinius, Edward, 61n107

Teoponte, 129
Texas City, Tex., 37, 53–54, 65
Thesis of Pulacayo, 34
Time, 77
tin
  Andrade efforts around, 36–37, 53, 67
  Bolivian dependency on, 4, 9, 94
  Bolivia's nationalization of mines, 4, 6, 43, 46, 47–48, 61–62, 64, 90
  falling prices of, 53, 70, 74, 156, 162
  Texas City refinery for, 37, 53–54, 65
  U.S. stockpiles of, 53, 95
  Washington policy on, 37, 52–54, 94
  during World War II, 25, 35, 37, 69
  See also mines and mining
Toro Ruilova, José David, 19, 20, 34
Torres, Juan José, 122, 128–29, 130, 176
  expels Peace Corps, 146–47, 148–49, 151
Tragedy of Bolivia, The: A People Crucified, 62
Treaty of Cooperation (1990), 166
Triangular Plan, 93
Trotskyites, 34, 47
Truman Doctrine, 48
Turkey, 48
Tydings, Millard, 62n111

unemployment, 162
Unidad Mobil de Patrullaje Rural (UMOPAR), 164–65, 168
Uruguay, 79
U.S.-Bolivian relations
  during Banzer regime, 11, 131
  Bolivian agency in, 1, 3, 5, 12, 92
  Bolivia's defense of sovereignty in, 148, 161–62, 167, 175–76
  Bolivia seen as source of raw materials, 14, 19
  under Carter and Reagan administrations, 154
  cultural differences, 11, 143, 150
  deterioration of during 1969–71, 10–11, 120, 122, 126–29, 131–32
  Evo Morales and, 3, 174–75, 177–78
  under George H. W. Bush administration, 166–67
  under Johnson administration, 100
  under Kennedy administration, 10, 93, 96
  during late 1950s and early '60s, 10, 54, 99, 140
  under Nixon administration, 132
  as patron-client relationship, 16, 19–20, 83, 161, 178
  prior to revolution, 36
  U.S. aim of avoiding Bolivian instability, 39, 49–50, 61, 83, 91, 93–94, 95
  U.S. cultural influences, 133, 151
  and U.S. nation-building efforts, 2, 5, 41, 92
  during Villarroel regime, 25–26
  and war on drugs, 160–62, 164–65, 166, 167, 174
  See also Andrade Uzquiano, Víctor; anti-Americanism; economic aid to Bolivia; military aid, U.S.; nationalization
U.S. Information Service, 128
U.S. Marines, 128

Valdés Subercaseaux, Gabriel, 124
Velasco, Juan, 122, 125
Venezuela, 69n141, 177
Verdesoto, Luis, 160
Vietnam, 107, 114–15, 140
  Bolivia as next possible, 108, 113n45
Villamil V., Elías, 35
Villarroel, Gualberto, 25, 59
  ouster and assassination, 35, 36
  reformist nature of, 34, 59
Villegas, Harry "Pombo," 108

Washington Consensus, 156
Washington Post, 67
water, 172–73
wealthy elite
  as beneficiaries of U.S. aid, 85
  control of Bolivian society by, 29, 42
  neoliberalism's benefit for, 158, 170, 174
Weissman, Marvin, 154
Whitehead, Laurence, 75, 85
Wiarda, Howard J., 119n71

women, 143
women's suffrage, 4, 43
working class
  under austerity plans, 9, 76
  neoliberalism and, 158
  prior to revolution, 27–28
  size of in Bolivia, 33
  strikes by, 71, 76
  unemployment among, 162
  See also labor unions
World Bank, 173, 175

World Labor Conference (1944), 59–60
World War II
  Latin America and, 21n30, 25–26, 35–36, 58
  tin production during, 25, 35, 37, 69

Yacimientos Petrolíferos Fiscales Bolivianos (YPFB), 24, 51, 126, 127
Yawar Malku (Blood of the Condor), 144–46
Yungas region, 166

www.ingramcontent.com/pod-product-compliance
Lightning Source LLC
Chambersburg PA
CBHW021404290426
44108CB00010B/376